*1,001 Ways to Connect with Your Kids* is cutting-edge truth based on age-old wisdom. It cuts through techniques and quick fixes to the core of why we have children in the first place: relationship. In a refeshing, insightful, readable, and applicable way, Jim Lucas shows us how to give our children what their souls really crave. This book is for every parent who has ever asked, "How can I have a real relationship with my child?"
    —**Terry Meeuwsen,** cohost of *The 700 Club*

There's no longer any excuse for not knowing how to connect with our kids. James Lucas has provided a proverbial gold mine of solid ideas for building the kind of relationships all parents long to have with their children.
    —**Les Parrott III, Ph.D.,** author of *High-Maintenance Relationships*

We knew we were going to read an informative, helpful, and loving book when the very first page we turned to was one of the most touching and uplifting dedication pages we've ever read. We could hardly wait to read the rest of the book. And read it we did, with a deep appreciation for the incredible amount of helpful information available to the reader. It affirmed much of what we did in our own child rearing, and it encouraged us to revisit Jim Lucas's positive gleanings with our grandchildren. We will be quoting much of *1,001 Ways to Connect with Your Kids* in the family and parenting seminars we present.
    —**Bob and Yvonne Turnbull,** authors of *Teammates: Building Your Marriage to Complete, not Compete* and speakers on marriage and the family

*1,001 Ways to Connect with Your Kids* offers some of the most practical and usable help I've ever seen. There's something here for every parent who wants to do it right—and that's all of us.
    —**Gayle Roper,** author of *The Decision* and *Caught in the Act*

# 1001 Ways TO Connect with your Kids

## JAMES R. LUCAS

Tyndale House Publishers, Inc.
WHEATON, ILLINOIS

Visit Tyndale's exciting Web site at www.tyndale.com

*1,001 Ways to Connect with Your Kids*

Copyright © 2000 by James R. Lucas. All rights reserved.

Author photo by Peter Lucas. Copyright © 1999 by Barrett Graphics. All rights reserved.

Designed by Melinda Schumacher

**Library of Congress Cataloging-in-Publication Data**

Lucas, J.R. (James Raymond), date
    1,001 ways to connect with your kids / James R. Lucas.
        p. cm.
    ISBN 0-8423-3154-9 (sc : alk. paper)
    1. Parenting—Religious aspects—Christianity.    I. Title: One thousand one ways to connect with your kids.    II. Title: One thousand and one ways to connect with your kids.
III. Title.

BV4526.2 .L815 2000
248.8′45—dc21                                                          99-055351

Printed in the United States of America

05   04   03   02   01   00
7    6    5    4    3    2

*To four wonderful friends:*

*Bethany:*
> *I see in you a love of words and people, your
> interest in life, your spunk, your joy, your smile.
> I see a world that is much better because
> you're in it. You challenge me with your
> bouncy, happy spirit. You encourage me by
> your desire to be involved in my work.*

*David:*
> *I see in you a balance of thought and feeling, a
> desire to learn much and apply it all, maturity,
> strong purpose, and determination. I see a
> man with a warm and engaging spirit who
> will affect thousands. You challenge me with
> your curiosity and out-of-the-box thinking. You
> encourage me by your care and enthusiasm.*

*Peter:*
> *I see in you the artist's heart, the love of the
> visual and musical, the responsibility and
> generosity and insight and great sense of
> humor. I see many who would do well to count
> you as their friend. You challenge me with your
> refusal to let me be an old fogy and drop off
> the cutting edge. You encourage me by being
> my friend and ally.*

*Laura:*
> *I see in you great enthusiasm, warmth and
> compassion, outstanding competence as
> teacher, director, thinker, persuader, and
> writer. I see no limit to the scope of your
> impact. You challenge me with your deep
> questions and ideas. You encourage me by
> being you, and being there.*

# Contents

# Acknowledgments

I appreciate the contribution of my children to this work. Laura read and edited the manuscript, offered ideas, reminded me of ways to connect that I used with her (ah, memory!), and found many of the quotes used in this book. Peter encouraged me on many occasions, including after a major computer-related glitch that resulted in the loss of some material. David provided office support, including entering the last round of changes, organizing the files, and printing the manuscript. Bethany was my daily encourager, who made the whole project more bearable with her regular cups of hot chocolate.

I thank Maryl Janson, my longtime friend, for her assistance and support. Her ideas and suggestions and corrections and examples made an invaluable contribution to this book. She's a terrific, interesting, and loving teacher and speaker, and mother of five. She pressed me to write my earlier parenting books, was the force behind the first Proactive Parenting Seminar, and has been a cheerleader for *1,001 Ways*.

My family was inspirational, especially during our robust family dinners (while out for dinner recently at our favorite Chinese restaurant, the server told us we laughed more than any family they had ever had there—I took it as a compliment!). Thanks to Pam and each of the rest of you for your love and care and confidence. I also appreciate the suggestions Anna Bourdess made to the project.

I owe a great debt to many parents and children who have helped me to see what works and what doesn't in creating parent-child connection. I am particularly grateful to those who have attended our Proactive Parenting seminars, asked great questions, and given their wonderful insights.

I appreciate the efforts of my friend Dave Horton in believing in this project and getting it in front of the right people. Thanks to Ken Petersen and Ron Beers at Tyndale House for their confidence in the type of book

I was trying to write and the impact it could have. My gratitude goes out to Dave Hoover for shepherding this project through the editorial process, to Susan Taylor and Annette La Placa for their fine editing and their tender loving care of the manuscript, and to Travis Thrasher for being an ongoing source of encouragement, information, and humor.

Finally, my thanks to V. H. for your inspiration and encouragement.

# Introduction:
## The Quest for Connection

**W**e want our children to be connected to us at the soul. We want them to know that in a tough and largely uncaring world, there's a place they can always go for understanding, insight, and help—us.

But how do we pull that off? How do we connect with these complex, rugged individuals? How can we train them, correct them, discipline them, and punish them—and still end up being their friends?

As a young man I became a youth pastor, both because I loved teens and because I thought it would be excellent training for my own future role as a parent. I was eager to observe. What were parents doing right? Where were they missing the point? What things drew kids toward their parents, and what drove them away?

What I discovered blew me away. I saw parents who were devoted to their children, gave their children opportunities, provided them with good guidance and direction—and ended up with poor relationships with their children, or worse. They loved their children, but not in a way that connected them soul to soul. I was stunned to see these parents' genuine care meeting with such apathy, resistance, and rebellion.

There had to be a better way, and I determined to find it. I asked teens what connected them to their folks. I asked parents. I held group discussions. I dived into the Bible and found wisdom in other works of philosophy and literature. After I had spent three years as a youth pastor, our first child, a little girl, was born.

So I began putting what I was learning into practice with my own children. I tried to find the way while working as a pastor, then as a corporate executive, and eventually as a consultant, a speaker, and a writer. Time has often been scarce, and the challenge was greater because of the age spread of our children. (At one point I had one in college, one in high school, one in middle school, and one in elementary school.) I found myself juggling college commencements with PTA meetings.

Each of our four children's personalities are in some ways dramatically different (a fact that all parents of more than one child discover). And all four children seem very different from me. I experimented as I worked to be close to them, and of course, I made some mistakes. But I began to find the common ground, the way to connect no matter how great the differences between parents and their children.

How? I saw that by becoming a person in authority who doesn't rely on power, a mentor rather than a boss, and a friend instead of a master, a parent clears the pathway to the heart of his or her child. By sharing faith and principles with authenticity and honesty, a parent builds bridges instead of walls.

The highest tribute a parent can give to a child is to say, "I want to connect with you." That's why I wrote this book. It's designed to be a launchpad for building a soul-friend connection with your children. Some of the ideas will remind you of things you've done already or have always wanted to do. Others may need some "customizing" to make them work for you. And a few may not fit who you are, at least right now. It's all right not to use those. This is a book of ideas, not rules.

Many parents think, *We're already connected; we make a big deal of occasions like birthdays and graduations!* But that's an illusion. True connection happens step-by-step, in small ways even more than in big ones. It's the consistent, frequent contacts, efforts, and traditions that create a tie that binds—forever. So choose an idea, and starting building connection with your kids.

Jim Lucas

# Part 1

# *What to Say:*

## Words

## That Create

## Connection

*Words are uniquely powerful for creating connection between parents and children. Although communication can be used for either good or evil, with proper use, words can be a marvelous bonding agent.*

*God created the world out of nothing—by the power of his words alone. According to the Bible, we're made in God's image. That means we also—on a small scale—have the power to create something new out of nothing.*

*This "something new out of nothing" can be the planting of wisdom, insight, understanding, encouragement, or comfort where before there was emptiness, ignorance, or discouragement. Our words can create life and relationship and mutuality where before there were alienation and disconnection. Just as we don't live by bread alone but need the words of God to live, so our children don't live by nutrition alone, but need—desperately need—what we can create with words.*

*The first and most important mission of parenting is to get on the inside—to crawl inside the heart of your child. That kind of connection isn't easy, but it's absolutely critical. Without it, we're just dancing around each other and going through the motions of life.*

*Because you're made in God's image, you can use your words to create a new thing—real life and a real bond with your child.*

# Establishing "Forever" Communication

## # 1  God-Powered Words

The book of Genesis tells us that God spoke, and voila!—the earth was there. No construction project—just very powerful words. Genesis also explains that God made people in his image. In some incredible ways we are like God. One way is that we have tremendous creative power. As a parent, you can use that power to *create* relationship with your child. And you can use it to create character traits in your child. Ask yourself, *What do I want to* create *in my child? Competence? Confidence? Compassion?* Then plan and structure your words so that your God-given power makes something where there was nothing.

## # 2  You're the Best

Three simple words: "You're the best." Said often enough and without elaboration or explanation, these words can build a mountain of self-worth for your children—and it will be hard for them not to love somebody who makes them feel so good. Best at what? Being who they were designed to be. And these words are so much better than "You're better than ____," the fatal disease of comparison.

## # 3  Think Big, Talk Big

Many parents could use a vocabulary transplant. We tend to think too small ("You're doing OK on that"). The impact of "OK" and "all right" and "pretty good" is close to negligible. Adopt some big words, words uttered too infrequently by parents: *terrific, outstanding, magnificent, incredible, extraordinary, dynamite, wow!* Think big and talk big—and maybe your children will behave "big" and your relationship will cast a long shadow.

# # 4 Friend to Friend

When you're looking into the face of your child, ask yourself this question: *How would I speak to her if she were a friend whose regard I wanted to keep?* Think of her as someone who, like a friend, has the power to walk away from your relationship—because she does have that power.

# # 5 Name Them

Parents spend a lot of time on a name for a baby and then usually stop naming. Don't stop. Name their strong points: You're responsible, you're upbeat, you're goal oriented. And name their virtues: You have integrity; you have compassion; you have loyalty. Help them see the best that is in them—and the best that is in you for noticing. They won't be able to avoid loving someone who sees what even they aren't sure of.

# # 6 Go Soul Deep

Tailor your compliments. Be specific, and comment on behaviors and events that are under your kids' control or that they have struggled to achieve. If you compliment only the superficial, you'll create an increased interest in the superficial. You'll lead your children to *become* more superficial. You want soul-deep children with whom you can relate intimately. You can't relate deeply to a superficial child, even one of your own creation.

# # 7 Don't Make 'Em, Don't Break 'Em

Few things in life do more damage to relationships than unfulfilled promises. Go ahead and make promises—but not very many, and always underestimate what you really think you can do. "We'll try" makes a better answer than "We will." When you do make a promise, keep it—even when it hurts (Ps. 15:4).

# # 8 No Excuses

When you do break a promise or miss a commitment, don't fall into the understandable but deadly trap of spouting excuses, justifications, and rationalizations. Your excuses may make you feel better about your failure by coating it with words, but it can make your relationship with your kids a whole lot worse. The simple, humble "I can't believe I blew this—please forgive me" is the pathway to a deeper bond.

# # 9 Overdeliver

If you really want to have your kids rely on you, do even *more* than you said you would! If you promise, "I'm going to get us a movie tonight," and then follow up the movie with a snack or game or story, your kids will know your words carry a lot of weight. Even better, they know *you* carry a lot of weight (the good kind, in the soul). The goal is for your kids to be able to *count* on your words so they can count you as trustworthy.

# # 10 Laugh Attack

Long after you're gone, your kids will remember your laugh—assuming you laugh. I can still hear my grandmother with her silly laugh that offset her usual seriousness. Most people laugh less and less as they get older, as life gets tough and takes its toll. Don't let it happen to you! Find something to laugh about—at life, at yourself, at the pomposities of others, at anything that's out of place or time. Laughing with your kids over life's absurdities will glue you together. Let them hear you laugh often—and, like the old comedians, always leave them laughing!

# # 11 Enough Is Enough

If you want your words to have more value, use fewer of them. It's supply and demand: "The more the words, the less the meaning, and how does that profit anyone?" (Eccles. 6:11). If you want your words to "stick," it's quality, not quantity, that does the trick. Kids remember sentences, not essays.

# # 12 The Vacation Principle

A good conversation is like a good vacation: It helps to know where to stop. Lots of relationships have been damaged by the "just one more thing" parental tendency: "Not only is your room a disaster, but you look like something out of *Invasion of the Body Snatchers*." Even a wonderful conversation can go too far. On the rare occasion that you make a point that goes all the way to the bone with your child, stop talking. If you keep going, you may diminish the memorability of the point and perhaps even negate it. When you see that what you've said has made a deep impact, pull off the road and order lunch.

# # 13 Hold That Thought!

"When I hear my children expounding on something and they're wrong," Maryl Janson, speaker, teacher, and a mother of five told me, "little alarms begin going off. I want to jump in, correct them, and show them the right way. But when I do, they just quit talking. I sometimes have to choose not to listen to those alarms." It isn't always best to offer corrections. Sometimes it's more important to keep the communication lines open than to try to make sure there's no dirt in the lines.

# # 14 More Early, Less Later

It's easy to talk too little when the kids are little—and too much later on. Babies are a captive audience; take advantage of that, even talking about life principles to young children. In an article titled "The Smartest Thing You Can Do for Your Baby," William Phillips writes: "Recent studies have found that how—and how much—parents and other caregivers 'converse' with a baby... can have a profound impact on her intellectual development for the rest of her life.... What promotes that development more than anything else is human speech" (*Parenting* magazine, August 1997). Even unborn babies will thrive on—and connect with—your words. As your kids get older, you'll have to decrease the quantity and go for quality, looking for those moments when your teenagers are actually listening.

# # 15 Pregnant with Meaning

Pack a lot of zip into your words. Think about what you want to say and how you want to say it. Laying out a detailed plan for a musical career may not be nearly as effective as saying, "You know, I was thinking about your music last night before I fell asleep, and it struck me that you could really affect people deeply with it for years." When a vision is planted, a child's appreciation for the one who planted it will be inevitable.

# # 16 One Memorable Sentence

When you give a note or birthday card, don't cop out and just sign the sentiments printed in the card (no connection there!). But don't wax on and on, either. Mathematician and philosopher Blaise Pascal once wrote to a friend, "Please forgive this long letter—I didn't have time to write a short one." The brief opening of the Declaration of Independence lives on, while hundreds of history books and other documents lay forgotten and untouched. It's better to take the time to come up with one memorable sentence.

# # 17 The Five "I's"

Public speakers make their communication meaningful with five "I" techniques. Try to talk with your children in a way that's

1. Informative—with real content and take-away value
2. Incisive—cutting below the surface to say something meaningful

3. Iconoclastic—knocking down myths and cherished baloney
4. Interesting—laced with stories and examples and humor
5. Inspiring—making your kids feel they can do it!

# # 18 The Back Door

We parents tend to come in the front door, blurting our instructions or desires directly, being honest and clear. Sometimes that's not the best way to capture children's attention. Don't forget that your kids are incredibly complex beings who want to think for themselves. Try approaching a subject through the back door: "I've heard three opinions on this subject. What do you think?" or "I read about this topic last week; isn't this interesting?" In the country, best friends always just let themselves in—through the back door.

# # 19 Validate Feelings

Your kids may bring you an issue or a concern, and then it's up to you to take it from there. You can fall back on the easy "dismissal": "Oh, don't worry about that." Or worse, you can communicate "I told you so": "If only you'd listened to my advice." If you want to connect with your kids, you've got to show them you identify with their feelings: "You sound angry. I know how you must feel. I'm sure you're frustrated. I'd be upset, too." You can dissect the problem later, if it's appropriate. But first, you've got to get invited into the laboratory.

# # 20 Free to Respond

Your children should feel free to "think out loud" when they're with you. You want them to respond openly and honestly, even if what they come up with is rough-edged or incomplete. If you edit too much along the way, you cut short what you hope to be a "forever" conversation with your children. Many good writers avoid editing during their first burst of creativity. They get their big ideas out, then they hone them. Correcting your children too much while they're "writing," so to speak, can make them feel foolish, shutting down both creativity and connection.

# # 21 Discussion versus Dialogue

People are wise to distinguish between discussion and dialogue, says Peter Senge in The Fifth Discipline (Doubleday, 1990). In a discussion, you present your position. As soon as you're done (or maybe just before), your child presents his or hers. Back and forth you go, stating and defending. There is no interweaving and little understanding here.

In a dialogue, you both open yourselves to new ideas, feelings, analysis, and synthesis. You share what you're thinking, including assumptions and things you're not so sure of. Your child does the same. The conversation becomes a tapestry as you both understand what you didn't before and as you become one heart—rather than two boxers.

# # 22 Get Repetitive

When your children tell you something that is obviously important to them, you honor them by saying, "Now let me see if I understand what you're telling me...." That communicates, "This is really more important to me." It also assures them that you really "get it"—or that you don't, which can open up even deeper conversation.

# # 23 Kind Words

Nasty words sting and hurt and wound, and you can spend a lifetime trying to erase them. But kind words soothe and heal and nurture, and they "live in the heart and soul and remain as blessed memories years after they have been spoken" (Marvea Johnson). The older I get, the more I appreciate kindness. Kindness is a way of life—and a way to relational life.

# # 24 Guided by Light

Like a top journalist, we need to package our words to have clout and truth. "Put it before them briefly so they will read it, clearly so they will remember it and above all accurately so they will be guided by its light" (Joseph Pulitzer).

# # 25 Golden Silence

Did you know you can speak with your silences? Correction, for example, can ruin our bond with our kids if we do it too much, too verbally, too long. A grieved look and a few tears sometimes speak louder than a lecture.

# # 26 A Parent's Voice

Find some "great words," or write some of your own, and record them for your children. Create treasure, on a tape. Many years ago, when my children were too little to read, I recorded most of the book of Proverbs for them, adding a bit of my own commentary to make it more understandable and more personal. They could listen to a chapter in bed before they went to sleep or in the car on long trips. These tapes were passed from one child to the next, and they listened to them again and again, long after they could read on their own.

# # 27 Truth in Story

Make something up out of nothing. Since you're made in the image of your Creator God, exercise your creativity and come up with unique stories that illustrate truths that are most important to you. Fictionalize Bible stories or other great works, or make up a brand-new story. As Howard Gardner says so well, "Stories go in deep" (*Leading Minds*, Basic Books, 1996). Stories from you, in your own words, can go in even deeper.

# # 28 Your Family Language

Create a few words and phrases that make up your own family's quotebook. Pay attention when your kids use your funny language, and egg them on. In our family, "blobbing" means saying no without saying *no;* "hook-e-dook" means nonsense or baloney, and "fantabulous" is a kooky mix of *fantastic* and *fabulous.* Those words reinforce your sense of family unity, and they'll bring back fond memories, far into the future.

# # 29 Just Imagine

Watch for the "imaginaries": ideas that can be talked about and used again and again to create a sense of shared family culture. When Peter was little, we teased him about having "hematosis hickley," a sickness characterized by forgetting your responsibilities and having a green spot on the back of your neck (Bethany came down with it more recently). Laura had an imaginary friend named "Jurdy," and David had a stuffed animal he called "Torture" (we never analyzed that one too deeply). These concepts are part of our family history—of who we are. Remembering them always brings a laugh and binds us to the past and to each other.

# # 30 The Mirror

It's frightening to realize that the way your children talk to and treat each other is a direct reflection of how you talk to and treat them. "Stop screaming at him!" we scream. "We don't criticize each other in front of others," we admonish her in front of her siblings. If you don't like what you see in your children, consider it time to look in the mirror. The wonderful truth is that communication patterns can be changed— starting with you.

# # 31 Flicker: Future Memories

Describe a time when your kids will be doing something far into the future. For example, "Honey, someday you'll be sitting at a large table having a wonderful Thanksgiving dinner. You'll look around the table at children, grandchildren, nieces, nephews, or friends, and you'll feel so grateful for all that God's given you. There may be a flicker of a memory of a time when *you* were a little child sitting at the table looking at me. Even if I'm gone and in heaven then, I'll be with you in that soft and pleasant memory. I'm trying to live with you now in such a way that when that memory comes, it'll make you smile."

# # 32 See the End from the Beginning

It's morbid and unhealthy to be overly concerned about death, but a healthy appreciation for the reality of death can inspire us to live well and to leave a legacy for our children. Ask yourself, *What do I want them to feel when they're standing by my grave?* When they're old enough to understand it without being punished by it, tell your kids, "Someday, I hope a long time from now, you'll be reading the writing on a stone, and you'll be flooded with memories and emotions. What I'm hoping you'll remember is . . ." Seeing the end from the beginning can bring color to the middle.

# # 33 Journal

Some parents find writing comfortable for expressing deep truths or emotions. Keep a journal that your kids can inherit someday. Even if writing isn't your strong suit, you could jot a few key thoughts down from time to time—when you or your child has learned something essential or made a big change, or just when you've thought of your child in a fresh and meaningful way.

# # 34 Respond to Intent

One way a parent's negative words do lasting damage is when the parent falsely judges the child's intent. So listen carefully for the feelings behind your children's words, for the intent behind the conversation. Perhaps a child is trying to work through the hurt of mean comments by another student at school and says, "Those horrible teachers just don't care what people say." You might respond to the surface comment with, "You're not allowed to disrespect your teachers," without finding out what's really going on. Don't "slam the door shut" by giving a quick response to your child's surface comments. Remember, it's really *hard* to judge what's going on in another person's heart and really *easy* to misjudge it.

# # 35 Don't Name It

It's easy to see a behavior in a child and miss completely what it is and what it means. You might say a child is being "rebellious" when really he just hates peas and would rather die than eat them. You might say she's being "disrespectful" in church when the service is so boring that most of the adults are considering pulling the hair of the person in front of them. Stop yourself and think, *What's driving this outward response?* You'll improve your connection with your child by taking the time to get the right answer.

# # 36 The Short and Long of It

To paraphrase Tennyson, "Life is short, but love is long." This has a two-part message for parents regarding their words to their kids. First, life is short: "Our time together will fly by; it will go so fast, so let's do it right, let's make it count." And second, love is long: "I'm far from perfect, I'm not even sure I know how to do it, but I'm certain of this: Long after I'm gone, you will still know—*really* know—that you were loved."

# # 37 Trustworthiness

Business organizations fail horribly when they demand commitment and loyalty from people whom they treat in a cavalier manner. Parents can fail at the same point. Trust is the basis of a close relationship. Your kids can bond with you when they know you to be trustworthy, a person of integrity. So do what you say you will—always! If you promised to read them a book at bedtime, but you forgot and now it's ridiculously late—read it anyway. If you said your teenager could use the car, but now you wish you hadn't because you want it yourself, hand over the keys with gladness and either stay home or take a taxi. Compromised words yield compromised relationships. The cost is too high.

# # 38 The Real Deal

Few things in life sound as tinny and meaningless as "token" words of love and relationship. Saying, "Love you," in a ritualistic, obligatory way does nothing to create bonds but rather dismantles them over time. Remember that it's better to say nothing at all than to say nothing when you speak. Put yourself into your words. "There is only one kind of love," said French writer La Rochefoucauld, "but there are a thousand imitations."

# #39 Heaven's Lieutenants

"The voice of parents is the voice of gods, for to their children they are heaven's lieutenants" (William Shakespeare). Measure your words, since even in little daily frustrations what you say can have long-lasting impact. The difference between "You delight me" and "You're a nuisance"—each three words long—is a man or woman who, fifty years from now, remembers you with rejoicing or resentment.

# #40 The Three-Way Super Glue

Using your words to include God in your connecting bond will make it that much stronger, since "a cord of three strands is not quickly broken" (Eccles. 4:12). While walking together, point out God's "eternal power and divine nature" (Rom. 1:20) and use them as a jumping-off point into who God is. When you feel blessed, give your children a high five, and thank God as you would any gracious old friend. The key is to talk about God in a real and pertinent way, to make God's loving, awesome, or righteous presence in the middle of your relationship a kind of glue between you and your children.

# #41 Celebration

Our "forever" ways of speaking won't end at the time when our children are away from us. "For what is our hope, our joy, or the crown in which we will glory in the presence of our Lord Jesus when he comes? *Is it not you?*" (1 Thess. 2:19, emphasis added). These words from the Bible are a wonderful and perfectly clear rebuke to those sad, hard-bitten souls who claim we won't know each other in the afterlife. It'll go far beyond "knowing" each other. We'll have an explosive celebration because the ones we love are there—our "hope" (that our relationship paid off), our "joy" ("I can't believe what a 'wow' it is that you're right here!"), and our "crown" (our "topping off," our "reward," isn't gold or diamonds, but *people*). Look into your children's eyes and souls as you tell them the next line: "Indeed, *you* are my glory and joy."

## Say "I Love You" like You Never Have Before

# # 42 Spiritual Spelunking

Hearts, even in little children, are incredibly complex. To find the right words, the ones that really say "I love you," we have to go on a journey into their hearts, like a spelunker who explores a cave. "You have to crawl inside your children's hearts. And it can be a very challenging journey" (*Proactive Parenting*, Harvest House, 1993). You have to find out who they are and what makes them tick. Only then are we really ready to talk.

# # 43 Like Is Love

"Like" is the earthy side of love. We can "love" people we don't necessarily like, but it becomes impossible not to love someone that we like. We should step away from parental "love" for a few moments and ask ourselves, *Do I really like her? Would I choose him out of a crowd to be my friend? How can I encourage more of the really likable stuff?* Kids expect their parents to "love" them. When we like them, too, it knocks their socks off.

# # 44 Playing Favorites

The next step after loving and liking our children is for each of them to become a *favorite*. A favorite is a someone we prefer over the crowds, want to hang out with, and really think is super. How does this fit in with the sound advice to not play favorites? Every one of your children is your "fave"! This is still honest, because the heart is a spacious place with room for all of your favorites.

# # 45 Mass Customization

In the world of manufacturing, one of the key concepts is "mass customization"—producing components in a large economy of scale (the "mass" part) but assembling them at the latest point in the process to meet the needs of each individual customer (the "customization" part). Words can be mass customized. We all speak the same language and share the same vocabulary—we have a "mass" of words in our warehouse. But you can "customize" them by putting them together in ways that really mean something to each individual "customer" (each child). Think of ways to communicate in a special way with each of your kids.

# # 46 Say It Loud, Say It Clear

There's a popular leadership principle that says, "Praise publicly, criticize privately." Too often in life, it's the other way around. Children need to be praised—sincerely, and for genuine accomplishments and character traits. If you praise them in front of others, they know you mean it!

# # 47 Just between Us

As you deal with your children honestly about their achievements, they'll expect you to deal with them honestly regarding areas they need to improve. Children need to be criticized—constructively, for their good—but the more private the better. Treating their failings with dignity communicates, "I love you: I love you too much to let you be wrong, and I love you too much for anyone else to know about it."

# # 48 Whisper

Whispering creates soul connection. The very act tells a child, "You and I have something special between us." Even criticism, when offered in a gentle whisper, has a bonding effect. Whispering says, "No one else hears me; this is from my heart to yours."

# # 49 "We Interrupt This Broadcast . . . "

You communicate "I love you" when you *don't* use your words to interrupt your children. You hate it (or should) when they do it to you, and they'll feel no different. To wait until they're finished speaking or to say, "Holler when you have a minute," communicates, "You're really valuable, and so is whatever you're doing." Respect is fabulous relational glue.

# # 50 Let Them Finish

Avoid finishing your children's thoughts for them. It's rude and annoying, it shuts down conversation, and some percentage of the time you're not going to guess right. A "hmmm" or an "I hear you" exudes care and appreciation to them, no matter how little they are.

# # 51 The Right Stuff

Parents can spend a lot of time working to change or redirect their children's behaviors and desires. Sometimes all that correction inadvertantly communicates, "You're not intelligent enough/good enough/acceptable," when really we need to tell them, "I love the real you!" Remember to affirm the good behaviors and desires you see in them. Say, with all sincerity, "All these good things you hope for are things I want for you, too!"

# # 52 Stamp of Approval

Your love for your children comes through loud and clear when you ratify their interests. When they say, "I'd like to learn to dance/take up tennis/travel to Europe," don't be quick to say no. Sometimes when you shut down an idea, children feel as if you're saying no to their interests, their values, or their ability to decide and act. Of course there are times when you'll have to say no, but as often as you can, say yes. When you do, you affirm their whole being.

# # 53 It's about You

When you say "I love you," where is your emphasis? Are you thinking about yourself ("You know I'm the one who loves you—look at how much I do for you")? Or are you focusing on the "you" in "I love you"—affirming each child's uniqueness, idiosyncrasies, and interests? Putting the emphasis on the "you" could add a whole new dimension to your relationship with this incredibly complex being.

# # 54 Overheard

You can deliver a strong "I love you" in a roundabout way. When you're talking with a friend at a holiday party or at church and your child is nearby, talk about your child. An overheard, heartfelt "You know, I can't even tell you how much I love my daughter!" can add so much to your joint emotional bank account.

# # 55 Overheard Again

Don't hesitate to talk to God about your child—in your child's presence: "Dear God, thank you for giving me this incredible bundle of energy and terrific friend. You know how much I love him, even though I'm sure I don't always show it or get it across. Help me do a better job of letting him see that I'm wild about him." Your genuine prayer to the Lord will also say "I love you" to your child. And when God answers that prayer, your connection can only be deeper and stronger.

## # 56 Harmonious Echo

Many parents talk about their children to others, stressing their kids' accomplishments. Other parents feel awkward talking much about their children at all. Just do it! Talk about your kids with everyone, but not just about achievements. Emphasize your love and appreciation for their being, their souls. As others begin to understand how deeply important your children are to you—just by being, not by performing—the echo of that depth of feeling will reverberate off your friends and find its way back to your kids. It becomes a symphony of affection.

## # 57 I Need You

Ever notice how friendships can feel one-sided when only one friend really needs the other? Your friendship with your kids requires that same balance. Too many children feel unneeded by their parents—especially by parents who need to be needed by their kids to feel good about themselves. At the opposite extreme are parents who "need" their kids so much they treat their children like employees or even slaves. But when you properly need your kids, you help them develop skills and knowledge, you let their capabilities supplement your weaknesses. Isn't it just like God to produce complementary families, where strengths and weaknesses among members work together to form a really strong unit? Saying, "I couldn't do this without you," is an awesome way to say, "I love you."

## # 58 Take a Risk

When your kids come up with some new plan—a lemonade stand, an educational path, a project, a new business—say "try it" instead of discouraging the new venture. Your willingness to join in the risk communicates, "I trust you and support you, even if I'm not sure how this will turn out." There's a time for giving advice and cautions, but it's too easy for parents to become risk-averse, lecture-dispensing machines. Saying "try it" can force you past loving just the *idea* of your kids rather than the actual flesh-and-blood dynamos that they actually are.

## # 59 Welcome Home

"You'll never have a second chance to make a good first impression," the proverb goes. Every day is like a resurrection; it's a chance to make a new "first impression." The first time you see one another each day, whether it's morning or evening, give a big, joyous—bodacious even!—greeting. It'll create its own "first impression." Everyone feels good when they're welcomed enthusiastically (remember the Prodigal Son?). A great greeting helps you celebrate your life together and strengthens your bond. Long after I'm gone, I want my greetings to still ring in my children's ears and remind them of my forever love.

# # 60 Come on In!

Love is often best communicated in the little things. When your kids drop in on your projects or work unexpectedly, be careful not to respond, "Not now!" That communicates that you put a low value on your relationship with them—especially if they see you respond much more enthusiastically to an unexpected visit from a friend. Lay aside your important work to listen or chat. "Come on in!" is a busy person's way to say "I love you."

# # 61 Hard Truth = Soft Love

It's easy to avoid telling someone a hard truth, especially if you don't care about the relationship or if you care more about looking bad yourself. But when you really love another person, there's always a push to tell the truth. You communicate "I love you" when you tell your kids the hard truth that no one else will. Where else will they hear it? If they do hear it somewhere else, will that person be kind or crush their spirits? If you take the time and tell the truth with compassion, heart to heart, even hard truths translate into really soft love.

# # 62 Survey and Feedback

It communicates "I love you" when you take time to "survey" what's going on in your children's attitudes and feelings about the family. "How do you think things are going in our family? Do you feel respected? Do we need to slow our schedule down?" However they respond, give their opinions full consideration and then give them feedback: "Your thoughts have made an impact on me. Here's what I want to do/be/change." Your children know without a doubt that you've listened to them—carefully! You cared enough to answer. That's love. And they'll know it.

# # 63 Withdrawal

No matter how "tough" you think you are, your kids can pierce you with stinging comments or coldness. Parents are people, too, and the most normal response in the world is to withdraw emotionally in the face of rejection. But fight that impulse to step back when they hurt you! Hold on, and keep communicating "I love you" loud and clear. They may not hear it right away, or even for a long time, but your upside-down response will remain in their hearts and resurface at a future time of change or growth.

# # 64 Cool Truth

You can say "I love you" just by communicating some cool truth about your child's maturing process. When you say, "You know, you're so responsible I'm taking you off the formal chore lists and trusting that you'll just keep on doing a great job," you breathe new life into your relationship. "I trust you" is always a baseline for connection.

# # 65 Neither Rain nor Snow nor Dark of Night . . .

Jim Rohn, a motivational speaker, once said, "Nothing is as lonely as an empty mailbox." Provide your children with their own mailboxes—a box or envelope on a wall or the inside of a door. And then put their mail—unopened, of course—into it. Better yet, send them letters—even if you're home. Tell them how you really feel. Getting a letter that's yours and yours alone is a fun, personal, meaningful experience. Letters can be read and reread, scoured for love and meaning months and years after the date on the postmark.

# # 66 Weave a Web

E-mail is a wonderful way to say "I love you" anytime, day or night. Get an on-line service where each of your children can have their own "mailbox." Then use it to say "I love you." Maybe some midnight when your kids are long asleep, you can sit down for a few quiet minutes and pour out your heart. Lots of parents find it easier to say "I love you" in writing than in spoken words. E-mail is another fabulous tool in the toolbox of connection. Stay on the cutting edge of connection technology, and let your kids hear those wonderful words: "You've got mail!"

# # 67 Paper, Paper Everywhere

In my work with business leaders, I recommend that they leave messages of appreciation at people's desks to be "discovered" when they come back to their desks or in the morning. You can try this with your children, leaving scribbled Post-its or paper-napkin messages on their beds, on their doors, or on the front door to find as they leave. Keep them simple; it's frequency that has a cumulative effect. You'll find it's easy to do it often, since it only takes a few seconds. A lifetime of tiny notes may never stack up in volume to your Sunday newspaper, but it is infinitely more valuable.

# # 68  And for Dessert . . .

Once in a while, make lunch an opportunity to show your love by slipping a quick note into their lunch or backpack. They'll be rummaging around, looking for that dessert, and . . . wham! Some *really* nutritious stuff.

# # 69  A Nose Is Not a Nose

Many children have negative feelings about their physical characteristics. Draw some positive, appreciative attention to their God-given design: "You definitely have my ears—and Dad's mouth. I'm sure those are your grandmother's beautiful eyes." These points of connection tie them to a long heritage. And you can note in a special way something that's uniquely his or her own: "That nose, though, is mysterious. It's just you!"

# # 70  A Reason to Splurge

King David, when offered items to sacrifice, boldly declared, "I insist on paying you for it. I will not sacrifice to the Lord my God burnt offerings that cost me nothing" (2 Sam. 24:24). He knew that real love and devotion cost something. So splurge on a little luxury once in a while. Send your son a telegram. Send your daughter candy or flowers (beat her first big date by being the first to woo her with special treats). Food and clothes and shelter are necessary and good, and they do speak love. But the little extras really impress your children with your extravagant feelings of love for them.

# # 71  Piggy Bank with Holes

Your kids' hearts are like piggy banks that need your daily deposits of love. It's as if the bank has a hole in it that makes it necessary to keep filling it every day. Avoid making big withdrawals (actions that show no love or grace) or too many. Make sure your kids have "money in the bank" every day, a series of deposits that will make them rich.

# # 72  If I Didn't Have You . . .

I once finished this statement to one of my children, "If I didn't have you . . ." by saying, "there would be a huge hole in my heart." Think about how you'd feel without your children. Find your own words, and finish that statement for them.

# Great Questions to Pry Open the Clam

## # 73 Tell-Me-a-Story Questions

Some children are tough as clamshells to open up, but don't give up trying. One approach is to ask questions that require a *narrative* answer—a story or description. Avoid questions that can be answered with simply a yes or no. Instead of asking, "Did you have a good day in school?" try "Who did you hang out with at lunch, and what did you talk about?" The resulting give-and-take becomes a real conversation, not just the appearance of one, and it advances your understanding of your kids.

## # 74 Keep It Relevant—to Them

For a question to be meaningful to your children, it has to be relevant to their interests, not yours. It's way too easy to ask questions just because you want to know the answers instead of asking the questions that open up windows to their souls. The key is to ask yourself, *Do they care about what I'm asking? Will my question grab their interest?* Relevant questions get them talking and show them we're trying to stay in touch with their world.

## # 75 A Day Older and Wiser

Pick a subject, like science, and then ask your child, "What did you learn today that you didn't know yesterday?" You could follow it up with, "How do you think that might apply to your life or future?" If you have more than one child, one answer can get the others going. And if they try to give you the standard "Nothin'," tease them by pretending you'll give them the same answer when they ask what's for dinner.

# # 76 Fascinating Ordinary People

Ask your kids if they learned anything new today about a person—a teacher, a friend, a sibling, a neighbor. "What did you think about that behavior/character trait/previous life experience?" This kind of question gets your kids thinking about people—who they are, what they do and why, what connects with them and what doesn't. And it creates a pattern for them to discuss relationships with you.

# # 77 Negative Possibilities

Sometimes your kids will answer your questions negatively: "School was boring—and so are the teachers, and so are my friends." Don't fall back on the encouragement lecture: "Honey, you've got a lot of interesting subjects. And I thought you liked Mr. Johnson." Instead, follow up with questions that dig deeper: "What's the most boring thing? What could the teacher do to make this more interesting [maybe you could suggest it, politely]. What could you do to make it more interesting for yourself? What is the *least* boring thing?" In this way you don't criticize their statements or feelings, but you encourage them to keep talking to you and thinking of solutions.

# # 78 Sneak Pique

It's great to talk to your kids about your childhood, but often older kids will respond with, "Oh, brother, here we go again!" So pique their interest by posing a question shaped by something that will interest your children: "Do you know what all of the boys in my class did to one boy when he told on them?" Once they're interested, offer a trade. You'll tell your story, if they tell you some school memory or something that made them laugh or made them angry.

# # 79 Change One Thing

Ask your kids, "If you could change just one thing about ...," then name a person or situation. This isn't to encourage griping, but to discover the things your children value—and don't value. As you pay attention to their answers, you'll build up a storehouse of knowledge you can use to help them in future relationships. ("You've always struggled with people who are blunt—are you sure you want to spend that much time with him?")

# # 80 If You Could Change Places

"If you could change places with any person, who would it be? Why? What would you do that first week?" Don't limit the trading field to male or female, old or young, living or dead. Your children's answers will expose their inner character and desired destinies. Ask it again over the years to gain a growing perspective on who your kids are and where they're heading.

## # 81 And If You Couldn't

Most of us feel dislike for some historical or biblical figure. So ask the flip-side question: "Who is the last person you'd want to change places with? Why? Where did he or she go wrong?" You'll discover the character traits that your kids like and dislike. (You might even hear something that leads you to make a few changes in your own habits!)

## # 82 If You Were . . .

Wise leaders make a practice of finding out what's working and what's not in their own leadership style. They ask their own followers. As your children react to their authority figures, good and bad, keep the discussion open. Ask, "If you were your _____ (baby-sitter, teacher, boss, pastor), what would you do differently? How would you lead the group?" This helps your children "walk in another person's shoes," and it helps them think out loud about leadership and personality styles and how best to work with others.

## # 83 In History's Shoes

Choose a topic your child is studying or interested in, and ask a "what if" question about one of the key players. "If you were Lincoln right before the Civil War, what would you do differently? If you were Harry Truman in 1945, would you drop the bomb?" A look into history can be a look into your child, opening up conversations, showing your child's thought processes, building critical thinking skills, and maybe even helping him love history.

## # 84 Take the Family Temperature

Ask your kids what they like best about your family life, and then ask them what they would like to change about the family. It takes some courage to ask this one, but, as a family leader, you need to hear their answers. This dialogue can lead to helpful changes or even to a positive reinvention of your family life.

## # 85 Friendship Questions

Ask a zillion questions about their friends—real or hypothetical: "Who are your three best friends? What do you most like about _____? What are his weak points? How would you describe your ideal friend?" It's important for you to get an inside picture of your kid's relationship values. As you learn what they love and respect in a friend, you can compare and contrast that with your own characteristics. In the future, when you have objections to a certain girlfriend or boyfriend, you've got a friendship litmus test your kids have established for themselves in many conversations with you.

# # 86 Difficult People

The flip side of questions about your children's friends is questions about people they like the least. Or you might ask, "How would you describe the person you would least like to have as your friend?" Again, you've opened conversation on the topic of what's important in a friend, creating a context for discussing future friendships and building your understanding of your child.

# # 87 Best of the Best

*Fortune* magazine produces a list of "most admired" companies that makes for interesting reading. Everyone likes to "look up" to others. Ask your child what he or she admires about certain leaders or organizations and ask, "If you could design a perfect leader or friend, what five character traits would that person have?" Your child's answers highlight values and interests and give you a clue as to what kind of person your child wants to become.

# # 88 What about the Worst?

Kids like to talk about the "stinkers"—the worst behaved, most obnoxious kids in school or the neighborhood. Keeping a spirit of compassion and avoiding lectures, talk to your kids about what's wrong with the behavior of these kids. How do they treat others? How do other kids react to them? As your children discuss these stinkers with you, they're telling you what they don't want to be like themselves. It's great to get an idea of your children's developing character clear in your mind.

# # 89 Antarctica

To get to the root of a problem area in a nonthreatening way, ask the question "If you could get just one _____ (teacher, classmate, coworker) to move to Antarctica, who would it be? Why?" To be honest, all of us have people who come into our lives whom we'd just as soon see disappear. This question can open the way to help you team up with your child to deal with the problem person.

# # 90 See the Past from the Future

It's great to get your kids to "think big" about themselves and about life. Ask them, "Someday when you're gone from this earth, what would you like to be remembered for? What character traits? What accomplishments?" Like the other questions talked about here, ask the question again and again through the years. We appreciate people who get us to "think big" about ourselves and about life. If you have a growing sense of who your kids want to be, you can become their best ally for helping them reach those goals.

# # 91 In the News

Another "think big" question is, "If a magazine ran a feature story on you in five, ten, twenty years, what would the headline read?" If they're interested, get them to write the article and bring it to dinner with the family. As you help them visualize the future, you're pointing the way to positive future choices.

# # 92 A Hard Time

Ask your kids, "Who gives you a hard time, and why? What is that person going after?" This opens a door to the areas where your children have been hurt or felt criticized or pressured. These are deep questions about real-life issues. As you talk with your kids about a subject like this one, you help them think about ways of dealing with difficult people or situations. You help them design an abundant life for themselves instead of just reacting or complaining.

# # 93 Who Are the Bad Guys?

Get courageous and ask, "Who makes you really angry? Why? Do you ever get really angry at me or at someone else in the family?" It's good for your children to acknowledge their anger and great to get these problems out into the open. As you discuss things humbly and genuinely, both of you gain insight and may modify your feelings. As you talk about anger and enemies, you demonstrate that "loving your enemy" doesn't mean having soft, warmhearted feelings about, say, Hitler. The psalmist writes to God, "You hate all who do wrong" (Ps. 5:5). Share their indignation over unjust behaviors; get to the nitty-gritty of real life with your kids. And don't inflict false guilt for being honest and human.

# # 94 Family Fix-It

Ask your kids, "What do you hate most about (school, work, the neighborhood)? Why? How could we try to fix it?" Just talking about it, even if there's no practical action that can be taken, can be a tremendous relief for your children. As you enter into their disappointments, you gain the chance to guide them into possible solutions and show how much you care.

# # 95 The Bright Side

The flip side of what your kids like least is what they like most about work or school or church. As you ask your kids to identify those positives, you teach them to look for what's good and what works. And don't worry if what they like most about school is recess! (I like recess myself.)

# # 96 Understanding versus Misunderstanding

Areas where your children feel misunderstood can leave them secretly brooding or even depressed. So open that door by asking, "When do you feel most misunderstood? Why don't you feel people understand this side of you? What is there about you that you think no one would understand?" Your children, like you, know they can't always be fully themselves around others. Be their ally in helping them clarify their feelings and learn to make themselves better understood.

# # 97 The Usual Suspects

The person who can't describe a criminal can still sometimes pick him out of a lineup. So when your children can't find the words to describe how they feel about something, line up some possibilities. "Does your dance class make you feel challenged? successful? graceful? free?" You can expand their thoughts by providing words and concepts. When you really connect and they respond, "Yes, that's it!" you can move on to even better discussion because you've built a bridge of understanding.

# # 98 One Step Further

Don't give up when you get a token answer or a child doesn't respond by volunteering a lot of information. Take a topic as far and as deep as you can take it. Stick with it. When a child stops offering input, ask a follow-up question; his ideas and feelings on the subject may go deeper. Whenever possible, tie your questions into your relationship or to relationship in general. Don't give up until you're sure your child has gone as far as he can for now.

# # 99 Why Does the Bible Have to Say That?

I've asked my kids, "If you could erase a Bible passage or verse, what would it be? Why?" Their answers have often provided an insight into how God is working in them, challenging them. And it helps them handle their questions and doubts. God is big enough to let us wrestle with him like Jacob and argue with him like Job and negotiate with him like Abraham and Moses. Come up with an answer yourself: Which parts do you find most difficult to deal with?

# # 100 Get Specific

If we want to open the clamshell, we've got to get into the details of their lives. Instead of asking, "How's school going?" try, "What did you do in third period history with Ms. _____?" It's in the details that you'll learn about how your children's lives are being lived. The better acquainted you are with the details of their lives, the better your ability to ask good, incisive questions. For reference, I keep a copy of my kids' school schedules in my file so I can keep mental track of where they are and what they're doing during the day. Love, as well as understanding, is in the details.

# # 101 Straight Talk—and Other Approaches

Sex must be an interesting topic, or so many books and movies wouldn't highlight it. Then again, maybe the media can exploit the topic because few parents talk about it enough while children are growing up. But parents need not be ashamed to talk about what God wasn't ashamed to create. Come at the topic straightforwardly ("What do you know about sex?") or qualitatively ("What's good about how people talk about and portray sex? What's bad?") or in a way that prompts analysis ("Why do you think our culture is so obsessed with sex?") Your kids are thinking about sex. The question is, Will you ask them what they're thinking?

# # 102 Deeper Levels of a Private Subject

Dig into the topic of sex by taking it through multiple levels. Level one: "What are the kids at school (or in the neighborhood) saying about sex?" Level two: "What do you think about that?" Level three: "How does that make you feel?" Level four: "What do you want to know about that they haven't told you or you don't understand?" Level five: "How do you think this knowledge should be applied in relationships?"

Sex is an intimate topic, and your kids will feel closer to you, the one who was able to connect with them deeply on this private issue.

# # 103 Not Just Any Body

Most of us find something to dislike about the way God designed our physical bodies. Children's feelings about their bodies are often magnified, partly because they're changing so much, partly because other children can be brutally critical, and partly because aspects of their bodies *can* look funny, especially when they're growing fast and unevenly. So the question for an older child is, "If you could change just one of your physical features, which would it be? Why?" If it's fixable (like crooked teeth), you can move ahead into loving action. If it isn't, you might help a child accept and even appreciate the offensive feature. Share what you've learned yourself through the years as you came to accept God's design of you.

# # 104 Can I Help You?

Benjamin Zander, conductor of the Boston Philharmonic, tells a story about his father, who was in his nineties and dying. Zander's brother walked into the room and greeted the blind and incapacitated man. His father's response was beautiful: "What can I do to help you?" His character was there to the end, showing this father to be a servant leader, others-centered, compassionate. Ask your children the same question, and wait quietly for the answer.

# # 105 Desert Island

For a fun conversation opener, ask your child, "If you were trapped on a desert island for a year and could have only one kind of food or drink with you, what would it be? Why? What would you definitely *not* want there?" Maybe get the child to brainstorm his or her "top ten." A follow-up question might be, "If you could have only one other person on that island, who would you choose? Why?"

# # 106 The Best Memories

You'll grow closer to a child if you can share in bringing positive memories to life. Ask, "What was your most memorable birthday (or holiday or family vacation)? Get your child to describe the memory in as much detail as possible. If you were there, share your memory of this child at that time. Living memories build living ties.

# # 107 Defining Moments

Life is like a long trip with lots of miles going by that you can't remember, but it is marked by interesting sights, milestones, and stops along the way.

Give your kids an example of some defining moments from your own "life journey" (I remember how I felt when my brother Johnny broke my prized drum set) and describe them in detail. Then go back through their years, chronologically perhaps, and ask what their milestones were.

# # 108 Ultimate Highs, Devastating Lows

As you discuss your child's milestone moments in life, remember to ask about times of intense emotion: "What was the highest moment of your life? the lowest?" These "extreme" experiences will provide clues about what moves your child deeply—what he or she cares about the most.

# # 109 Beautiful versus Ugly

Making value judgments together gets you talking and learning together about what is valuable and how to value. Ask, "What is the most beautiful thing you have ever seen?" And, on the other end of the scale: "What is the ugliest thing you have ever seen?" The goal is not to judge but rather to learn how each other thinks. Take the conversation further, and get your children to list their "top five" beautiful or ugly things.

# # 110 Smart Stuff

We can dig into the issue of savvy. "What's the smartest thing you've ever done? The smartest thing you've ever seen anyone else do?" As you discover what your children consider "smart" in themselves and others, you get to the heart of what they value.

# # 111 Dumb Stuff, Too

You get a conversation full of insight and laughter by asking this question: "What's the dumbest thing you've ever done?" (You could get this dialogue rolling by sharing some disaster of your own.) "What's the dumbest thing you've ever seen anyone else do?" The goal is to crawl inside the evaluation system of your children and into frail humanity.

# # 112 Seeing Red

For insight into your children's personalities, find out what makes them the angriest. If a child's answers are all self-related (personal mistreatments, insults, being misjudged, etc.), the child is overly self-conscious and possibly self-centered. You can subtly counteract such a personality trend by helping the child consider the feelings and needs of others around him or her. You can't connect with a narcissist.

# # 113 Likable You

Dig into the souls of your children by asking: "What are your three most likable traits? Why do you think people would like you for these?" It's illuminating to discover what your kids think about the world's "take" on them.

# # 114 And Less Likable You

It's equally important to discuss your children's ideas of their three least likable traits. Ask, "How do you think these problem areas might cause people to react to you?" Be prepared to get this conversation started by asking first: What are your own three least likable traits? Ouch!

# # 115 A Time to Laugh

Ask, "What makes you laugh the most—jokes with friends, a certain TV show, a kind of movie? What makes it so funny to you?" The old saying about laughter being great medicine is true, especially in a pretty frustrating world. Once you know what makes your kids laugh, you can fill a future "prescription" of that particular medicine. Knowing how to make children laugh is a brilliant point of connection.

# # 116 And a Time to Cry

When you know what makes your children cry, you've gotten deep into the heart of who they are. There are ways to approach the subject. Try asking, "What makes you cry when you're watching a movie? What makes you the saddest about other people?" Share your own feelings with your kids. Let them know that sadness and grief are a valid and valuable part of their lives—and that you're not embarrassed by their tears.

# # 117 Could You Give It Up?

What a person clings to the most is a good indication about what is going on in his or her soul. So ask each child, "What would you have the hardest time giving up if God asked for it?"

# # 118 Plans and Dreams

What are your kids thinking about? dreaming about? Ask your older children, "What's one thing you want most to do in the next five years?" Then ask the questions that can help them fit workable goals to those dreams: "How will you spend time on that? What can I do to help you make it happen?" Kids can't resist connection with a parent who knows their dreams—and will go all out to help them achieve them. Soon enough, they'll see that their dreams are your dreams, too.

# # 119 Big Ideas

All young people appreciate the challengers and mentors who help them "think big" about themselves and their future. So ask your child, "What's the greatest thing you'd try if you knew you couldn't fail?" Then talk together about what would have to happen in order for him or her to give it a try.

# # 120 Twenty-Six Hours a Day?

These days all family members—young or old—tend to get really, really busy. But that doesn't mean they're passing the time with activities that matter the most to them. Ask your kids, "If you had two extra hours a day to spend on something you're not doing now, what would it be?" Think about the question yourself, so you can have a great dialogue. Who knows? It could even result in actual changes in the way you spend your time.

# # 121 Who's Our Neighbor?

Together with your kids, read the story of the Good Samaritan, and then ask, "Who do you think is our neighbor? Who could we help? What could we do together to help them?" Real bonding comes as you discover things you can do together that neither of you could have or would have done alone.

# # 122 Heartfelt Conviction

Personal convictions are a touchstone of character. Many children have convictions about which their parents are unaware. So ask your kids, "Which of your beliefs are you most comfortable talking about? Why is it easy? How about the most uncomfortable?" You're dealing with the real, deep-down person when you deal with their convictions.

# # 123 Research Your Thoughts—and Theirs

The thoughts that dominate your consciousness tell who you really are and who you are becoming. Ask your kids, "What do you think about the most?" It might help to make ballpark estimates of percentages of the time a child spends with certain thoughts. For example, Thinking about School—40 percent, Daydreaming about the Future—20 percent, Pondering the Opposite Sex—25 percent, etc. This can create a whole new area of discussion: Are these percentages OK, or would your child like to work at disciplining her thought life to increase some areas of thinking and decrease others? This is a great way to work together at thinking about "whatever is true ... noble ... right ... pure ... lovely ... admirable ... excellent or praiseworthy" (Phil. 4:8).

# # 124 Believing

Everyone wrestles with doubts about spiritual realities. Talk with your kids about their doubts: "Which of our teachings or our church's is hardest for you to believe?" As they understand that it's OK to think out loud about their doubts, they'll understand that they're no longer struggling alone—you're in it with them.

# # 125 What Do They Think of You?

Don't worry and wonder, "She loves me, she loves me not." Occasionally it clears the air to get straight to the heart of who you are in this relationship. Ask a child, "What do you think of when you think of me?" It can be a bit awkward at first, but if you can hang in there past the discomfort, you'll generate relationship-changing input.

# # 126 Fishing for Adjectives

One way to discover how your children are thinking about you would be to ask for describing words: "When you think of me, what's the first word that comes to your mind?" You might be pleasantly surprised—or unpleasantly disappointed (maybe you're hoping for "caring" or "brilliant" and you get "demanding" or "nitpicking"), but either way you're collecting construction materials for your relationship.

# # 127 Me and You

You can also get straight to the heart of the "us" in your relationship. Ask your child, "What do you think of when you think of us?" The key is to wait for the answer. Then, after you've gotten something real, you can ask, "Why?" This may lead to a discussion of memories, of past times together, good and bad. This is a beautiful way to discover how your child sees the tapestry of your relationship.

# # 128 Mental Exercise

Ask your child to come up with a quick mental essay: twenty-five words or less on the subject "Who We Are." The tight word count forces him or her to boil your relationship down to its essence, with fascinating results.

# # 129 On a Scale of One to Ten

Ask your child to rate herself on a "How much do you like yourself?" scale. Often it's amazing to discover a low sense of self-worth in a person you love so very much. Listen carefully, without judging. Then ask, "What do you think would help increase your rating? How can I help?"

# # 130 Giving Courage

Encouragement can be hard to come by in a down-and-dirty world. Ask your child, "What are the ways people—friends, teachers, pastors, family members—have encouraged you in the last month? What did you like about the way they did it? How could I encourage you more?" Encouragement is a gift your kids can have—every time you choose to give it.

# # 131 Me versus You

Find out what your children perceive as the biggest disagreements the two of you have ever had. Ask why they think you had the disagreements. Talk about what each of you contributed to the disagreement. Ask, "How did that make you feel?" As you discover where the "sore points" are, you can slowly work toward healing—and toward avoiding those same holes in the road.

# # 132 Conflict Resolution

There are many approaches to resolving conflicts: cooling-off periods, give-and-take discussions, negotiation, mediation by a friend or pastor. Go ahead and ask your older children directly which seem to work best for them. Then do your best to resolve conflict using their preferred method, which removes tension and allows you to focus on binding up wounds.

# # 133 Listen to the Small Stuff

When your kids start talking to you—even if it's about trivial topics—keep 'em at it: "What else happened? Tell me more!" Your simple interest and encouragement convince them that even their smallest thoughts and feelings are safe with you. "Because you have been trustworthy in a very small matter," said Jesus, "take charge of ten cities" (Luke 19:17). Or one heart.

# # 134 Accept Their Gifts

When your children talk to you and answer your questions, treat their ideas and feelings like gifts—and say thanks: "I'm so honored that you'd tell me that, that you'd trust me with your deepest thoughts." They'll want to give you more.

# # 135 Brainstorming Eternity

Seeing the end in great detail can make "now" seem even more meaningful. Talk about spending eternity in heaven with God. Ask your kids, "What do you think we'll do together in heaven? What would you like to do?"

# # 136 This Life in Perspective

Talking about heaven, the "afterlife," with your kids can give it wonderful reality—and it puts life on this earth into perspective. So have fun with your dreams of what heaven might be like. Ask, "If you could have any job when you get to heaven, what would it be? Who in history do you want to have dinner with? What do you want your home to look like?" It's *new* life, not afterlife.

# # 137 Connection versus Correction

Connecting requires real vulnerability. To ask these deep questions, you have to take the lead, giving answers yourself and exposing your own doubts and failings. Beyond vulnerability, it takes loving self-discipline not to critique or edit your children's answers once they begin to share themselves with you. Remember, your agenda is connection, not correction. Avoid the sound of a door, slamming shut.

# # 138 What Will You Do?

Put your kids in *your* shoes: "What will you do differently as a parent from what I'm doing? What will you do to connect with your children? How will you make sure they know you love them?" Trying to answer these questions can bring them closer to you—and their answers can give you pretty good clues about how to get the job done with them.

# # 139 Good, Better, Best

You can spur your kids to greatness—now. Help them think idealistically: "How can you make the world a better place—even now, at your age?" If they need ideas, be prepared to offer small steps they can take right where they are (pick up litter in the park when they see it, replace the toilet roll when it's empty). As they begin to see themselves as difference-makers, their idealism will be elevated to greater acts of service. They'll feel good about their service—and about you, the one who inspired it.

# # 140 Great Kids

You see their potential. Share their big dreams for themselves. Ask, "What do you think being great would be like? feel like?" Then, "What can I do to help make you great?" Your support and drive to see them fulfill their potential is irresistible to them. And you will be too.

# 4
# Something to Talk About

# # 141 That's Not Fair!

Even very young children have a keenly developed sense of what's fair. A concern for justice is not something you need to implant in your child—it's already there. So make it work for opening conversation between you and your child. You can wait until you hear the inevitable "That's not fair!" or you can describe a scenario and ask for your child's reaction. The search for justice—or injustice and the eventual return of justice—is a theme that resonates throughout history. Bond with your son or daughter by digging into justice deeply and finding its treasure together.

# # 142 Reality versus Illusion

If you take time to explore illusion and deception with your children, you'll build your relationship as well as hand them a skill that's critical for living well: discernment. Max DePree once wrote, "The number one job of a leader is to define reality" (*Leadership Is an Art*, Bantam, 1990). Start by talking about simple illusions, like optical illusions: "How much taller do you think the St. Louis Gateway Arch is than it is wide?" As it turns out, both dimensions are exactly the same, although it doesn't look that way in a picture or in person. As they get older, your kids can discuss with you the illusions people create. All of us, to some degree, are reality-impaired—our perceptions don't align with reality. Developing alignment together can be a wonderful adventure (see my leadership book *Fatal Illusions*, AMACOM Books, 1997).

# # 143 Contradictions

Your kids are noticing the many contradictions in life around them—maybe in church life or politics, maybe in the way two Scriptures seem to teach opposite viewpoints, maybe in their social interactions. If it feels uncomfortable to talk about these contradictions, we can avoid them, but you can provoke some interesting conversation by openly discussing the contradictions your children are observing. Tell them about the ones you note, instead of sweeping them under the carpet. As you build a bridge to their hearts by talking with them, you're also modeling for your children an honest way of wrestling with events and ideas.

# # 144 Separate or Salt?

Should you as a family be separate from secular culture, protecting yourselves from danger and temptations? Or should you be salt in the culture, staying involved so that your Spirit-led choices make an impact? The answer to both questions is yes, which opens the door to wide areas of discussion: When should you be salt? When should you be separate? Is it back and forth, or is it both at the same time? Working out the gray areas of this topic will bring richness and maturity to your family and its relationships.

# # 145 Eyes Wide Open or Closed Tight?

How do you guard your heart, yet at the same time remain open to new experiences? When is it best to open your eyes, and when should you shut them? When is it best to dig into a situation, and when is it better to run away? Your kids will gain discernment by talking with you about making wise choices in complex situations. Talk with them about the futility of a closed mind, yet the danger of keeping it so fully open that it becomes an "open sewer." Your kids will someday be adults grappling with life around them. Talking about choices and various scenarios will help your kids become both interesting and moral, street-smart and innocent, savvy and realistic.

# # 146 Respect for Authority versus Mindless Obedience

"Any fool can make a rule, and every fool will mind it," said Henry David Thoreau. Our kids need to respect those in authority over them—just as we all do. But how can they strike a balance between healthy respect for authority and healthy disrespect for foolish, stupid, or wrong authority? This is a highly nuanced topic, but it will delight you to see your children rise to the challenge of discussing these ideas. Put the questions in terms of history ("How do you think blind obedience played a role in creating the horror of Nazi death camps?") or present-day realities ("Given a certain situation, would you do what your boss tells you, or would you report him to his supervisor?"). Deal with the moral questions of responding to authority so that your kids don't end up "making it up as they go along."

# # 147 What Is Forgiveness Anyway?

Don't let your kids be satisfied by surface platitudes about forgiveness; the topic is too important, too foundational. Talk with them about handling wrongdoing when actions have been taken against them. Should they confront it? ignore it? forgive it? Forgiveness is a complex subject; you won't mine it quickly or easily. Ask your kids, "Is it even possible to 'forgive and forget'?" (this amply distributed advice is not even found in the Bible). Ask, "Do we have to forgive when the person who has done wrong isn't even sorry?" (see Luke 17:3). The real wrestling you do with this topic, avoiding the platitudes, will pay off in your family life and in every relationship of your child's future.

# # 148 Good or Evil?

Another rich topic to discuss with your kids is human nature: Is humanity basically good or basically evil? Popular culture often seems to argue that we all start out good but circumstances make us bad. But where did those "bad circumstances" come from? On the other hand, if we're all sinful from the day we're born, how does that jibe with the teaching in Genesis that human beings are created in the image and likeness of God? Could people actually be *both?* This is another topic that won't run dry—whole religions and denominations have been built around the answers to these questions. Dive in!

# # 149 When We All Get to Heaven

Talk about heaven with your children. Is it just wishful thinking on the part of people who are scared to die, or is it real? Bone up on Scripture yourself so that you will be prepared to talk about the subject with your child. Discuss what you both imagine heaven will be like, whether you'll know each other there, what you might do, and in what ways it will be different or similar to life on earth. Encourage creativity in imagining out loud what your extended life with God will be like.

# # 150 What about Hell?

If heaven is real, what about hell? Does the punishment really go on forever? A discussion of eternal punishment can lead you and your child directly into a discussion about God's character: If God is gracious and compassionate, why does he allow eternal suffering and punishment in hell? This is important stuff, so don't dish out quick, flip, dogmatic answers here. Explore the truth—together—with your child.

# # 151 Are Things Evil?

Good versus evil is the drama that makes the world go around, so it makes wonderful conversation material. Talk with your kids about the nature of evil. Can things be inherently evil, or are things neutral until people use them for good or evil? The various media make solid examples: TV, movies, the Internet, certain magazines. Discussing the nature of evil can take you and your children into the topic of what it means, really, to be human.

# # 152 Fate or Freedom?

Is everything that happens to us in life predetermined—all of it fate or destiny? Or is there variability because of our freedom to choose? Is the "end" all predestined, or is it open-ended? Does God decide everything, or do people? The answers your children settle on will create a foundation for their own future lifestyle, establishing how or if they pray, how they'll respond to pain and crises, and whether they'll lean toward being proactive, reactive, or inactive. Build a connection at this foundational level!

# # 153 Principle or Practice?

Are there principles to live by? What are they? Where do we find them? How do we apply them? Is everything black and white? Or are there some areas of gray? Which are the immovable principles, and which are flexible practices or opinions? Explore this topic together, and build your relationship on true principles and flexible practices.

# # 154 Sharing Beliefs

What is the best way for believers to share their faith and beliefs with others? What are the worst, or offensive, ways? Talk with your children about how to connect with people when discussing beliefs. As you talk with them, they'll be honing their own skills. You should see them becoming more reasonable and "connected" as they think out loud with you about their beliefs.

# # 155 The Case for Singleness

Is singleness a phase, just a stage on the way to marital bliss, or does God particularly value singleness? God starts everyone out single, so he must think it's a good option. Talk with your kids about singleness. What are they supposed to do with it? How will they use it wisely? Start this discussion as early as possible; it takes some of the pressure off the dating/marriage scene, and it will promote the best use of their years (however many) of singleness.

# # 156 Bad Reasons to Get Married

Talking about marriage always promotes lively interaction. Brainstorm with your kids all the lousy reasons why people get married. They'll have their own ideas, from couples they've seen or from their own amazing insights. It may feel like an absurd way to come at the subject, but it drives them to real-life thinking and to second questions. ("If people marry for so many bad reasons, should it be harder to get married?" or "If there are lots of bad marriages, should it be hard or easy to get divorced?") Keep 'em talking with you on this most interesting subject.

# # 157 Don't Marry That One!

Change the angle of discussion about marriage. Ask your kids, "What kinds of people should we avoid marrying? What are their characteristics? How will we identify them? What will happen to us if we get involved with them?" Exploring life through this reality-lens can broaden their perspective and give them a healthy fear.

# # 158 The One

There's another, related marriage topic. How will your kids know when they've found "the one"? Create a great conversation discussing whether there is only one Ms. or Mr. Right or whether they could successfully marry almost anybody if they have good preparation and relationship skills. Talk about how it happens—is it magic? logic? Are there right or wrong ways to meet, fall in love, and marry? Keep talking about this topic at different ages and stages with your kids—you'll never exhaust the subject!

# # 159 Relationship Lab

Consider the people and relationships around you to be a "learning lab" where you and your kids can dissect together the friendships, marriages, and families with which you're both familiar. The goal is to unite around some ideas of what really makes good and bad relationships. Be careful not to misjudge or slander others, but caution shouldn't keep you from looking together for truth about relationships.

# # 160 Family Evaluation

Be courageous and turn the "learning lab" microscope onto your own family. Getting your kids' view on how things are going will clear away the illusions. Ask them, "How do you think our family is doing? What are our strong points? weak points? What are our biggest problems? What could we do to change them? What are you bringing to the mix—good and bad? What am I contributing—good or bad?"

# # 161 People to Avoid—Period

Here's a "hot topic": What people should we avoid? Christians can disagree on whether it's ever right to do this, but I once dug into Scripture and came up with thirty-eight types of problem people we're instructed to avoid. You could have a general discussion on this subject or make it a family Bible dig—searching for those people types to avoid.

# # 162 Money

Your home is the perfect environment for your kids to learn about one of the key issues of life: the handling of money. There are numerous topics here: How should we get money? How should we spend it? Do we give until it hurts, or do we give until it feels good? Is money evil or just the love of it? How do we find the balance between a "poverty" mentality and materialistic greed? Connected parents can clear away their children's confusion about money.

# # 163 Economics 101

Along with talking about money, try discussing the economy. Although called the "dismal science," and may in fact be more art than science (U.S. President Harry Truman once said that if you lined up all the economists in a row, they wouldn't make a straight line), the economy is "where we live" every day. How does it work? How *should* it work? Why do some systems produce good results for many, while others seem bent on waste and destruction? How can we profit from our knowledge? Join hands and go on a voyage of discovery.

# # 164 The Lifestyle Tour

Take the kids to various places where people live differently—ethnic neighborhoods, rich or poor neighborhoods, crime-ridden or virtually crime-free neighborhoods, areas of dynamic growth or of decay. Talk about the people who live there, and ask, "Why do you think they live this way? What are their values? Would you like or dislike living in this area? Why?" The "tour" will be enjoyable and will broaden your children's perspectives; even better, it will help your children solidify their own values.

# # 165 Great Leaders

Your kids can learn a lot by analyzing the people history has called "great." So pick a great person and dig in. Was Prime Minister Winston Churchill a defender of freedom or a stalwart of imperialism? Was the Russian czar Peter the Great actually great, or was he a lunatic? What about Jesus? Was he who he said he was? How can you know?

# # 166 The Music Connection

Music has always been a continental divide in the generation gap. Kids think their parents' music sounds hokey and dated; parents think their kids' music sounds obnoxious and incomprehensible. Bridge the gap—to your relationship's advantage. It's more important than you may think because music has a way of speaking to the soul of a young person, sometimes helping them express feelings and thoughts when they don't have the words. Try to understand their music; even try to *enjoy* it. It helps to find out what it means to them, so ask: "What do you like about this song? How does this music make you feel?" Remember that, odd as their music may seem to your ears, some of the popular stuff from past decades was pretty strange, too. Remember "The Flying Purple People-Eater"?

# # 167 Wave That Magic Wand

Get creative in unleashing your kids' imaginations. Ask, "What would you do if you had a magic wand?" Be prepared to offer your ideas of what you'd do: "I'd make self-cleaning dishes. I'd declare that Mondays wouldn't start until noon. I'd make all the traffic lights turn green as I approached." Have fun with this! Enjoy observing your children's sense of humor; you may even get a real glimpse of closely held hopes or dreams.

# # 168 If You Had a Flying Carpet

Get your kids thinking about the great big world: "If you had a flying carpet, where would you go?" For help, investigate with a map or globe. Explore the places your children choose by getting books and pictures and videos. Check them out together—sitting on a carpet, of course.

# # 169 Get Hysterical

Discuss your own most hysterically funny moments—then those of your family. Think about the craziest thing you've ever heard about. And then ask your kids, "What about you? What are your funniest moments?" Humor opens a door to fellowship with your kids.

# # 170 Better Than the Birds and Bees

When your kids are old enough, don't hesitate to talk with them openly about sex. Discuss whether sex is good or bad in itself, about whether it can be used for good or for bad, about whether it should be a duty or a pleasurable pastime of play and exploration. Though Hollywood would like to dominate this subject, it was really God's wonderful idea. Don't let this topic get overnourished everywhere else and undernourished inside your home.

# # 171 Afraid of What?

Scary stories have been around forever, and scary books and movies abound. How come? Because fear is an endemic part of life. Fear is a common human emotion that unites us—we're all afraid of something. Get your kids talking about the things that scare them the most. They'll find security in knowing that you know and care—and can help to protect them or help them handle their fear.

# # 172 Good-Bye, Comfort Zone

Find out the things your kids consider risky by asking, "What would you like to do but would be uncomfortable trying? What would encourage you to take the risk?" Help them analyze themselves by asking, "Do you see yourself as a risk taker? At what times and in what situations?" As you discover their self-imposed limitations, you can lovingly help them break free and step outside that comfort zone.

# # 173 The Whole Truth and Nothing But the Truth?

Talk with your kids about honesty. What is it? Do they always have to be completely honest? What if their honesty would hurt other people? Should they always tell others exactly what they think? Could people be honest with bad motives? Let the conversation get personal: "What makes it hard to be honest about yourself? Do you think it's good to keep some things private or secret?" Honesty is a virtue but one with many facets. Come to an agreement about what honesty is, and you'll open avenues of understanding between you.

# # 174 God's Searchlight in the Soul

Discuss "conscience" with your kids. What exactly is it, and how does it work? What is a clear conscience as opposed to a guilty one? Is a conscience always a trustworthy guide? Discuss the possibility of false guilt and bogus hangups. Discuss the possibility of a conscience that becomes numb or is even killed. *Conscience* is a word that's often bandied about without careful definition. Delve into the concept with your kids.

# # 175 Approval: Gains and Losses

It's so basically human to crave the approval of others. Help your kids think about the intricacies of gaining or losing approval. Do they really have to have it? How far should they go to gain or keep someone's approval? Is it always their fault if they lose a person's approval? Is it ever good to lose someone's approval? Take a lot of time, and listen carefully on this one.

# # 176 R-E-S-P-E-C-T

Respect—find out what it means to your kids because this is a crucial subject. People of all ages, races, and nations can find themselves disagreeing or even fighting because they feel disrespected. So what is respect? How is it gained? What takes it away? Discuss this with your kids. Do they have to respect everyone? How do they gain respect in their lives at school? How should they show others respect? Step up to dignity together.

# # 177 The Powerful Tongue

Explore together how people use their tongues to build up and tear down. Analyze gossip (saying things behind people's backs that you'd never say to their faces) and flattery (saying things to their faces that you would never say behind their backs). Talk about encouragement. Discuss what kinds of words lift people up and what kinds bury them. In this conversation, you will see your friends, and relatives, and schoolmates, and neighbors—and possibly yourself.

# # 178 Family Vision

Discuss often and in great detail what you all think your vision of the family is and should be. Ask, "What is our family like? What's best about us? What's worst? How can we use our strengths? What can we do to make a difference?" Talk about how you might become great. In the glow of a distant vision, you'll see each other's faces more clearly.

# # 179 Low on the Totem Pole

They say a society is judged by how it treats its weakest members. Talk about this idea with your kids: "How is our society treating the helpless? the homeless? orphans? widows? the elderly? babies? disabled people? people who are just "different"? Make it personal: "How are *we* treating them?" This can sensitize your children to those who are fragile and help them appreciate their own fragility—and yours. We really do need each other.

# # 180 Value of Life

With all the social commentary these days on cloning, fetal research, euthanasia, and other topics, it shouldn't be hard to broach the subject of what life is worth. Ask your kids what they think. "Is human life an accident or a purposeful creation? Are humans animals or the greatest of God's creations?" Connect over these foundational issues.

# # 181 Purpose of Life

While you're on the subject of what life is worth, consider what its purpose is. Bring it up with your kids by asking, "Do you think the purpose of life is to have fun or to serve God? Could it possibly be both? Could you have fun serving God?" You talk about these issues now—your kids will live them for decades.

# # 182 Daydreams and Nightmares

Dreams can launch you and your kids into a myriad of interesting conversations. Ask them, "What's the scariest dream you've ever had? the most colorful? the most triumphant?" Or try, "What do you daydream about when you're supposed to be studying math?"

# # 183 Play-by-Play

Do your kids' biographies in play-by-play, third-person narration: "And then Jim heroically overcame the unrequited love of Sherry and went on to …" Then let them do yours. The exercise encourages both of you to see life as an unfolding adventure and to avoid taking every disappointment too seriously. You'll laugh as you gain perspective. It's your history in the making.

# 5
## Sharing Your Personal Story

## # 184 Ancestor Stories

Other cultures do better than we Americans do at helping their children
see themselves in context. Maybe we've thrown out the baby with the
bathwater—we so carefully avoid worshiping ancestors, we completely
ignore them. But God very deliberately places children in families—in
families that stretch back to a distant horizon. Talk about your ancestry
with your kids. Who were these people? What good and bad things did
they do? Brainstorm with your kids how the actions of those earlier
generations affect your family today. Is there anything you can learn
from their successes or mistakes? Family ties you together—keep
building on that connection.

## # 185 Happy Days

Hearing about what you did as a child—hearing that you even *were* a
child—can bond your kids to you. As they identify with your experiences
and feelings, they will come to understand that you can identify with
theirs. So tell them what you liked to play, where you liked to go, who you
played with, and what those friends were like.

## # 186 I Disobeyed, Too

One day when I was about five, I went, against my father's orders, into the
alley behind our house. I walked about three or four houses away until I
was next to a free-standing garage. A couple of big kids jumped me and
locked me in the garage. It felt as if I were in there for about two weeks.
Somehow, I managed to get out. As I ran toward home, I saw my dad
standing by the gate with a strap. That's when I learned that sometimes

there is more than one consequence for disobedience. My kids loved to
hear that story. They could relate to it. It made me and life more real.
Years later, they were delighted when we found that old garage. Through
that story, it belonged to their history and memory as much as it did to
mine.

# # 187 Tales of Terror

My kids' eyes nearly bugged out when I told them how I'd nearly been
kidnapped. One winter evening when it had gotten dark early, a friend
and I were standing by the road when suddenly a car screeched to a stop
in front of us. A huge man leaped out of the backseat and tried to force
me into the car. I resisted—even harder when I saw a gun lying on the
seat. He knocked my glasses off, breaking them and cutting my forehead.
Finally, the driver of the car hollered at him to go, and they sped away. I
didn't know it then, but as I told the story to my kids I could convey to
them that this was a crossroads for me. I could have been hurt badly or
killed. My children saw it, too, and felt a reverence for God's provision
and deliverance from evil in that moment in time.

# # 188 Wounds That Cut Deep

The world is full of people who will trash our heart, return evil for good,
and throw away our friendship. Your kids need to know that betrayal
cuts deep, that you understand what being betrayed feels like, and what
to watch out for—and they need to know they can survive it, just as you
did. For me, the sting of betrayal by two "friends" in sixth grade is still
painfully sharp in memory. Tell your kids a similar true story from your
past, letting your kids climb inside your hurt. Your bond with them will
grow tighter.

# # 189 Temptation Tales

Your children can learn, from you, that temptations are a reality and that
a tendency to fall into temptation is part of who they are as human
beings. Without giving too many gory details but providing broad strokes,
you can forewarn your kids and help them be prepared to deal with
temptation by telling them true stories of when it happened to you. I've
told my children about the cousin who first showed me pornography—
about the mixed feelings it raised and the battle for my mind it started.
Your kids will learn from your experiences.

# # 190 Stories in Your Scars

Few children escape childhood without one or two physical scars to show for it. These make great fodder for conversations and for building your children's compassion for you. The surgery, the fall, the cut, the repaired tooth—they all have a story. Let your stories become your kids'.

# # 191 Respect the Past

Even if your childhood was troubled, be careful not to express continual contempt for your past. Not only will that produce self-contempt in you, it will alienate your kids from your family, their history, and even from you. Find a workable combination of truth and respect for the past, and it will yield your children's respect for you. The more links to the past that you share, the stronger your connection with your children.

# # 192 Sing a Song

Every family has songs that just seem to belong to them. My Irish grandfather used to sing "Won't You Come Over to My House?" and "School Days," and I remember my German grandmother singing "Polly Wolly Doodle." Their voices and their personalities still ring in my memory decades after they've passed away. Those songs are like magical superglue for bonding kids to family; they're heirlooms to pass along. If you can't remember any songs from your own family history, get started on some songs for the family you're growing now. Every time your kids sing them to your grandchildren, it'll renew their bond with you all over again.

# # 193 Pet Names

'Fess up and tell your kids all the nicknames you were called as a child; they'll love it. One grandparent used to call me "Snicklefritz," and another regularly referred to me as a "pistol." Think back and remember the pet names your parents and relatives had for you. Have you been using them on your kids? Laugh together about all the funny or loving names that have been part of your history.

# # 194 Real Places

Many years after my father's death, I went back to St. Louis with my two sons. We went in search of a place from my memory: a hill under a big tree, where my dad and I had lain and lazily watched a crew resurface a street leading into a park. When we found it, the scene was much as I remembered it. I sat under the same tree with my sons and described that long-ago day, feeling the thread of connection weaving from my father through me and into my boys. Don't underestimate the power of place.

# # 195 Memories

Get out the photo albums if you've got them; but with or without pictures, take the time to describe your memories—the good times, the times when God laid his hand on your life. You'll be amazed at how your kids listen, spellbound.

# # 196 Hearts of Flesh

Think back to events or times that made you laugh or cry, and talk about those experiences with your children. As they grapple with their own ever-changing feelings, it will encourage them to see that you also have a heart of flesh and not a heart of stone (Ezek. 11:19). This is crucial, because they can't fall in love with a rock.

# # 197 Necessary Grief

No matter how much joy we find in life, there are always losses that can and should be grieved. Take your kids back to a time when you experienced a loss—a job, money, a reputation, a loved one—and lead your children through your sorrow. In this way, your children learn that grief needn't be hidden or kept as a secret worry. As they realize you've cried, been angry, rallied, and grown, they'll be prepared to grieve themselves. And they'll love you more for showing them the way.

# # 198 Bringing Work Home

Many parents shield their children from their experiences, not wanting to burden their home life with the challenges of their work life. Resist this impulse! Don't shield your kids from valuable insight, and don't shield them from being close to the whole you. Let them see God's hand moving in your work and ministry. Your experiences are valuable, but only if you transplant them into your children's hearts.

# # 199 "V" Is for Victory

"My dad can beat up your dad" is typically spoken contemptuously, but the idea behind it isn't so bad. Kids like to know their parents are strong. So your victories are their victories. Share your experiences of triumph or success, and let your kids feel strong because they're connected to a strong family.

# # 200 Whoops!

Your kids will love to hear about your goof-ups. Your failures become a bonding agent because it's a lot easier for your child to connect with someone who is human and fallible (like they are) than to relate to SuperMom and Perfecto-Dad. As you remember your past mistakes, you're letting your kids know they don't have to be perfect, that mistakes aren't fatal, that they can learn from mistakes and laugh about them. All in all, kids think parents who make mistakes and live to tell about them are pretty cool.

# # 201 True Confessions

Perhaps you're reluctant to talk about your personal temptations, as if you're the first person ever to struggle with jealousy or lust or discontent. But if you never talk about these temptations, your children will feel that you're far off on some mountaintop, not down here where they live, where real life happens. If they can never see you handle temptation, they'll feel isolated and weird when they experience temptation themselves, and they may never learn to handle it. Without sharing unneccesary detail, you can show your kids you've been fighting in the very same fight for self-control.

# # 202 At Your Worst

Though there are some things you shouldn't talk about and some details you should leave out of what you do talk about, you'll build relationship with your children by letting them see you at your worst—and see you forgiven and making restitution. When I was a teenager, before today's tight airport security, a friend and I simply walked onto some flights without purchasing tickets. The day I described this to my children, their eyes got bigger and bigger; somehow, so did their perspective of me. That's because I told them that later, as an adult, I went to the offices of that airline and paid for all the flights plus interest. I told my kids about the overwhelmingly positive reaction of the airline executive I met that day. I let my kids see me at my worst—and doing something about it.

# # 203 Choice and Consequence

It's hard to teach your kids moral principles without tangible evidence that they work. So let your kids see the consequences that come from following right principles—and from not following them. My kids love this story about me: When I was in fifth grade, I faked being sick (because I didn't like school and there were several nasty people who were harassing me). I missed 110 days. The longer I stayed out, the harder it got to go back. Although I kept up my schoolwork and got promoted to sixth grade (a positive consequence), the negative consequences vastly outweighed the good. My classmates virtually ostracized me. After that year, I almost never missed another day—not at school or even later on the job. My kids identified with a little boy who was too scared to go back to school—and they learned something about the consequences that follow choices.

# # 204 A Search for Dignity

There's a lot of indignity in childhood. Athletic failures, getting picked last, name-calling, being bullied. Ever wonder how you survived? Your kids sure would like to know. Tell them about your journey to becoming a person who expects to be treated in a dignified way. Show them it can be done without becoming tough and cynical or brutal to others in return. Your children need to know what it takes to step up to dignity, so let them identify with your brokenness and healing.

# # 205 Sore Spots

A young man I know once heard his father remark to his mother, about him, "You know, he's really weird." Ouch! Talk with your kids about the words your parents said to or about you and how those affected your image of yourself and your life, especially the painful words. Tell your kids how you felt. Then take a deep breath and ask the more difficult, but more bonding, questions: "Have I hurt you with my words? When?" Sometimes a throwaway comment or slip of the tongue has done some damage. You can use your story to ferret it out.

# # 206 Family Values

More and more, world-class business organizations are emphasizing shared values rather than creating lengthy policy manuals. When a group is heading in the same direction, there's less demand for rigid rules. Don't assume your children know your family's values; explain them. Without direct conversation about your values, your kids could even misinterpret them. Say you encounter a beggar but don't give him any money. This may be because you suspect he'll spend it to get drunk. But if you don't explain your action, your kids might assume you're not generous or that successful adults don't bother with down-and-outers. So build on good values, and show them how to bring their values to life in their actions and choices.

# # 207 Where Are You Going?

In a recent survey in *Inc.* magazine, 87 percent of the executives responding said that vision and mission were critical to their success. A vision is nothing "spooky"; it's simply a clear, compelling picture of a desirable future. Where is your family going? What is your family's purpose? If you haven't considered what your own personal life mission is, it isn't too late to start. How is vision playing out in your family? Everyone needs to know they're part of something greater than themselves, that there is a common goal that joins them to others.

# # 208 Relationships

If "a person is known by the company he keeps," let your children understand your "company"—why you hang around with the people you do. Distinguish between people you're spending time with to help and peer friendships. When your kids understand what you're looking for in friendship, what you appreciate and don't appreciate about other people—you've invited them further into your heart.

# # 209 Open Decision Making

When you make "adult" decisions and then announce them to your children, you shouldn't be surprised when the distance between you grows. It's alienating to be left out of decisions that affect you. Describe your decision-making process to your kids, and bring them into it as much as possible. This gives them a sense of "ownership" (you won't have to "sell" them on the decision; it's already theirs). When you shut them out of decisions, you're acting distant, like royalty, not like closely connected friends. It's better to let your children participate in adult decisions and see them respond with maturity and support, rather than immaturity and resistance.

# # 210 Trouble with a Capital T

Draw your children into the inner part of your life by telling them about your problems, new ones or ongoing, unresolved ones. When you share your problems—problems at work, at church, with money, with friends, or with family—you communicate that you trust them, and you make problems seem normal. This will make it easier for your kids to share their problems with you. Sharing common problems and concerns says, "We're in this together," and can't help but bring you closer.

# # 211 The Old Victoria Cross

Remember the "general" elephant in the Disney movie *The Jungle Book*? He regularly boasted about having won the Victoria Cross—the highest military honor possible. Don't puff up your past when you talk with your kids, making it better or worse or bigger than it really was. Faking is nearly always detectable by children and is sure to damage trust. Honesty is the basis of bonding.

# # 212 Admit It

As you work toward deep connection with your children, perhaps it's taken quite a bit of courage to be vulnerable with them and open your heart. Tell your kids how scary it is for you. Let them see that though real conversations can be difficult, even messy, you care enough to open up.

# # 213 My Own Identity

Have a healthy, air-clearing discussion to explain to your children how you've grown to know your own identity and don't need them for "validation"—that you don't need to drain the life out of them to fill the empty spaces inside yourself. Explain what your source of personal strength and courage is and how you've conquered any need to "leech" off their lives. Mutuality, not dependence, is the key to solid connection.

# 6

# Painting with Words

## # 214 Earliest Memories

Describe your earliest memories to your children—in as much clear detail as possible, creating word pictures for even very small children. My earliest memory is of a vacation trip by un-air-conditioned car from St. Louis to California when I was about three. I remember seeing what looked like a tornado way down the road and the beaches and giant (to me) waves in California. As I shared these stories in vivid detail, along with my feelings and reactions, my little children were lit up with interest. I'd been there. They could relate. That's connection.

## # 215 Childhood Dramas

Share the exciting stories of your childhood with your kids, especially ones about when you were hurt. Such stories make you seem more human, more real, more like them. My children were enthralled with the story of how the front wheel of my bicycle collapsed when I was riding fast down a hill and the resulting scratches and scrapes that made blood pour from a thousand wounds. My children could see the whole thing in their imaginations. They felt it—and cared about the boy I was—and am. That's connecting to the whole me.

## # 216 Collected Insults

Both sympathy and pity are reactions that bind us to one another in our humanity. So go ahead and describe times when you were insulted— maybe about a school or athletic performance or for an awkward physical feature—and watch your kids respond with sympathy ("I'm glad that didn't happen to me!") and pity ("I feel bad for you"). Even those insults are part of your history. Make them part of your relationship.

# # 217 Popularity

Think back to a time when you felt popular—or at least the center of attention. Maybe you made the big hit, excelled at a recital, won the coveted spot on the cheerleading squad, or were part of a cool circle of friends. Talk to your kids about the feelings that accompany popularity—and also describe how it felt when the popularity faded away (which always seems to happen). Talk about hanging on to the people who really loved you—even when you weren't so popular. Those people may not be peers; they can be very unexpected. They can even be parents, like you.

# # 218 Dorky Days

Can you remember a time you felt like a big dork—someone who wanted to be "in" but couldn't even find the door? My classic experience as a dork goes back to the ninth and tenth grades. In 1965, at the end of ninth grade, the accepted dress was a sports shirt, slacks, loafers, and *white* socks. But when I went back to school in the fall, *I was the only one wearing white socks!* Fashion dictates had changed over the summer when I wasn't looking. I can still feel the embarrassment, the torture of enduring my bright white socks all day with no way to escape. As I told them this story, my young teens squirmed right along with my discomfort. That picture of me makes me real to them—and like them.

# # 219 In Five Years . . .

Out loud, picture a shared future. Describe, in great detail, an event five years in the future where you and your child are sharing something special (a graduation celebration over dinner, a planned summer trip). Make that event seem so real that your child builds it right into his expectations. Don't let your child imagine a future with only his peers and without you—paint yourself in.

# # 220 The Door to Change

Children crave to be treated as individuals, with dreams and ideas in a soul of their own. So approach your desires for your kids' futures from an encouragement standpoint, not as a determination to force change. There's an old French proverb that says, "The door to change is opened from the *inside.*" Explain to your kids that when you have a good idea for their lives, you're going to come up to their door and knock. Tell them, "If you really invite me in—and I'll know by the warmth from your fire and the light in your eyes—I'll come in and tell you what I know. And when we're done talking, I'll wish you a pleasant good-bye and leave the decision with you." Promise that you'll never try to force the door open or knock it down. Your kids will remember that affirmation of their boundaries.

# # 221 Wrapped Around

Yes, your children need you to be an authority figure, and, yes, boundaries and rules are important. But you'll have to take the relationship further if you want connection. Paint a word picture together by describing how completely you are "wrapped around your kids' little finger." Say, "You probably don't even *know* how much power you have over me, to influence me, to get me to do things for you because I love you so much." And then, once in a while, bend the rules. Demolish a bedtime and go out for ice cream. Give them a day off school. Cancel chores. Let them know it's because you just can't help yourself. It's important for your kids to feel they have both access to you and influence with you. Let them know they've got you.

# # 222 A Perfect Fit

The Bible says, "He determined the times set for them and the exact places where they should live" (Acts 17:26). Paint that word picture for your kids: "God scanned the world with you in the palm of his hand, checking out families to select a perfect fit." Tell them, "He had you and our home planned for years, from forever. He zoomed you in, right here, right now. We may not be perfect, but we were God's choice for you. We're trying to make sure that neither you nor God is disappointed with that decision." When they know they're in the right home, it'll be easier to bond with the others who live there.

# # 223 Now—and Later

While cutting food for your young children, here's a great picture that can connect them to you far into the future: "You know, I'm cutting your food for you now because you can't do it for yourself. Someday, there might come a time when I won't be able to cut my food for myself. Will you do it for me then?" You'll probably get an enthusiastic "Yes!" Help them get started loving the you that is yet to be—and help them accept your help right now.

# # 224 To Bed We Go

Remember that delicious feeling from childhood of falling asleep in the car and having a parent carry you to bed? You half awaken and then sleepily melt into the bed, thankful for the tucking in. If they don't remember being carried off to bed, tell your kids about it the next morning. They'll enjoy that picture of your care and physical touch. If you want, tell them you hope they'll tuck you in someday when you are old or ill and need their help. Prepare them to care and still be connected decades in advance.

# # 225 Read to Me

Another way to remind your kids that you're hoping they'll love you your whole life long is to ask them to read to you when you get older. Bring it up when you're reading to your kids and they're enjoying the closeness with you and the fun of the story. As you paint these "old age" pictures of yourself, you're expressing humility—you need them as much as they need you.

# # 226 In My Father's House Are Many Mansions

I was once upgraded by a wonderful desk clerk into the top suite at the Fairmont Hotel on Nob Hill in San Francisco—and it changed my picture of heaven, which is often described as a mansion with many rooms. My suite at the Fairmont was huge, elegant, and gorgeous, with an entryway, living and dining and office areas, a large bedroom, two sitting rooms, and three bathrooms. There were breathtaking views on three sides, from the Golden Gate to the Bay Bridge. It was world-class, and I know heaven-class will be even better!

Just for fun, tip a bellboy to take you and your kids to the best suite in a fancy hotel—just for a look. While you're there, talk about your hope of heaven: "Can you picture us celebrating in a place like this? I hope the 'place he's prepared' for you is close to the one he's prepared for me! Will you have me over often?" Give them that fabulous picture, and enhance their expectations forever.

# # 227 Make a Music Memory

When you find that the kids like one of your favorite songs, or you come across one that you all enjoy, plant the seed of memory: "I'll think of you whenever I hear this song. Whenever you hear it, you think of me, too, even if I've passed away by then. That way, I'll still be as real to you then as I am right now." I imagine my kids will remember being with me whenever they hear my much-loved Strauss waltzes—even though they tease me about them now.

# # 228 Silly Stuff

Repaint any pictures that make your kids laugh. My kids love to be reminded of the New Year's Day when I made a mess of the living room and a mess of my knee—to my family's great amusement. I'd loaded up a paper plate with chips and nacho cheese in the kitchen, while the rest of the family was in the living room. I don't know what came over me, but on my way back I started making a bugle sound and came charging in with a leap, intending to land on the couch. I missed. I careened off the end of the couch, landed on my own plate of chips and cheese, and slid across the floor. It was so ridiculous, even I was laughing. Every time we relive those details, the bond with my kids is somehow strengthened. If you don't have any stories of silliness to replay, I suggest that you go right out to the store and buy some nacho cheese!

# # 229 Take Them Back

Set the stage for some of your memories by actually taking your kids back to the places where the victories and defeats of your memories took place. Your kids can picture you in these places as a child, as a teen, or as a college student, and you'll blend your past with their present. "Here's where Jimmy D. and I had a down-and-dirty fight." "When I was sitting in this very pew, I could almost hear God whispering my name." "This is where Joni told me she didn't want to be my friend anymore." Share your memorable stories and places—and your kids will know you in a way they don't even know their peers.

# # 230 Get on a Role

Some stay-at-home evening, surprise your kids by showing up dressed like a very old person—makeup, clothes, the whole shebang. Role-play the part of your child as an old person who is telling her grandkids stories about her relationship with her parents (you) when she was growing up: "When I was sad or had a bad day, my mom would . . ." "You know what my dad used to do when I made a mistake?" Your words will show her you understand some of her feelings—and some of your foibles. It'll help you set a lofty standard for how you'll want to treat her.

# # 231 Protect the Shine

Parents have a twofold challenge: to protect their kids and to encourage them. Explain it to your kids this way: "When the wisest and most caring people have corrected me, it was like they were stepping on my shoes without messing up my shoeshine. They slowed me down, but I didn't feel any less positive about myself. That's what I want to do with you. If the shine starts to go, you let me know that your shoes are getting messed up!" This way you'll open the door for them to express their feelings when you've been correcting them. You can always ask, "How are your shoes looking?" and really be asking about their hearts.

## # 232 Food for Thought

Select a value that you really care about, like "compassion," and write it in icing on a cupcake. Then give your kids this picture: "I want the good things in me to be part of you. I want the good things I give you and that we have together to get into you and then be fed to your kids. So let's eat!" Eating "compassion cupcakes" is a small physical ritual that helps bond your kids to your values—and, of course, to you.

## # 233 Never the Last Bite

Next time you're out indulging in ice cream or frozen yogurt, remind your kids of the pace of life. "When you first dig in, you eat great big bites. As you get near the end, the bites get smaller. At the very end, you scrape the sides to get one last little taste and are grateful for it. Life is like that. You can eat big bites at first; whole summers go by, and you cram them in and hardly notice the details. As you get further along, you start to appreciate it a bit more with each bite." Apply this word picture to relationships. Tell them you don't want your relationship to be that way—taking a lot out and scraping their heart until there's nothing left. Promise you won't do that to your kids: "Every time you take another bite, I'm going to add a scoop of affection." Real love is like a never-ending sundae.

## # 234 Soft Snow versus a Blizzard

Samuel Taylor Coleridge once wrote, "Advice is like snow; the softer it falls, the longer it dwells upon, and the deeper it sinks into the mind." Tell your kids you hope your advice will be like soft snow for them, and ask them to tell you if it ever turns into a blizzard.

## # 235 Heart

Some stormy night, tell your kids a story of a little girl (or boy) lost in a dark and unfamiliar landscape. Scary sounds come from the woods around her. The people she passes look unfriendly and refuse to help her; some even laugh at her plight. She begins to panic: *What should I do?*

*Where should I go? Doesn't anybody care about me?* Then she sees a house with a light. As she gets closer, she's amazed to hear her favorite music from inside. On the door is a sign with her name on it and the word Welcome. She goes in to love and safety.

Tell your kids that house is your heart—the music will always be playing, and the welcome sign will always be out for them.

# 7

## Maximizing the Magic Moments

## # 236 Show and Tell

From the time they're very little, kids have a built-in need to show Mom and Dad ("Look what I painted on the wall, Mom!"). Don't miss the moments when your kids are trying to show you something. Ooh and aah and ask questions. Be thrilled with their creative efforts, and affirm them for doing it, creating it, finding it. Don't tell them, "Not now" (unless you're performing open-heart surgery or something equally important), and don't demean their efforts. The goal is *connection,* not perfection.

## # 237 Start Small

The ancient Chinese philosopher Lao-tzu once wrote, "Lay plans for the accomplishment of the difficult before it becomes difficult; make something big by starting with it when small." So pay attention to those magic moments with your kids when they're small, and they'll keep coming back for more of them when they're older. Their little projects and interruptions may seem negligible or annoying to you, but this is where the pattern is set. That project may seem like nothing when it is actually the key to a future of connected moments.

## # 238 Memory Pockets

Memory is odd; people remember minute details, while whole years can get lost in the shuffle. Get your kids conversing about the past over dinner, and pay attention to the things you thought were no big deal but seem to be the things that are "sticking" for them. It may have been the walk in the park rather than the last vacation. When you know what's hidden in their memory pockets, you can plan to make more of those kinds of memories.

# # 239 Carpe Diem

Sometimes you'll be busy when your kids are ready to talk; sometimes you're eager to talk when they're not ready. "Carpe diem"—seize the day—is the operative phrase. Encourage an easy openness both ways—keep the channels open, as far as it depends on you. "Sure, I've got a minute," says that you're open. If it turns out the conversation is something that can wait, get the "executive summary," and then set a time to talk about it later.

# # 240 Windows of Opportunity

Nobody runs around with his soul exposed all the time. It would be exhausting, and our soul would get battered. Most of the time we go about our business—work, school, homework, housework, chores, leisure—and the deepest part of us remains hidden. So when you see an opening—a small window of relationship opportunity—jump on it, ever so gently. Whenever you can, create those windows. You can do this by recreating times when conversation really opened up for you in the past. Were you out one-on-one in a restaurant? Were you going for a walk? Pursue those same activities to make windows of opportunity. Meanwhile, don't miss the ones that come up, surprisingly, on their own.

# # 241 When the Worst Doesn't Happen

Whenever something bad almost happens and doesn't, express your thanks to God, and grow closer in that moment. Once David and Bethany and I were cycling down a hill toward a busy street when David didn't start braking soon enough and went skidding toward the front of a fast-moving car. I screamed—too late—and watched as he headed in what seemed like slow motion toward disaster. Just inches before he went under the car, he came to a sudden stop and the car completely missed him. I have no rational explanation; in fact, everything logical in me says David should have been hit. We felt closer as we discussed what this adventure meant to us and as we imagined the work of an unseen angel's hand.

# # 242 Teachable Moments

Sometimes you'll know for certain that you've "got 'em." Your kids are in close, listening, paying attention. Never waste a moment like that by lecturing or rambling or talking about trivialities. That's the moment to maximize that valuable time with one or two statements that would ring the truest and penetrate most deeply—right then. Not overdoing the talking is the hardest part of capitalizing on teachable moments, but it's important to leave space in the moment for them to internalize what we've told them. Pack a wallop with a few well-chosen words, and the memory of that moment will keep them connected to you.

# # 243 Don't Go Home before the Finale

Magic moments have their own pace. So if things get quiet in the middle of a special conversation, don't be quick to tidy up loose ends and get on with life. Don't be so linear that you miss the roses just off the path. A quiet space can sometimes be two souls resting before ascending to the next level.

# # 244 Ten Minutes or Ten Rules

You can try to "manage" your children with rules, or you can lead them with vision and by example. When you reach a "defining moment" in your life—the loss of a job, an assignment with an impossibly short deadline, a setback in ministy, the betrayal of a friend—don't leave your kids out. You've got an opening, say ten minutes long, to show them who you really are and how you really live. Don't waste it with complaints and moping. Share your feelings, thoughts, conclusions, and revised plans. Your kids would rather follow a noble leader whom they love and trust than an impersonal list of rules. Ten minutes beats ten rules—ten times out of ten.

# # 245 Elevator Speech

Great salespeople can deliver a complete presentation to a buyer in the amount of time it takes to ride up a few floors on an elevator. Even complex business deals are tailored into a concise format. It's a couple of minutes, win or lose. But of course, these folks are prepared. So give your best ideas some thought, and consider how you can succinctly but effectively tell your kids your visions, dreams, and hopes for your relationship. Prepare a three-minute, heartfelt "presentation." Then when you get a spontaneous three-minute opening, you'll be ready.

# # 246 Bits and Pieces

There's an old negotiating rule that says, "If you can't get a steak, get a sandwich." You won't always be able to sustain really special times with your kids. But don't fall into the trap of thinking that the quick moments and short periods of connection don't count or aren't meaningful. Connection isn't about "all or nothing." Just as a puzzle is made up of a thousand pieces, connection can be constructed from a thousand little interactions. Don't moan about the pieces that are still missing—use the ones you've got right now. They'll add up into a beautifully finished whole.

# # 247 The Unplanned Plan

A great and memorable time of connection can flow from a deliberately unplanned day. A whole day, you and one of your children, doing whatever comes to your *collective* mind to do. And you don't have to pack a lot into that day. The Roman writer Cicero said, "To live long, you must live slowly." It's just as true of a relationship. Let it unfold like a rose.

# # 248 Curious about You

There are times when your kids will initiate a conversation about you—maybe out of their own curiosity or because of a school project or because a friend asked a question. My daughter Bethany once interrupted me to ask, "Daddy, how many states have you been in?" I could have short-changed the conversation ("Honey, I'm too busy writing this book on how to connect with your kids!"). Or I could have given her a quick answer and gotten back to my work. But I saw a chance for her to crawl inside my life. So we made a big deal of figuring it out. It turns out I've been to forty-four states. Later she presented me with a checklist of the six states I haven't yet visited with a line by each one to mark off when I go there. You better believe I'll report it to her when I do. My journeys have become hers.

# # 249 Clinging at Bedtime

Bedtime is a day's closure, an ending for a small piece of your lives. Children can become "clingy" when the day is over and they're about to be alone. Make room for those few minutes, and let them cling. Don't let putting them to bed become just another detail to wrap up ("Brush your teeth") or just a time of relief ("Thank heaven they're going to bed!"). Stretch that connecting time together, just a little.

# # 250 When to Ignore Bedtime

Of course regular bedtimes are important, but they don't have to be set in concrete. Once in a while, at the end of a day, when all the hubbub ceases, there's an amazing opening—a chance for deep connection with a child. Don't get so hung up in your routine that you miss it. Peter and I had one of those times recently. We'd watched a movie together, and Peter seemed ready to say good night. But I sensed it was one of those moments, and we ended up talking until about 3:30 A.M., covering a mountain of issues, questions, concerns, and frustrations. About 2:00 A.M. we cranked up the microwave with pizza rolls and mozzarella sticks. Magic moments can be canceled by practicalities ("We all need to get some sleep"). Sometimes what you really need is to break out the food and turn those moments into a party.

# # 251 Transitions

Transition times can be pressured, but they can be magic, too. Daily transitions, like mornings, can be tense or full of welcome. Sit on their beds, play cheerful music, and make the first greeting of the morning happy. Kiss them awake, or tickle their necks. See what you can do to find connections in the weekly transitions—from weekday to weekend and back again. And watch for the big transitions—like the end of a semester or the start of a new one. When you're out of the routine and into a transition, all sorts of good things can happen—if you're paying attention.

# # 252 A Very Merry Unbirthday to You

Regular birthdays and holidays are great for connecting, but why not instigate a random act of celebration? Look how the Prodigal's father threw a huge party—when that son had been *naughty*. Celebrate a time when your kids have been good, or gotten along, or earned a good grade (not necessarily an A), or helped out around the house without being asked. Let them know you really *appreciate* them. Put on the music. Go out to dinner. Have pizza delivered. Make a big deal—out of *them*. When all is said and done, it's people, not events, that need to be celebrated.

# # 253 Volunteer Blessings

When your children do something kind just because they want to—serve you breakfast in bed, cook a meal, bake cookies, straighten up a closet, clean a room—you're onto something special. Thank them, of course, but also praise them in front of others; write them a note. Stretch it out. Don't let that magic moment when a heart has generously opened pass unnoticed. There are too few Good Samaritans.

# # 254 When You're Happy, I'm Happy

Romans 12:15 enjoins us to "rejoice with those who rejoice." As a parent, that means when your kids are happy, you want to get in on it. "That girl finally smiled at you? Wow! Cool! The bully is moving to Cleveland? Let's party! I mean, let's *dance,* and *sing,* and eat stuff we normally shouldn't!" These things might seem like small potatoes to you, but they loom large and joyous in the souls of our children. Don't miss a happy moment. What could be better than being bound together by joy?

# # 255 The Court Jester

The court jester was a critical figure in medieval politics. Back when kings and queens thought they were the big enchilada, what with "divine rights" and all, the price of disagreement with them could be really high—like death. So how did people let these big shots know they were way out of line? In stepped the court jester. Through humor and jokes and rhymes and stories, the jester poked fun at the dumb ideas and follies of the person on the throne. The royalty would often laugh the loudest—and, when the laughter died down, make some changes to policy. Let your kids be court jesters—put on skits and plays and tell jokes and poke fun at "house rules" and the dumb things that can creep into your family life. A joker may be just what the doctor ordered.

# # 256 Take a Long Walk

Few things are as conducive to producing magic moments as a long walk—out on a beautiful day, walking without a plan or destination in mind, just enjoying the pleasure of each other's company. No force—just let the moment come to you. God did it first—with Adam.

# # 257 Hikes

A hike farther from home could give you and your kids the sense of being away, but doing it together. The shared experience allows ample time to dip into each other's soul. On foot is the best, since it's hard to commune while riding bikes. Once again, don't plan an agenda—let the moments come at their own time and pace.

# # 258 Spontaneous Play

Connected relationships are often playful ones. It takes some measure of security in the relationship to be comfortable playing games, but playing can bring even more security and closeness to the relationship. Tag, hide-and-seek, pillow fights, water fights, kite flying, "last one to the car is a rotten egg"—all can add to your sense of unity. Go with your intuition—especially if it seems silly.

# # 259 A Special Place

Places and settings have power to bring about connection. Maybe it's a fireplace with a roaring fire and music and marshmallows and sparkling apple cider. Maybe it's a tucked-away spot in a park that seems to belong to you alone. Maybe it's that vacation spot that you return to over and over again. Remember your favorite times of sharing, and try to re-create that same mood. You may have to experiment in different settings to find the ones that work for you, but they're out there!

# # 260 Down on the Carpet

It's hard for a little person to have a magic moment with a giant. "A great man is always willing to be little," wrote Ralph Waldo Emerson. Get down on your kids' level, wherever that is, and look them in the eye. When your eyes are locked into theirs and theirs into yours, you've got 'em.

# # 261 Speaking Their Language

With very small children, new talkers, you can make a bit of relationship magic by repeating their sounds and funny words back to them. Your interaction improves their language skills, of course, but it also develops your relationship. As they grow, their words, ideas, hopes, and dreams spoken back to them can deepen the relationship while affirming their thoughts and dreams. It's hard not to be close to someone who "sounds" like you.

# # 262 The Clarifying Question

When you're faced with the urgent, daily rub of life, and one of those connecting moments arrives, you've got to ask yourself the clarifying question—the big one, the $64,000 question: In five years, which will matter more? Paying these bills or my relationship with this boy? The laundry or her soul? When you train yourself to ask those questions, you'll still pay the bills and do laundry, but not at too high a price.

# Part 2

# *What to Do:*

## Actions

## That Create

## Connection

*What* you do to create connection with your kids is just as important as the words you use to build that bridge. Healthy traditions play a role, projects can build relationship, and activities can show your pride in your kids (without turning them into arrogant megalomaniacs or self-esteem junkies). What you do can hone your empathetic skills, your ability to walk around in their shoes.

Maybe more important than anything else you do will be powersharing and mutual learning. And you'll bond with your children while helping them find the best that they were meant to be.

In the seminars I present on parenting, I cover "A Proactive Parent's Ten Commandments." Several of those relate to our actions: number 2—I will listen more than talk and do more than preach; number 6—I will abandon control and rely instead on influence and relationship and consequences; number 10—I will start my children as apprentices and grow them into friends. Not surprisingly, these are the best approaches—as well as the most effective— with all people in all forms of organization.

Our actions can bring us closer—or drive a mighty wedge between us. Read on, and be closer.

# 8 Powerful Traditions

## # 263 We're Outta Here!

Get away from home, just the two of you, and share time in a way that pleases both of you. It can include "razzmatazz," like bowling or miniature golf or tennis or going to a movie, but to be connective it also has to include some quieter, face-to-face, one-on-one time. Talking about the action part of the outing can lead to some heart-to-heart stuff. It's tough to do in a busy life, especially if you have a number of children, but it's worth the fight. Let them see you put it on the planner, just like you would any important meeting. The more regular—the more it becomes a tradition—the better.

## # 264 Home Alone

Hide out sometime with one of your kids for an at-home adventure. Crawl into bed with lots of supplies, and play fort or house. Rent a bunch of movies, and have a marathon with all sorts of goodies to eat from a run to the store. Whatever you do, it's just the two of you—no phone, no cleaning, no responsibilities, no interruptions. A once-a-month at-home adventure can become a refuge for you both.

## # 265 Debriefing

Many spouses try to find a time in the evening when they can unwind and debrief their day with each other. Why not create a time like that with each of the kids? Just ten minutes alone can keep the relationship open and can occasionally lead to a full-blown discussion that would never occur on the run. Trying to do this all together at dinner just isn't

the same as connecting one-on-one in private. Some things aren't meant
for a group.

# # 266 Festival—Party On!

"The life without festival is a long road without an inn," said Democritus
of Abdera. A festival is "a joyful celebration or occasion." The ancient
Hebrews actually collected *three* tithes—the Lord's tithe, the poor tithe,
and the *festival* tithe. God is apparently very serious about the cry in the
human soul for "fiesta"! So declare your own festivals. My family
celebrates St. Patrick's day (in part, because of my strong Irish roots) with
corned beef and cabbage, Irish soda bread, Irish potatoes, green butter,
green milk (colored, not old), my festival green tie (a gift from my mother),
Irish music in the background, and the big finale—a screening of *The
Quiet Man.* Choose a holiday—Groundhog Day, April Fools' Day, First
Day of Summer, All Saints' Day—or declare your own. A regular festival
is a cozy inn on a long road and a planned time of connection.

# # 267 Breaking Bread

There is something about eating together that relaxes a relationship and
brings out graciousness all around. Dinner dates with spouses and
friends are fine, but why not try dates with your children? Make it a
tradition tied to some regular cycle of life: Go out for frozen yogurt after
the first day of school every year; have dinner at a nice restaurant to
celebrate the end of the school year; eat breakfast out on teacher
in-service days when there is no school. It allows life to develop a
"feel"—and in their hearts, they sense closeness to you, this person who is
so in tune with their schedule.

# # 268 Come and Get It!

"A dining-room table with children's eager, hungry faces around it," said
Simeon Strunsky, "ceases to be a mere dining-room table, and becomes
an altar." Many families have lost the connective power of dinner
together, but you can get it back. Even if you can't arrange it every night,
one or two regular evening meals together can work wonders for your
relationship.

# # 269 Rise and Shine

Once or twice a year wake up your kids for a surprise breakfast out—and
make it long and leisurely. Come up with enough enthusiasm of your

own to get even the grumpy ones going. It would be hard to find a better way to open a day—and perhaps a heart.

# # 270 Earn It

I have occasionally tied responsibility to reward by letting the children "earn" a dinner out with me if they complete their chores. On a monthly basis, they'd track their chore accomplishments with stickers on a calendar. If they filled up the month, we filled up an evening (and our stomachs). They earned it (it was their "treat") and felt good about it, and we ate and laughed and grew a little closer.

# # 271 Bring It Home

Adults typically eat out far more often than children do, whether it's over business or with adult friends. Let your children in on your activity by bringing something home for them—leftovers, or something saved or ordered just for them. Tell them about your time at the restaurant or banquet, and make them part of the evening's fun. This reinforces the idea that the time you spend away from them isn't meant as an escape from them. Don't ask for a doggie bag—ask for a "little girl" or "little boy" bag!

# # 272 Giving Thanks around the Table

Sometimes, instead of saying a standard grace before a meal, I rotate the thanksgiving around the table and let each person "free form" their thanks. I'll lead with "Laura is thankful" or "Peter is thankful" and then turn it over to them. Try it at your house—you'll get a chance to hear what's on their minds, and you give them the chance to set the tone for your family meal.

# # 273 Saturday Ice Cream

Regularity is so much a practical part of building connection. Pick a day of the week that works, and go to an ice-cream shop or bakery for a treat. Dawdle over the snack, and let the conversation meander and evolve. It becomes a bright spot in a *life*, not just a day. C. S. Lewis talked about the importance of those nice, comfortable, familiar places and traditions. He called them "drippings from Heaven."

# # 274 A Weekly Sabbatical

Weeks have their pattern, and all weeks have an end. What a wonderful time to draw together, find some peace, lick your wounds, get revived, and strengthen yourselves for the battles and opportunities that lie ahead.

Don't ignore a day of rest and renovation, or the cost will be measured in your mental and physical health and in the drifting of your relationships with your children.

# # 275 Saying Good-Bye to the Day

Bedtime is a natural, cyclical time of closure. It makes sense to use that time to evaluate and measure, to clean up relational messes, to make sure you don't let the day end with anger still brewing. It's a perfect time of reconnection built by God right into the fabric of daily life. Lead your children into that time of connecting and reflecting. Encourage them to ask two or three questions about anything they want, and take time to answer. With older children, allowing a few minutes for them to respond to "Tell me about your day" could work wonders. Finish each day strong, regardless of what mess you've made during that day.

# # 276 Past Your Bedtime

Make the most of the time when your children are older and stay up even later than you do. If they're coming in late, it's OK to wait up as long as you're intending to deliver a hug and a snack, not a lecture. Even better, leave the light on and a note where they're sure to find it. Tell them you're glad they're home, how much you love them, and mention something specific about the next day. A love note beats a lecture ten times out of ten.

# # 277 Life Day

When that child first came into your life, it was a momentous occasion, a life-changing event. Tell your child about when she came into being—when you first knew you were expecting, when the doctor confirmed it, when you saw her on the sonogram, when you picked out clothes and furniture. We shouldn't let her forget that her relational impact started long before her birthday.

# # 278 The Birthday Journey

It's easy to let birthdays be a time of presents and cake and singing the most-sung song in the world. Create some tradition that's unique to your family to help you put some "oomph" into birthday celebrations. Maybe show a young child her baby book or his baby clothes. Talk about the actual birth day. Maybe you can sit down with an older child and remember the milestones he's passed on the journey from the day of birth to this birthday. Birthdays don't just honor the individual; they can lift up the entire family, even the generations that came before.

# # 279 One-on-One Birthday

Do your best to find some one-on-one time with a child to celebrate his birthday—apart from the cake-and-presents event. Mark the birthday milestone by deepening your relationship. Go out on the town, or just for a long walk around the block. Party events make a kid feel special, but that one-on-one time convinces him he's *loved.*

# # 280 Birthday Bashes

We've had a long-standing birthday tradition in our family: The birthday person gets to pick a restaurant and take us out (I pay, of course) for a birthday bash. We all quiz the birthday kid days or weeks ahead about where she's going to take us. And once we're out, we take a long time, really drag it out (we practically move in). We talk about the past year, past birthdays, where her life is going. We ask the waiters to sing happy birthday and tip them more if they really get into it. We did this even when we were broke. Try it with your kids. Go for the time, the connection, and the memory.

# # 281 Make It a Birth Week

Where is it written that the celebrating can only take one day? Birthdays can be an extended fiesta, with special activities scattered throughout the week. Don't neglect the big deal on the actual birthday, but also have a blast during the birth week. We're even talking about making it the birth month! Isn't that ... too much? Are you kidding?

# # 282 Vacations: Living On

I've heard people warn against the danger of "overvaluing" vacations, of living for them and not living the rest of the days of the year. But I don't think it's *possible* to overvalue vacations. I say, look forward to them, plan for them, drool over them—and still have plenty of suds left to live passionately the rest of the time, too. Vacations live on as bonding agents forever in the memories they create. They're something you share as a family that no one else has or can get in on. With every remembrance, old bonds are strengthened, and new bonds are formed.

# # 283 Picture Perfect—and Plenty

A vacation is a giant memory pocket. So snap so many pictures that you won't be quite sure you'll have the money to get them developed or the time to sort them into that nothing-in-it-except-the-vacation album. As you peruse your vacation photos, you relive the connections you made. You'll enjoy those photos for years and years—so invest.

# # 284 Amassing Mementos

Don't stay so busy snapping photos that you miss the other "scrapbookables" you can collect on vacation. Brochures, mementos, hotel bills, parking tickets—save it all. The scrapbook details make the vacation come back to life with shared experiences and laughter and lessons.

# # 285 One More Time

It's great to help your children see the world, but there's something connecting about going back now and then to a vacation spot that holds wonderful family memories. So hit the same location, the same hotel or motel or campground, the same restaurant. In a sense, that place belongs to your family. Claim it.

# # 286 Splish Splash

I *still* really like summer, even though as an adult I don't get the time off anymore. What a great time to connect—especially with long, lazy days at the pool. Our family drags all kinds of paraphernalia off to the pool—bathing suits and trunks, towels, sunscreen, and practically everything else! Snacks and drinks, and books and projects. It's hard for a day like that not to produce some connections with the kids—as we share what we're reading or working on, chat at leisure, and enjoy the beauty of the day. Don't waste a day at the pool by treating it as a chore or "duty."

# # 287 I Need a "Daycation"!

Even on short notice, plan a day off work so you can spend the day on a mini-vacation. Build in drama, and build in quiet. Breakfast cooked together, something athletic, a stop at the library, lunch out, a trip to that little town two hours away, dinner on the road, sunset at a lake, a movie back at home. Mix and match, add and delete—but share a day that leaves you both with a "Wow!" and feelings of love for the ones you shared it with.

# # 288 Happy New Year

Our family often shares New Year's Eve with others, but New Year's Day belongs to us. We welcome the year in a cozy but festive atmosphere. We play games, watch games, watch parades, build a fire, and eat lots and

lots of stuff we really like (and feel guilty about, if we eat at other times).
We talk about the year past and look ahead to the year to come. We don't
make "resolutions," but we do set goals and share them with each other.
Start the year with a bond.

# # 289 Be My Valentine
I've always wanted to use this "sweetheart" day to sweeten my
relationship with my children. Broaden your idea of romance ("idealized
love") to include your kids. Talk about the original St. Valentine. Write an
unforgettable "Be Mine" card. Buy candy and flowers. Don't let the day lie
vacant until some young upstart with a different idea of "romance"
claims the day. With your experience, you can out-dazzle any upstart.

# # 290 Declaration of Independence
July Fourth is a great day to talk about independence—and
interdependence. Celebrate with deep, mutual understanding of what
these concepts mean to you as individuals and as people who need other
people.

# # 291 Halloween
Many people get hung up over Halloween, but why let weirdness rule?
The word means "holy eve," so make it a time for connection. Start some
new tradition, like giving candy to each other after a great meal. Build in
some fun. Draw or carve each other's faces on pumpkins. See who can
take the pumpkin seeds and spit 'em the farthest—well, maybe not.

# # 292 Thanksgiving
Who should we thank on Thanksgiving? God, of course. But thanksgiving
is a perfect opportunity to thank God for each other and to thank each
other for each other. Write notes all around, or go around the table so
each family member can tell what he or she is thankful about related to
others, or simply thank those others. In most families the only thanks
given on Thanksgiving Day is one person's prayer before eating. You can
do better than that!

# # 293 Christmas
Christmas can turn into a present-orgy where we get more presents than
any one of us has time to enjoy. At our house no one is allowed out by the
tree (and presents) until everyone is up and ready; then we start with the
Christmas story (I read it while our two older children act it out with

pieces from the manger scene, complete with angels, who swoop like Batman). Next come the stockings, one at a time. Then presents, also one at a time, rotating around. Food starts showing up along the way. We talk in between presents. The gift-opening can take hours. The time and the day feel like "ours." We traditionally finish it with a movie, like *It's a Wonderful Life.*

# 294 Holiday Greetings

Make card-sending an event of its own, whether at Christmas or some other time of year. Choose the cards together, split up the duties (addressing, stamping), sign them, and put in pictures or a newsletter. While you're working together, make it fun with special treats and good background music. Reach out as a team.

# 295 Adopt a Family

For a day or weekend, or the same day or holiday every year, adopt a needy family. Make them cards, make or buy decorations, get presents that are chosen carefully for the individuals, make or buy a dinner, bring noisemakers. Don't just drop it and run. Fiesta with your friends. Give yourselves along with your other gifts.

# 296 Regular Video Events

A regular "appointment" to watch a favorite TV show gives us a point of collection and a shared experience, whether it's Nickleodeon oldies such as *Dick Van Dyke* or newer, more serious shows. Discussion can take place at commercials (thank God and the inventor for the mute button!) or once the program's over. A special movie time can work well, too—the matinee on the weekend.

# 297 Audio Drama, sans Cassettes

Don't let reading together become a lost art in your family—and don't stop the reading out loud together once your children begin to read. Meet them at the door when they come home from school with an entertaining book and plenty of cookies and milk. Or find a time just before or after dinner. You read or take turns. Leave time for talking about what you read and how to apply it to your life together.

# 298 Tickling with the Funnies

You can't overestimate the value in laughing together. Reading a comic strip or funny column at dinner could tune you into each other and generate conversation. For years I've clipped Dave Barry's column out of the paper and saved it to read toward the end of a weekend meal (at home or out). It works with the whole family or one-on-one.

# # 299 The Best Book

After dinner is an excellent time for digging into the Scriptures. For variation, try reading some great Bible story together, then ask each person to draw a picture illustrating whatever stands out the most to them. Then go around the table and find out what each person drew and why. As you discover what speaks the most to each child, you can use that knowledge to build a joint spiritual journey.

# # 300 Memory Marathon

From time to time have a marathon review of family photos or home videos. Do it slowly, with plenty of time for questions, comments, and humor. Celebrate with dinner out afterward.

# # 301 Scrapbook for Two

Start a photo collection in an album that just contains the two of you—a whole book that says, "We're connected." Get the kind of album that lets you write in thoughts and feelings about some (if not all) of the pictures.

# # 302 Me-and-You Video

Make a videotape of just the two of you. No other people, no pets, no family activities. Just you and her. Hand the camcorder to kind strangers and thank them for blessing your relationship. If you don't have a camcorder, borrow one or save your dollars. You won't come this way again.

# # 303 Sounds like . . . Sounds like You!

Over the years, keep a cassette recording of your children talking, singing, and laughing at different ages and stages—one tape per child. Whenever you pull them out to listen, it's a warm experience for both of you as you bring back the past. Your kids are older, and you didn't start when they were young? Get out the tape player—it's never too late.

# # 304 Banners High

Buy or make a homemade family banner. Then fly it at the front door or on a pole whenever there are special events—birthdays, graduations, accomplishments, successes, milestones. Use your surname or some other family motto or catchphrase. This is guaranteed to make everyone in the family feel, "We're something special."

# # 305 Coming and Going

Develop some traditions for your comings and goings, your hellos and good-byes. It could be a high five, a salute, blowing and catching kisses, or drawing the outline of a heart in the air with your fingers. Let them know you're glad to see them or that you'll miss them when they're gone.

# # 306 Bananas Day

Every once in a while, have a Bananas Day—when you "go bananas." Splurge all day. Go to three movies in a row. Eat things banished from your diet. Buy some "useless" trinket. Give money to every needy person you encounter. It was the so-called weeping prophet, Jeremiah, who said, "Rejoice in the bounty of the Lord" (Jer. 31:12). You can't go bananas every day, but for one glorious day it's an unforgettable blast.

# # 307 Bethany Day

There's a Martin Luther King Day and a Columbus Day, so why not create a David Day or a Bethany Day? You're the parent—you can declare a holiday! Declare one in honor of your child, and celebrate it to the fullest. Take them out of school or work. I don't even know Columbus. I prefer to celebrate David and Bethany and Laura and Peter.

## Make and Do:
## Projects That Build Relationship

# # 308 First Things First

When planning activities or projects with our children, it's easy to get caught up in plans and logistics and forget the whole point. So, first things first! Stop and ask yourself: *Is there anything about what we're planning that holds at least the possibility of enhancing our relationship?* Nearly anything you do with your kids should be able to add, at least modestly, to the connection you're already building between you.

# # 309 Avoid Narcissism

Projects that put children at the center of the universe are generally not healthy for your relationship or for your children. It's not about "Here's what *I* want to do"—that's using each other, not relating to each other. It's not about giving them anything they want. It's about two people connecting. Remember that, and you won't end up creating a child with an insatiable ego, complete with a demanding, whining spirit.

# # 310 Family Tree

A family tree can connect you to your children and to a long heritage. Even the skeletons in the family closet can teach you something about the strengths and weaknesses in your family. Chart your family tree on poster board or using a computer program. With a scanner, you might even incorporate pictures, including the ancient ones. Talk about these characters as you write them into the family tree: Who were they? How did they affect who we are? What do we like and dislike about them? Looking backward can be an excellent precursor to looking inward.

# # 311 Coat of Arms

Design a family coat of arms together. Selecting words and symbols and layout can take you deep into who you are as a family, what you believe in, and where you want to go together.

# # 312 Vision Statement

Writing a vision statement for your relationship can be both bonding and elevating. A vision is simply a written statement of what your purpose is, how you intend to carry it out, and your shared values. One page is about the right length, but if you do it right, you could work on it over months on outings and at other times.

# # 313 SWOT

Organizations that want to stay on the cutting edge constantly evaluate where they are versus where they want to be. One simple method they use is the "SWOT" analysis:

Strengths. What do we do better than anyone else? What are our "core competencies"? our "core passions"? Build around strengths.

Weaknesses. What are we not so good at? Should we learn or get some help? Work around weaknesses.

Opportunities. Where can we best use our strengths? How can we maximize our impact? Feed opportunities.

Threats. What things or people are likely to hurt or damage us? How do we prevent it? Starve threats.

A relationship is a form of "organization." Both depth and good decision making can come from a relational SWOT analysis.

# # 314 Living Legacy

Take your children to a tree nursery and let them pick out a tree they like. Then plant it together—dig the hole in alternating spurts, fill it back in, water the tree, put a support in the ground, and tie the tree to it, then love that tree together. In fifty years, even if they don't live in that house anymore, they'll think of you every time they pass that tree. It remains a natural statement of a love planted long ago.

# # 315 Good Deeds

Doing a good deed for someone outside your family is a marvelous way to build family relationships. All of you feel good about being in a relationship that actively makes the world and other people's lives a little better. Acts of kindness or service broaden and deepen your friendships.

Brainstorm with your children to come up with a list of possible good deeds. The decision to do it, along with the brainstorming itself, will be a connecting experience.

# # 316 Grocery Delivery

One act of kindness might be to take a quantity of food to a needy person or family. Talk about this with your family. How can this be done graciously, without embarrassing them? What would they like to eat? And when you drop off the food, take time to talk respectfully with the recipients. Afterward, you can dissect how it went, what you will do differently next time, and how the kids felt about what they were doing.

# # 317 Meals on Wheels

Make a meal to take to a shut-in, making enough so that you can stay and eat with them. It lets the shut-in person be the host or hostess, even if that person is no longer able to cook and entertain others. Much connection can come from giving one of God's people both physical and spiritual food.

# # 318 Doing unto Others

Another arena of service might be helping an elderly person or single parent by taking care of some basic maintenance projects that they don't have the time or capability to take on. Pack a cooler, and launch into yard work, painting, cleaning—whatever you can do—and do it *together.*

# # 319 Seeds of Kindness

If planting a tree works for you in your own yard, why shouldn't it work elsewhere? Affirm another person and show you care by choosing and planting a tree for her. You'll bind her with that symbol of hope for a living future. And that tree may belong to someone else officially, but you and your kids will know it will always belong to you.

# # 320 If I Had a Hammer

There are all sorts of building projects you can do with your kids, depending on your skill level and time—hanging a picture or shelf, enclosing a room, putting up a storage shed, or putting in a little fountain or bird feeder. Choose a project whose size and scope permits you to take it on with your children. It's fun if other do-gooders are involved, but for deep connection it helps if the service project can be done by just you and the kids.

# # 321 A Friend in Specific Need

Our family once heard of another family who had to wash their clothes in the bathtub. We had a blast shopping around for a decent used washing machine, delivering it, and setting it up. While focus-on-me projects never build relationship, Good Samaritan projects can hardly fail to do so.

# # 322 The Great Defenders

Find some way to fight for or get justice for someone else. Strategize with your kids how to fix a situation where someone operating in good faith was ripped off (like a widow who was sold a shoddy product and can't get the seller to take it back). Wouldn't it be great if it could be said about you that you "defended the cause of the poor and needy, and so all went well" (Jer. 22:16)?

# # 323 Adopt an Ancient

If you become aware of a very elderly person who is alone or mostly alone, adopt him or her. Visit, bring a meal or favorite snack, talk about your values. Bring your camera and take a "family" picture, with the elderly person in the photo, to put beside his or her bed. Put your children's pictures on the dresser. Develop a sense of compassion together for a young heart in an old body.

# # 324 Goofy Gourmets

Try out a really complicated recipe. Get adventurous in preparation and ingredients. If the dish turns out to be more experimental than edible, have a good laugh and try again. If it turns out all right, share it as something you made with your own hands. If it turns out great, decide to whom you might best give it away.

# # 325 A Little Business

Lemonade stands are one of my favorite businesses. When we were visiting my mother in St. Louis, we took a walk and came across one that had "entrepreneur" written all over it. They had two lines drawn on the street where you had to stand in an orderly way in line. The kids/owners told us we could drop off the cups on our way back for recycling. I loved it. There was only one thing missing: an adult. Some parent missed all the fun of connecting and teaching kids about business and money. My son Peter once started his own lawn-care business ("Clean Cut Lawns") which he turned over to his brother, David, on his way to starting a photography business instead. Turn your collective imagination loose.

# # 326 Voting with Mom or Dad

Your kids can connect with you as you care together about what goes on in the world. When an election is coming up, study the issues and positions of the candidates with your kids. Think out loud about how your votes should be cast; take an informal vote at home. Take the kids along when you go to vote; get them absorbed in the process. The sense of making a difference is a strong bonding agent.

# # 327 Take 'Em Along

As my children were old enough, I watched for opportunities to take them with me to meetings (business-related and church committee meetings, seminars, etc.). I'd discuss the issues with them before and after, respectfully treating them as full-fledged business partners. Watching you do it is how they'll learn to join with you to take on the world.

# # 328 Fight a Good Fight

Standing up for a good cause can join you and your kids in your shared values. A protest or picket campaign reminds you that you're strong and your opinions are meaningful and carry power. Even if others insult you for your beliefs, you'll find yourself pulling together even more closely. And there are *so many good things* to stand up for.

# # 329 Personal Shoppers

Let your kids help you pick out clothes, furniture, even cars. My son Peter is determined not to let me get out of style. If you bring them into your purchasing, they'll feel more comfortable having you along when they're buying or picking things out.

# # 330 Friendly Competition

Get close to your kid through friendly competition. Whatever grabs the two of you—chess, checkers, Scrabble, Risk, basketball, tennis—connect by doing it together. At the same time, you'll be showing how to win graciously—and lose graciously. When they beat you and you're glad, you've shown them how to live and made them glad to know someone who can respond in such a sensitive and caring way.

# # 331 Housework Teamwork

Household chores can become an area of hostile warfare or a building block to family unity. You can't work as a team by barking out orders and continually critiquing. And you'll rile their sense of justice if you sit and read the paper or talk on the phone while they're working hard at their chores. You'll accomplish both housework and relationship-work by attacking chores together: You move the furniture while he vacuums; you wash the dishes, and she dries; you scrape this end, and they scrape that end, until you meet in the middle. Sometimes they'll have to do chores by themselves, but hopefully they'll be missing you.

# # 332 That Spoonful of Sugar

Turn some aspect of a chore into play. Raking leaves alone is depressing, but doing it together lightens the load and gives some sense of togetherness, accomplishment, and even fun. Together Bethany and I raked leaves into big piles but then split the tasks: I manned the bags; she stuffed the leaves. We raced to see how fast we could get a bag loaded and tied. When that "game" ran out of gas, we tried to guess how big an armful of leaves she could pick up at one time and then rated them. We decided we were "leafers." I told her she was the Mark McGwire of leaf gatherers. We had a thoroughly enjoyable time on an activity that had all the initial allure of water torture.

# # 333 Tea for Two

Sharing can be both fun and bonding. When you go out to a restaurant, don't order separately and leave it at that. Make it a connection. Order two meals that you both like, then split everything. My daughter Laura and I have done that since she was a little girl, and we're still doing it today. It makes the whole table—and the experience—seem more personal and interconnected.

# # 334 Food Assault

Get some king-size portion of something, and eat it together from the same serving dish. Old-fashioned ice-cream sodas used to come with two straws (the only rule is no blowing into the straw—although that could be interesting). Somehow those two straws will intertwine.

# # 335 Happy Victory to You

You know how waiters and waitresses come out to sing to patrons on their birthdays? Try getting the waiters to come sing their very bad but wonderful rendition of "Happy Victory to You" for other victories or milestones in your family life. You'll have to tip them to do it, and it could cost a lot to get a decent "choir." But it's worth it for your child to feel celebrated and special.

# # 336 Interior Designers

Redecorate a child's bedroom (or yours) together. Look at magazines, window-shop, pick out the materials, do what you can together, and decide who will do the rest. For it to bond you, you'll have to avoid being controlling or critical. This project leaves your imprint on your child's room, where he spends such a big part of his life.

# # 337 Time-Out

Plan for naps—time apart. If you want to keep reconnecting with your child, you'll have to have times of separation to make it so. Sleep isn't necessarily required. What's important is getting a regular break from each other, which is beneficial to your relationship. A short separation can lead to a happy reunion. Build some "time-out" into the ebb and flow of your lives together. Constant anything—even togetherness—can breed boredom, lack of appreciation, and even resentment.

# # 338 Time-In

"When a parent needs a break," says my friend Maryl Janson, "she can schedule a 'time-in' for the children.' This is a time in their room with toys or other items from a 'time-in' box that are not accessible any other time of the day." Time-in isn't a punishment. Make it fun. Select interesting items to go in the time-in box, and ask your kids to tell you what they took out, and why.

# # 339 Solve a Problem

Discover a problem area you both care about, and set to work together to solve the problem. Maybe there's a bias in your local newspaper, sleazy businesses in the area, speeding drivers in the neighborhood, a congressperson voting the "wrong way" on a critical issue. The key—both for connectedness and effectiveness—is to find something that makes both of you righteously angry. Shared indignation can be a powerful glue.

# # 340 Pet Connection

Selecting and caring for pets—fish, turtles, birds, cats, dogs—can bring softness to your relationship. My son David has a terrific collection of hamsters, rabbits, and fish. We've shared many ups and downs together as we've worked on this "living project"—picking out pets, working through illnesses, playing with and watching them. There's no way to pour out your collective love on God's creatures and not feel closer to your "partner in compassion."

# # 341 Fond Farewells

The burial of an animal should not be done with embarrassment or sloughed off ("Just put it in a box and stick it in the trash"). The ending of life can be a point of connection if you say good-bye together. Through the tears, the conversation, the digging, the picking of an appropriate box, and the inclusion of things the animal enjoyed, the empathy and comfort you offer a grieving child is a strong connector. Life presents many endings, all of which can be significant for your relationship.

# # 342 Cartographers

Assuming you're following the suggestion to take a lot of vacations and "daycations," try making a map showing everywhere you've been. Either make a map yourself, or buy one that you can mark with stickers or markers. Chart your adventures on a map of the United States and also on a map of your local area (blown up so you can identify lots of detail closer to home). The map provides a sense of place and time and of common journey.

# # 343 Salad Bar

Plan a trip to a salad bar in a restaurant or grocery store. Load up a "snack pack," with all the good stuff you both like, and then eat it all out of the container while sitting in your car or at the park.

# # 344 Amateur Hour

Work up some kind of musical duo that you can perform for family or at church. Working to get good at something and to get over "stage fright" can be a wonderfully unifying project.

# # 345 Harmonizing

By its nature, singing requires us to at least attempt harmony. It is a natural builder of connection. And its success isn't dependent on sounding like an opera star. Jam around the piano—or guitar, or drums, or kazoo, or comb and tissue paper. The point is *fun and joy,* not readiness for Carnegie Hall.

# # 346 Singing in the Car

Trips, whether long or short, are tailor-made for singing, which is a lot more fun than bruising backseat battles. "He Touched Me" can give way to "The Magic Touch." Some of my best memories of togetherness when I was little involve singing in the car: "Daisy," "I've Been Workin' on the Railroad," and "You Are My Sunshine." Classic or silly songs, slow or fast, with the radio or a cappella—it's about passing the miles and making some memories.

# # 347 Whistling While You Work

"Whistle while you work" works. Singing can make a humdrum task into a soul-full project. Put some rowdy music on and sing along, or just blend your voices. When I sing with Bethany, sometimes I'll sing or hum the first line, and she'll answer with the second. I follow with the third, and so on until the last line, when we try to finish with a harmonious crescendo (the neighbors haven't asked us to move—*yet*). The house—and the heart—is alive with the sound of music.

# # 348 Project Discipline

A lot of closeness is killed by nagging, so avoid lecturing and nagging and other "Big Brother" activity. Get your kids involved in determining what kinds of consequences will help them cooperate, and then follow through. Missed chores might mean early bedtime. Toys left lying around at the end of the day may disappear into your room for a week. Returning home past curfew might mean no car next weekend. When you've decided on the consequences ahead of time, then you can sympathize with their predicament. This "project" also builds your children's ability to make intelligent decisions and their sense of personal responsibility.

# # 349 Events Planning

Plan a dinner party together, with the goal of creating together a diverse, interesting, eclectic group. Plan the seating as well, with the most potentially dynamic and even conflicting people next to each other. Prepare questions you can alternately throw into the fray. Afterward, you can dissect how your soiree went. You'll give your guests an unforgettable evening and yourself and your child an enjoyable adventure in people.

# # 350 The Paper Trail

A lot of teachers make students bring their school papers home and request that parents "sign off," indicating that they have seen them. Don't rubber-stamp those school papers without really seeing them. Block out time to look them over with your kids—not to correct or criticize, but to help and praise and take a walk through the paper trail of their day.

# # 351 Personal Files

Buy or make a file box together for preserving each child's important papers and projects from school. A good rule of thumb is, keep about one in ten. This helps your kids value and prioritize as they choose what they'll keep—and teaches them not to be mindless packrats who keep everything. Sort and decide together, agreeing that some of the good stuff, though beautiful, still has to go.

# # 352 Treasure Chest

What do you *do* with all the stuff they build and give to you? Stash it on shelves and in closets and throw some of it away when they're not looking? It becomes a problem of time and space. I recommend buying an inexpensive, sturdy plastic box, label it with your child's name, and store as much as possible in there. As they see you treasuring their "treasures," they'll sense how important they are to you themselves. Down the road, as you unearth all those old treasures, you'll connect all over again.

# # 353 It Takes Two, Baby

When you notice that a child is floundering with a project—a wood project from school, a costume, his income taxes—go ahead and join the effort, but let your child lead. You be the "gopher"—go for this, go for that. Or divvy up the work, intertwining your efforts and your hearts.

# # 354 Proof for Perpetuity

Whenever you've completed some project together—small scale or large, silly or momentous—have someone take a picture of the two of you with your finished work. On the back of the picture, each write a short sentence about what it meant to you—and to your relationship.

# # 355 Procedure Review

When I work with business leaders, I recommend that every procedure come up for review at least once a year. This gives all staff members an opportunity to critique and correct bogus or ineffective practices and provides all the team members with a better sense that the organization belongs to them. Try procedure review with your children. Let them know that every year, on some planned schedule, all "procedures"—chores, house rules, weekly schedules—will be reevaluated and modified. Planning together how the family should be run in daily practice is relationship superglue.

# # 356 Paint by Number
You can get a "Paint by Number" set and alternate the work over time—they do the "1," you do the "2," and so on. The same alternating joint effort can be made with original art work, sculpture, pottery, or even puzzles.

# # 357 A New Song
Make up your own song together. Collaborate, or alternate lines of music. Or one of you write the music, the other the lyrics. Even if you can't read or write music, you can use a tape recorder to put in notes and measures, first you and then her. Playing it back will be sure to bring a laugh!

# # 358 Repetitive Reading
Select favorite stories that contain excellent relationship themes as well as great narrative drama. These are the ones to read over and over to your children. Kids of every age love to hear the "old stories," and you'll be deeply ingraining the value of close relationship while you're entertaining the troops.

# # 359 Faith Project
When a faith issue comes up—a need for guidance, illness, loss of a job—make it a joint project to pray together consistently. Going through the doubts and the ups and downs and praying together can draw you close. You'll rejoice as God answers your prayers, and when he doesn't seem to respond as you'd hoped, you can wrestle together with that disappointment and search together for what it means.

# # 360 Formal Portraits
Kids have their individual school photos taken yearly, and families often have photos taken of the whole gang. But once in a while, have photos taken of just the two of you. Dress up, go out for dinner before the photo shoot, and have dessert afterward. You'll have a great visual reminder of

your strong bond to keep in your wallet or on your desk: a photo of the dynamic duo.

# # 361 A New Name

You and your spouse picked out your child's name. Ask your child what she likes or doesn't like about that name, and let her pick a new name to add to her other names. It may be simply a nickname, or it can be a real middle name or third name. Make sure the initials work together. Try out her new self-chosen name, and put it up in lights.

# # 362 All the News You Can Use—and Then Some

Creating a joint newsletter makes for interesting connecting times—and with user-friendly computer typesetting, you might even make it look quite good. Cover the highlights of what you're doing *together* (not individual efforts or accomplishments). Write articles and columns about each other, not about yourself. If more than one child gets in on the project, dole out assignments to each reporter. A collection of newsletters becomes a journal of your relationship. If you like, share the newsletter with family or friends. Broadcasting what you're doing as a team says to the world, "We speak with one voice!" Do it as a one-shot newsletter, or make it a regularly appearing serial.

# # 363 Biography

Ask your child to write a brief biography, not of you or him, but of your relationship. What you can feel and learn from hearing a child explain your relationship in his own words is of great value. Here is a portion of Bethany's (age eleven) about us: "One hot summer day, Bethany and Dad went paddle-boating. They saw a tiny passage, and they decided to go through. They got to a fallen log and a little waterfall a few inches high. There was a tiny rainbow. They just sat there for ten minutes, speechless, and then they hugged each other."

# 10

## Proud—
## and Proud to Show It

# # 364 Self-Worth versus Self-Esteem

The goal of praise is to build your relationship with your child and to build and bolster your child's self-worth. Self-worth says: "I was made in the image of God. I have value. I can make a contribution. I don't have to be self-conscious, self-contemptuous, or apologize for my existence." This is different from self-esteem, which says: "I am great, even superior, no matter what I do."

A recent study looked at "inflated self-esteem, the kind that can come not from actual achievement but from teachers and parents drumming into kids how great they are.... Unjustified self-esteem can trigger hostility and aggression.... Schools often contribute to the problem [by] viewing self-esteem as a cause of success, rather than the result of achievement" (from "You're OK, I'm Terrific: Self-Esteem Backfires," *Newsweek*, July 13, 1998). Praise in lieu of reality builds narcissistic self-esteem; praise rooted in reality builds invaluable self-worth—and appreciation.

# # 365 The 9 to 1 Ratio

Catch your children doing good much more often than you catch them doing wrong. Seek a ratio of 9 to 1. It's too easy to catch them messing up—you can focus on the one bad grade out of eight, the 10 percent of the chore that didn't get done well, and the one time this week they spilled the milk (but never mention the twenty times they *didn't* spill it).

# # 366 Track Record

Keep a pocket log on yourself, noting the times when you criticize and correct and the times when you offer your children praise and appreciation. Make two columns where you can tally check marks. You might be surprised that you're focusing on the negatives more than you think—and you don't want to turn into somebody *you* would hate to have as a parent! You'll want to affirm your kids year round, so keep a log for a week or two a couple of times a year to see how well you're meeting your own goals.

# # 367 Time to Party

When a child gets a smashingly good report card (either A's and B's or a big improvement), throw a family party—complete with his or her favorite foods, a luscious cake, and an exciting video. You can do it at home or go out and splurge.

# # 368 Two-Minute Praise

Write a note—a two-minute note (sounds easier already, doesn't it?)—that tells your child in fifty words or less how proud you are of him. Leave it on his bed or tape it to his mirror—he'll find your notes when you're not around, but you'll still be there.

# # 369 Get Specific

Focus your praise *on a very specific effort or action.* Praise has deep meaning only as it values the other for a unique contribution. A generic, "I'm really proud of you" seldom has the same sense of authenticity as something you've really put some thought into, such as, "I saw you give the Murphys' toddler one of your Matchbox cars. That was really generous."

# # 370 There's Something about You

My friend Maryl Janson likes to focus praise on specific traits she sees in her children, even if those traits are just budding in their development. "I want to encourage the development of their character. I might say things like, 'Responsibility is your trademark,' 'I love the way you throw yourself into projects,' 'Your thoughtfulness for others is a rare virtue,' or 'You're the most organized person your age I've ever seen.'"

# # 371 Nickname Them

An old saying goes, "The much-loved child has many names." Don't be like Archie Bunker and come up with a pet name like "Meathead." Let your playful pet names carry positive identifiers for your kids. Just for fun, call him "Samson" because you think his character is strong. Call her "Betty Crocker" when you're proud of a meal she's prepared. Tell her she's

"Rose"—sweet and beautiful and a pleasure to have around. Call him "Renaissance Man" because his artistic interests take him in many directions. Play with nicknames, and make the play count for praise.

# # 372 Personal Praise
The most meaningful words of recognition or praise are the most personal ones. Tailor what you say to the specific individual child: "Honey, with your quiet personality, I know it took a lot of courage for you to get up in front of the whole church—and you really pulled it off with poise. Good for you!" Or, "I know you've been really working at self-control. I was really proud of you this morning when you were patient with your brother and didn't fight back." Then make the reward personal—personal time together, doing something you both enjoy. Time and relationship are the truly valuable rewards.

# # 373 Up in Lights
Make a list of all of the things you like about your child. Mail her a copy, and post the other on display in a prominent place (the front door? your desk at the office? hanging from the dining-room chandelier?). Proudly display a headline with your child's name and "daughter of (your name)." Show her you're proud to be the parent of such a fabulous person.

# # 374 Crazy for You
Whoop it up. Choose to get totally passionate about something your child has done—or just the fact that he's yours. "Every child needs at least one person who's crazy about him," says Fran Stott.

# # 375 A Little Goes a Long, Long Way
Henri Nouwen wrote, "A little praise raises my spirits, and a little success excites me. It takes very little to raise me up or thrust me down," (The Return of the Prodigal Son). Don't save your praise for only big events or accomplishments. Mark the little steps along the way.

# # 376 You're Just Too Marvelous
You might share a common genetic makeup, but you'll discover right away that each soul stands alone, uniquely created. Emphasize the originality of each child. "We should say to each of them: Do you know what you are? You are a marvel. You are unique. In all the years that have passed, there has never been another child like you," wrote the famous cellist Pablo Casals (quoted in Chicken Soup for the Soul).

# # 377 You Are Somebody

Tell your children why it's so terrific to be *around* them. "I can't believe how generous you are!" "You amaze me with your responsible attitude," or "Your courtesy is so pleasant; no wonder I love spending time with you." Help your kids value the good things about themselves; that's giving them self-worth. They'll find it terrific to be around you, too.

# # 378 Superkid!

Create stories where your child is the hero. And, of course, the hero of the story needs a faithful sidekick, an understanding friend like Sancho Panza to support their Don Quixote heroic efforts. And Sancho, of course, should look and sound a lot like you.

# # 379 Actions Speak Louder

You can tell your kids you're proud of their musical abilities, but you'll show them your love and praise by showing up for the concerts every time you possibly can. Speaking uplifting words is important, but loving "with actions and in truth" (1 John 3:18) is more important. Bring action and truth to all your praise, and you'll strengthen that strong bond with your children. Even when it is hard or inconvenient. *Especially* when it is hard or inconvenient.

# # 380 Employee of the Month

In my work with organizations I discourage "employee of the month" programs, in which one person "wins" and everyone else loses. But you can plan a monthly achievement program so that your kids can all win. Make it a chance to better the household chores record—or maybe a reading program. When kids attain a full month of success, reward them with a night out with you.

# # 381 Upside-down Praise

When your children do something special or well, it's a no-brainer that this is an opportunity to offer praise. But your kids need encouragement just as much when they've messed up or failed. So reaffirm their good qualities that are still there, even though their failure is shouting shame. Look for what was positive in their attempts, even if a plan or project hasn't succeeded. Bob Moawad says, "People are in greater need of your praise when they try and fail, than when they try and succeed."

# # 382 Look 'Em in the Eye

Send your praise deep inside by delivering the message when you've linked souls through the windows of your eyes. The first few times you try to talk eye-to-eye, it may feel uncomfortable. But do it anyway. You'll like what you see.

# # 383 Hands-on Praise

Whenever you can, add a gentle touch to your words of praise. A pat on the back or a squeeze on the arm holds relationship value. Outward touch is a symbol of inward connection.

# # 384 Standing Ovation

An idea I've used to show appreciation for people in an organizational setting works just as well at home. Walk into the room where they are. Take note—silently—of something excellent that they're working on or have recently accomplished. When you're sure they've noticed what you've noticed, just start clapping. Give them a standing ovation. Then walk quietly away—without saying a word.

# # 385 Stand Up!

When one of your kids has done something terrific, announce the good deed at dinnertime. Then rise, like the king at Handel's *Messiah,* to acknowledge the excellence with a round of applause. The public praise for a private act will encourage your child to do more—and will make him feel very good about you. Few people feel really appreciated. Your child can be the exception.

# # 386 The Hero Board

When your kids have shown true excellence (like standing up when an elderly person enters the room, or caring unasked for a baby brother or sister), write them a short note. But don't give it to them. Instead, post it on a "hero board" in the kitchen or some other place for two weeks. It adds to the effect if visitors can see it. When you put their name in lights, they won't need to look "out there" for approbation.

# # 387 Trophy Room

Make room somewhere in your home for achievement recognitions: certificates, diplomas, degrees (at least copies), blue ribbons, letters of appreciation, artwork, poetry. Find a place to showcase their excellence, especially a place accessible to visitors. When Peter got super comments on his writing from two different college professors, we printed up the quotes with some graphics—and on the "trophy wall" it went.

# # 388 Trophy Case

If you can, save up to buy an actual trophy case to capture and preserve all those recognitions that can't be hung on a wall—trophies from athletics or other school competitions, the "game ball" from an event where your child was the team hero, whatever brings back the memory of an achievement. Don't give each child his or her own shelf in the case; you don't want comparisons to shortchange one child. Intermingle their trophies.

# # 389 Put It on the Fridge

Many families use the refrigerator as a combined message center, schedule posting, and place of honor. Clean up your fridge front by making part of it the "business" section and part of it the "honor" section. Then make it the "way station" on the way to the trophy room. Agree with your child on which things are important enough to make the "honor" section.

# # 390 Photo Album

When your child is being honored or is participating in some special event, photograph the whole scenario. Like a reporter, ask questions to get all the details. Then create a photo album with the child's name on a personalized "plate" on the front. Include the photos from the event together with descriptive sentences that preserve the occasion. Let the first picture, of course, be one of the two of you.

# # 391 Pass It On

When you attend teachers' conferences or have an informal chat with a Sunday school teacher or day-care provider, you'll sometimes hear great things about your kids. Do *not* forget to pass those encouraging words along. Make a note so that you don't forget the glory and substantiating detail. Then show your kids the great things someone else saw in them—and show them how pleased you are to be the bearer of such good news.

# # 392 Test with Praise

A person is "tested by the praise he receives" (Prov. 27:21). Watch how your children respond to praise. Is it building bridges to them—or just building an inflated ego? A big clue is whether they share credit for achievement with you or others who helped them. You're looking more for interdependence than self-satisfied independence.

# # 393 The Truth and Nothing But the Truth

Praise your kids with authenticity. You don't want to make a big deal out of things they know aren't really that big a deal. And you don't want them becoming dependent on the opinions of others. Your kids know when they've worked hard, tried hard, and accomplished something. So put your mind to it: What would your children agree that they have done well? We want to praise where they already have a sense of accomplishment. Unbelievable praise, disconnected from real virtue or achievement, rings false with your children and leaves them feeling empty. The goal is recognition, not a false reality.

# # 394 Showing Up

A construction worker once told me that the hardest part of his job was "just showing up." Parenting can be like that. There are just so many events—and so little time. And let's admit it: Some of these sporting events and band concerts are painfully disinteresting. But show up for everything, and look for what's good about these events and how they're good for your kids. The harder it is for you to make the time to show up, the more your kids will appreciate it.

# # 395 Bragging with an Audience

Brag about your children to other people in the presence of your children. Some parents try this, and it doesn't seem to work. Usually they've failed to make their praise specific and undeniable. If you give a vague, overarching statement like, "He's really artistic," the child can deny it. Instead, say something like, "He painted this picture of the San Francisco harbor with excellent perspective and color. I couldn't believe the emotions it brought out of me." Try reinforcing your "brag" with a true comment from some other respected adult: "His art teacher said that he's in the top 5 percent of students he's ever worked with." Bring your child into the conversation, if possible: "Honey, would you tell them what you told me last night about how you created your composition?"

# # 396 It Pays to Advertise

Take out a "brag ad" in your local paper. It makes much better reading than ads from car dealers and department stores. You can do this for the

big events—graduation, other big achievements. Or use it to
communicate congratulations on everyday successes: a good report card,
a church ministry, a sacrificial act. The praise needs to be specific. You
might want to make it an announcement: "The parents of _____ are
pleased to announce that..." Or prepare your entry as a press release:
"The Lucas family today added another name to the winners of writing
awards...."

# # 397 Make Praise a Commodity
In some families, praise just doesn't happen. In those homes, children
hang on to even minor "nonpraise" praises like, "Well, you didn't mess
that up!" or "You look better than usual." Don't make praise a rarity; make
it the everyday currency of your household. Praise should be a
commodity (like wheat) rather than an investment (like a rare work of
art). With praise, philanthropy beats hoarding every time.

# # 398 Pay Up with Thanks
In his book *Up the Organization,* Robert Townsend called thanks the most
neglected form of compensation (Alfred A. Knopf, 1970). Many bosses
figure, "I shouldn't have to thank them; they're supposed to do their job."
They couldn't be more wrong. Thanks is a very ordinary form of
praise—which brings extraordinary relationship value. If you want to
build bridges, thank your kids as often as you can.

# # 399 The Praise Litmus Test
"If a child lives with praise, he learns to be appreciative," wrote Dorothy
Law Nolte. True praise, well received, begets appreciation—for the child
and for you. If your child seems to appreciate you, your praise has been
the right kind and is working its magic. If she takes your affirmation for
granted, there's something wrong—your praise isn't specific enough, it
isn't meaningful to her, or perhaps your other words and actions are
negating its effect. A second clue that your praise is effective is when
your child is able to pass along praise to others. If she can't, authentic
praise is too scarce a resource.

# # 400 The Comparisons Pitfall
Avoid using comparisons to praise one child at the expense of another
(especially if the other is another child in your family), as in "Thank
goodness you're better at math than Francesca." Such comparisons are
almost certain to breed arrogance, competitiveness, and a strong dose of

sibling rivalry. If a child achieves "first place" in some area, overcompetitiveness may make him feel compelled to fight for it. Focus your praise on each individual child and his particular talents, skills, and accomplishments, and avoid the "better thans."

# # 401 Labels

Labels are usually deadly. They're especially so in praise. "He's a typical firstborn: hard-driving, conscientious, loyal, and a perfectionist." The problem with a comment like this is that you make his actions "uncontrollable" as if he were typecast from birth. If siblings hear such a comment, they may give up pursuing those same strong qualities, since they aren't the firstborn. Such labeling doesn't qualify as praise; it's more like compliment by horoscope. Remember that your son or daughter is a one-of-a-kind human being, and resist the labels that accompany some of the discussions about personality (birth order, personality type, strong-willed, right/left-brain dominant).

# # 402 Voided Interaction

If you try to offer praise or encouragement when your general tone toward your children is judgmental, harsh, and nitpicking, you might as well not bother. They'll completely discount the value of any praise to zero. When parents complain that their children's behavior toward them is angry and nasty, I want to ask, "Are they mirroring the way you treat them?" One family we had in our home for supper appalled us with their dinnertime "conversation": "Sit still. Straighten up. Eat that vegetable. You may not have any more. Stop staring." It made me wonder what their comments would sound like when they were home! Then one of the parents offered a word of so-called praise: "I took _____ with me on a business errand, and she was such a little lady." Believe me, that praise didn't sink in for that little girl. It couldn't.

# # 403 Lofty Achievement

Someday when someone asks you, "What's your greatest accomplishment?" forget about professional success. At work or in the community, the best answer to give is the name of your child.

# 11

## A Walk in Their Sneakers

# # 404 Respect Their Dignity

If you see your children as undeveloped, unformed, immature, incapable servants or as blank tablets to write on, you're missing something essential in your relationship. These are fearfully, wonderfully made people, designed by God even before birth (Ps. 139). Respect their dignity, and remember the common bond that unites you in your humanity, your struggles, and your victories.

# # 405 The Nuisance Factor

Many things your children want to do with you will seem like a nuisance. Time-consuming games, uninteresting topics, and other interruptions can take you away from "important" adult stuff. A seven-year-old invited his mom to search some nearby woods for crickets to feed his frog. For him, that activity was a "ten" on a one-to-ten scale. For some mothers, it would rate in negative digits. This mom would rate it about a "one," but she went. And she actually had a wonderful time because it built her relationship with her little boy. See the power in a nuisance.

# # 406 Sympathy and Empathy

Know the difference between sympathy and empathy, and make sure you don't stop at sympathy. Sympathy says, "That is really tough. I know you must be struggling. I'll pray for you." In the midst of parenting on a bad day, even sympathy can be hard to muster. Empathy goes the next mile. It says, "I know how you feel. This is killing me. I *am* as anguished as you are." Sympathy shows a child that you care. Empathy shows a child that you understand, having been a child yourself, and that you know his feelings—up close and personal.

# # 407 Judge Not

Everything a child does has some reason—maybe not a good one, or a reason we can like, but there *is* a reason. So when annoying or disturbing behaviors crop up, stop yourself from jumping in with a quick judgment: "What's the matter with you? We don't hide report cards in this family! Don't you know that's dishonest?" Instead, start with your desire to understand what feelings or reasoning led him to his wrong behavior. You can work on the discipline aspect, too, but put your relationship and understanding first. There could be interesting reasons behind a child's hiding a report card. Maybe he's disappointed over getting a B, when that grade in that subject is acceptable to you. Maybe his report card was great, but he's worried his sister will feel bad about her less than spectacular one. Or could he be hiding the "evidence" out of fear of being beaten down by your cross-examination? If a bonded relationship is your first goal, you need to understand your child. The Roman philosopher Seneca said, "If you would judge, understand."

# # 408 Understanding and Praise

Remember that it is more satisfying to your child to be understood than to be praised. "There is much satisfaction in work well done; praise is sweet; but there can be no happiness equal to the joy of finding a heart that understands," wrote Victor Robinson (quoted in *12,000 Religious Quotations*, Baker Books, 1989).

# # 409 Always Ask Why

Some parenting "experts" advise parents never to ask their children why they did something. "You'll only get excuses and rationalizations," they say. But even if your child begins by replying with an excuse, it's worthwhile to ask why. Ask because you respect your child and because you're willing to get down to the motives that underlie their actions. Don't be like King David, who "never interfered with [Adonijah] by asking, 'Why do you behave as you do?'" (1 Kings 1:6). It's no good trying to achieve some sort of tyrannical surface control; your child's willingness to serve and obey will grow only out of your child's relationship with you.

# # 410 First Aid for the Heart

She comes to you with a wound so tiny that it's not observable with the naked parental eye. "I need a bandage," she whimpers. With all your parental knowledge, don't come back with, "Are you kidding? No blood, no bandage." You'll miss a chance to put empathy to work. Don't belittle a child's small problems. That little wound is huge to her—or maybe she just needed some first aid from you for her heart.

# # 411  Why Don't They Come to Me with Their Problems?

Business executives often complain that employees cover their mistakes, their conflicts with other staff members, or other problems. Many parents feel the same way when they're the last to find out about their children's problems. The answer in both cases may lie in the management structure. Are employees or kids penalized for telling the truth (in trouble for "snitching" even if their brother is pounding them)? Does the management/parent spend more time fixing the blame than fixing the problem? Does the management/parent ever admit they make mistakes or errors in judgment? Sometimes the person who hesitates to fess up is really acting in his own best interest. Maybe it's time for some restructuring.

# # 412  Listening Is Loving

"Listening is loving," says Zig Ziglar. When you listen, you ratify a child's value at a high level. Believe me, your children will notice the difference between the attentive listening you provide a visitor or neighbor and the 20 percent of your attention you give when they are talking. Five or ten minutes of real listening beats hours of pretend.

# # 413  Huh?

Conversation can either bring you closer or drive you crazy. Communication is difficult because of perception (how two people can interpret the same data very differently) and semantics (how differently people can define the same word); writes Stephen Covey: "Through empathic understanding, both of these problems can be overcome" (*Seven Habits of Highly Effective Families,* Simon & Schuster, 1996). My daughter Laura and I talked for three and a half hours about the role of government in everyday life, with lots of dialogue about the truth and meaning of historical information, and not finding out till the end that most of our disagreement came from different understandings of the words *regulation, oversight,* and *equity.* When you feel like your child is speaking a foreign language, keep that conversation going until you begin to understand what your child is seeing and saying.

# # 414 Paradigm Shift

Don't expect your kids to respond with instant insight and agreement to your Parental Proclamations. Every person has "paradigms," ways of looking at and understanding the world, and you can't expect your kids' paradigms to turn on a dime. Nothing big changes fast. Empathy dictates that you state your ideas, listen to theirs, and then give the subject a rest. Over time, your kids may alter their paradigm. Or yours.

# # 415 Are You Listening?

When children are toddlers, trying out their newfound vocabulary, they may not need your full-fledged, eye-to-eye attention. They're content simply to have you somewhere in the same room, someone to respond with a smile once in a while. But your older children will be sensitive to whether or not you are really listening. So stop what you're doing, even if it's just for five minutes, and listen to them with ears tuned-in for understanding. Or make an appointment to talk when you can.

# # 416 Listen for Understanding

When your children talk to you, they're communicating on several levels. So don't be the kind of parent who is "hearing but never understanding" (Matt. 13:14). An older child will be keenly disappointed if you're absent while present. So tune in—completely—to catch the levels of feelings and ideas that come through your child's conversation. It's the spirit, not the letter, that counts. Ask him, "How do you feel," not just, "What do you think?"

# # 417 Don't Pretend to Listen

There are times when you listen to kids but your mind is somewhere else completely—while driving on a dark, unfamiliar road in a storm, for example. But be honest about it. If your kids say, "Hey, you're not paying attention!" admit it. Don't ever just pretend to listen when your mind is focused elsewhere. Your kids are sharp enough to pick up on your mental absence, and you'll have betrayed their trust by "faking" with them. Admittedly, it's tough always to be "present in the present" in the middle of a busy life, but you've got to show up to a conversation with your mind, heart, and ears if you're really going to connect with your kids.

# # 418 Avoiding Selective Listening

Be careful to hear more than just your hot buttons—those words or phrases or requests that send you into a well-rehearsed negative script. Maybe you hear "borrow the car," "old enough to date," "cut class," or "I hate _____," and that's all it takes. It's like pushing "play" on a CD player: out come your preprogrammed lyrics. This is dangerous because you're listening selectively, reacting to your hot buttons without paying attention to the context of the conversation. Very often you'll misjudge your child's intentions. Listen to everything your child is telling you, including the intent and overall meaning.

# # 419 Jumping-Off Point

Sometimes a joint project—building a model, sewing a dress, painting the house, planting the garden—gets you talking over the details. As you work, you talk mostly about the project, but the project doesn't have to dominate the conversation. Other topics can be part of that concentrated time together. The best is when you tie the project in to life and love ("We could just paint over that rotted section, but that's as effective as trying to smile when you're bitter").

# # 420 Deep Listening

At this level of listening, your goal is to know your kids more deeply—to know them so well that you pick up what they *mean*, to see what they see. Achieve this empathetic listening through eye contact, making notes, asking questions (for understanding, not to make your own point), paraphrasing to make sure you're getting their drift. When my daughter Laura was going over possible educational/career directions with me, I took extensive notes—to show her I cared, to force myself to listen closely, to have a record to build on the conversation later on. Care, have a servant's heart, and be "completely humble and gentle" (Eph. 4:2), and you'll achieve deep listening.

# # 421 Passionate Listening

"You can listen like a blank wall or like a splendid auditorium where every sound comes back fuller and richer," says Alice Duer Miller in *Promises from Parents*. You've reached the pinnacle of good listening when you pour yourself into the topic at hand and into the person who's talking to you. It's when you listen with your heart as well as your head, when you let yourself get visibly and truly excited, when you can hardly stem the flow of give-and-take—that's when you've taken listening onto the level of an unbreakable bond.

# # 422 Crystal Ball Imagination

Inside the son you're talking with today, no matter how young, is the seed of the man he'll become. In some sense, he's already the great writer or the committed parent or the spiritual leader. Inside that daughter, no matter how small, is the seed of the woman she'll become. In some sense, she already is the doctor caring for indigents, a speaker teaching a roomful of people, a grandmother telling stories of her youth—of *right now*—to another little girl. Use your imagination to see that and you'll parent your children with passion—and better—today.

# # 423 Looking for Respect in Right or Wrong Places
Much of human motivation grows out of a search for respect or from dealing with disrespect. Everyone has a need to be deeply respected. If you can afford your children real respect, giving them the same courtesy and attention you would give to a church leader or learned visitor, they won't have to journey away from you to find it. They'll make you their heart's home.

# # 424 Fixing Isn't Freeing
When you think you're showing love to your kids, but they seem to be resisting it, a basic reason could be that the way you're showing love isn't the way they receive love. Or it could be even worse. It may not be driven by what's best for that child and may not even be real love. It may be an issue-driven need to nurture, fix, and control. If your kind of love makes your kids feel helpless and dependent or behave in ways that are self-centered and demanding, give your "loving" a makeover. You aren't raising a mature and responsible individual—or one who will ever be able to treat you with healthy affection.

# # 425 Break the Mold
It's fine to study physical or psychological or moral "stages" of growth that most children pass through. But don't believe everything you read. This categorization fails to encompass the truth that kids don't always pass through stages in the prescribed sequence—that there are as many "exceptions" to these rules as there are different children. The best way to help your children grow and mature in every way is to know their uniqueness and know it well. Then you can work with their individual strengths and weaknesses with the originality God has given them.

# # 426 Keep Up with Transitions
A lot of married couples stop "courting" once they marry, figuring they've achieved the goal of togetherness and failing to realize that their marriage will have to keep flexing as they both continue to change and

mature. Parents often do the same thing with their kids. They figure they've reached a great level of mutual understanding and love, and they "lock in," assuming they can move ahead on cruise control. But children are constantly growing and changing; there are seasons to life and seasons to relationships. So stay flexible. Be prepared to try different approaches to discipline, conversation, and conflict resolution. Your relationship is like a living organism—it's going to keep on transitioning.

## # 427 Are They Kids or Adults?

One transition that parents must recognize and deal with is "the big one"—the jump from child to adult that takes place sometime during those preteen and teen years, depending on the child. Suddenly you'll think, *Do I treat this twelve-year-old girl like an older child or like a young adult?* Be prepared to answer, "Young adult," or watch your relationship crumble. You can't try to keep your child "little." You have to treat her respectfully by seeing her as she see herself—as a young adult. Dealing with a young adult means a shift from strong direction to discussion and negotiating options. It's a good idea to talk to your teen as the mature adult you want her to become.

## # 428 Take the Offering

If your child sweetly offers you a "peanut butter and green bean sandwich," don't answer rationally ("Are you kidding? No way!") unless you can see that he's deliberately joking. If you believe your child is sincerely offering you something, it is better to respond *relationally* ("Of course, sweetheart. I love how you come up with new recipes"). Once the child leaves the room, you can discreetly dispose of it. This is not a dishonest response, because what you're accepting when he offers the peanut butter and green beans is actually his love offering to you. When you look at that sandwich and what you see is your child's "heart" on that bread, it's honest to respond, "Thank you, baby."

## # 429 Honor the Difference

Empathy involves laying aside your own needs, desires, and preferences in order to understand and respect the needs, desires, and preferences of your children. You can't expect them to be good at the same things you are or to like what you do just because they're *your* children. If you want the best between you, honor your differences and give them equal respect.

# # 430 Build on the Differences

It's your differences, after all, that make your relationship exciting. If both of you think and act the same, one of you is unnecessary. So instead of minimizing your differences, try to identify them and build on them. Make your differences complementary rather than a source of annoyance. If you like it quiet and your child likes it chaotic, don't try to convert each other. Instead, agree on how your child can benefit from quiet times with you (like focusing on a problem) and how you can benefit from chaotic times with her (it'll keep you young). Recognize that God must have had something in mind when he matched you up.

# # 431 Become like a Child

Jesus said, "I tell you the truth, anyone who will not receive the kingdom of God like a little child will never enter it" (Mark 10:15). This makes empathetically taking a walk in your kid's shoes sound, well, *important!* So try shedding your adult pretensions so you can think and feel with the sincerity of a child. Get into your child's games. Focus on fun and joy. Once in a while, refuse to be distracted by responsibility. Give yourself an evening "break" to play with your child. The bills to pay, the dirty tub to scrub, the laundry to fold—they'll still be there tomorrow. Are children irresponsible—or do they just know the value of recess?

# # 432 What Do You Think?

Even little children can teach you about how to live if you'll let them. I've been amazed at the fresh and diverse insights my children have given me on people and situations where I had the "normal" adult perspective. It builds your children's confidence (and builds your bond) when they realize their opinion counts with you.

# # 433 Take Mommy/Daddy to School Day

Sometimes, take a walk in your kids' shoes more literally. Volunteer for the activities related to their lives—attend a field trip, be an assistant Little League coach, take tickets or usher at their school play. Join in activities with a goal to be part of things, not to be in charge or "monitor" activities. Read your children's school newspaper and talk with them about what it says. Go to classes one day, if you can—maybe even on a day when they're home sick (if there's someone else to stay with them)—so there's no pressure or embarrassment. You can talk more specifically about their activities, schoolmates, teachers, and friends when you've come in contact with them yourself. You've deepened your soul connection.

# # 434 Your Home, the Truck Stop

One day at school or out in the neighborhood can beat all of the love and confidence out of a child. Just like you, when they come home at the end of the day, they're coming in to "gas up"—to refuel for another day. Think of your home as a refuge. You're the high-powered attendant at a service station, not a siphon.

# # 435 Protect Their Privacy

Every person needs a private life—even fairly young children. So afford your children consideration—when they're using the bathroom, changing clothes, or just need a break from family members or visitors. Don't read their mail or snoop through their rooms or belongings. Don't eavesdrop on their conversations. If you make your home like a prison camp, will they want to love the guard?

# # 436 Be a Confidant

We all have things that we need to tell . . . somebody. Most parents desire the role of confidant; they want to be the one with whom their children share their deep hurts and joys. Why do so few parents become that person for their kids? It's less about a generation gap than it is about a *trust* gap. "A trustworthy man keeps a secret," says the old proverb. Do your kids trust you with their confidences, or are they afraid you'll tell others or use them later against them? Are you listening with intent to care or with intent to fix? Start being a trustworthy confidant while your children are young, and maybe they won't need a therapist later.

# # 437 Be Their Comfort Zone

Feelings need an outlet, and you can become that "comfort zone" for your children. As you understand and accept their feelings, they'll bring up their hidden hurts or frustrations. And you should share your own feelings and experiences on the same issue or situation. When both of you are genuine, you can't help but strengthen your bond.

# # 438 Provide the Words

Have you ever been in another country, struggling with a foreign language, grappling for the word you want? It's a frustrating experience. Sometimes your children feel that same frustration when talking with you, so they say, "I hate you," when what they really mean is that they're irritated, annoyed, offended, exasperated. So guard your reactions. Being empathetic gives you time to explore their feelings and suggest other ways to express what they mean. Give them the vocabulary, trying one word or phrase at a time until you understand what they're really trying to express. Helping them express how they feel about something, and why, can make for incredible connection.

# # 439 Ratify Their Experience

Your words, tone, and body language communicate, "It's safe to express your feelings. It's OK. I understand." When you empathize with them ("If that happened to me, I'd feel like breaking things, too!"), you're accepting instead of judging their feelings. You validate that they're reacting in a normal and human way, and you open the door to help them handle those feelings productively.

# # 440 What to Do with Their Feelings

Part of growing up is learning which feelings can and should be acted on. As your children let you into their experiences, you're in a prime position to shape the actions that grow out of their feelings. Don't just blurt out specific directions on what they should do. Help them reason their way to discovery. Give them time to let their feelings play out. Then move into a rational, problem-solving time by asking questions: "Do you think hitting him back would make you feel better? Would you feel better right away—and also later—when you thought about your own behavior? What might happen if you did hit him back?" Shape their self-discipline; show them how their minds, and not just their feelings, can dictate their behavior.

# # 441 Kids' Impressions about People

Without encouraging judgment or nastiness, ask your children about their feelings regarding other people. Start with their feelings about their relationships with their siblings. Move on and talk about how they feel about other relatives, teachers, people at church, friends. When you ask, they may unburden themselves of unpleasant feelings they've hidden—negative feelings they believe are shameful or wrong. As you discover how your children are relating to the people around them, you will be able to help them process fears and dislikes, longings or discomfort.

# # 442 Mood-O-Meter

My friend Travis Thrasher sent me a rectangular Mood-O-Meter chart, with thirty-six moods represented on it and appropriate cartoon faces to illustrate. It hangs magnetically on my file cabinet, where I can move a smaller magnet around the thirty-six moods to indicate to all my office visitors that today I'm happy, crabby, angry, whatever. But instead of metering my moods, it has become a way for me to tune in to how others are feeling. People find it impossible to walk by that little chart without moving the magnetic marker to indicate their own mood. This might be something fun to buy or create and keep around your house. Kids especially might find it a nonthreatening way to express what's really going on inside.

# # 443 Get Down!

Recently I had a conversation with a well-known author and speaker who towered over me—and I'm fairly tall. It was a bit disconcerting. It served as a good reminder that "talking down" from a standing or seated position that's higher than the person to whom you're speaking can be intimidating, a sort of power play. So make it a practice with your child to sit or lie down on the floor. Squash into the toddler chair. Sit on the edge of your kid's desk when he's standing. Go to where he is.

# # 444 The Whites of Their Eyes

Some folks are more comfortable with eye contact than others, but whether or not you're naturally disposed to look your kids in the eye, it's something you can choose to do. Then use your eyes to respond to what they're saying, without having to interrupt their flow of conversation with words. You "listen" with your eyes and even talk back with them. If you find that you or they are deliberately avoiding eye contact, your relationship is troubled. The solution is not to say, "Look at me," but to search your children with your words and eyes to discover whatever is dividing you.

# # 445 Be Patient

Never walk into a room where children are playing or talking and just take over, interrupting the conversation or activity, giving orders, shaping them up. It's unempathetic and socially disrespectful (you wouldn't behave with such discourtesy to a person outside your family). Judge yourself. Ask yourself, *Would I be happy to see me coming into the room?*

# # 446 Do You Hear What They Hear?

Demonstrate your desire to be empathetic by listening to the music your kids enjoy—whether it's the sing-song stuff of toddlers or the raucous nonmusic some teens like. Discovering which songs delight or move them uncovers what your children value because people generally listen to music that expresses their own feelings, longings, or dreams. *Their music is a clue.* Wise parents listen and learn and use that music as a password into their children's heart.

# # 447 Emphasizing the Learning, Not the Grades

Report card time can be a massive disconnecting point for parents and their kids—but even poor grades can become an opportunity for better parent-child bonding. Don't emphasize the letter grade—C or B-, which can be a slim representation of what's going on in the whole class. And don't compare one child's grades with a sibling's or with your own performance in school at that age. Instead of driving a wedge between you, dig into the whole class experience your child is having—the subject, the teacher, your child's defeats or heartaches. Find out how you can get involved in the subject (to help pull up the poor grade, but more important, to help him master the area of study). Go with a child to the library to help with research (make sure he's still in charge of his own project). Stay up late with the kid who's preparing a makeup paper, and bring him a cold drink or snack. A poor grade is a signal for parents to get in there to bolster that area of school life. You can holler and divide, or help and build connection.

# # 448 Collaborate

Ever been floundering with a big decision? Ever felt unable to pick yourself up after a big mistake or error in judgment? These are the kinds of stresses your kids deal with almost daily, since their judgment is still forming and they have an unusual capacity for messing things up (just as we do). Think what it's meant to you in your own struggles to have even one person come along with a word of encouragement instead of criticism—with a second chance instead of dismissal. Help your kids the same way: Collaboration beats condemnation every time.

# # 449 In over Your Head

Once in a while you'll find yourself caught up in some project with your child that's taking up a lot more time and energy than you'd anticipated. Maybe it's a science project for school, a building project at home, a thousand-piece puzzle. When the hours go by and you start getting antsy—probably too aware of the 101 other important tasks awaiting you—hang in there. While your child's project isn't that important to you, it's crucial to your child. Because it's important to your child, let it be important to you. Parents who want connection leave out the complaints and finish strong.

# # 450 When I Was Your Age . . .

It's so easy to raise children by categories and formulas, falling back on the rules your parents applied to you or the ones that worked for older children. But rules aren't sacred—relationships are. Be prepared to modify applications of principles for each individual child. Great people and organizations thrive by constantly reinventing themselves. So don't hesitate to venture away from "This is the way it's done in our family."

# # 451 What's Your Child Good At?

Real empathy involves discovering and helping to develop a child's values, interests, and strengths. You may hope your kids will be good at everything they try, but it just isn't going to happen. Minimize your focus on your child's areas of weakness (except for encouraging perseverance to do their best in a required school subject they don't enjoy). Instead, celebrate the strengths and passions.

# # 452 Clip and Share

Keep your child's interests in mind by clipping articles you discover that touch on them. Find an interview with a soccer player for your soccer fan at home. Clip a newspaper article on inner-city housing for your teen who's planning to participate in that kind of work over the summer. You might personalize the effort by highlighting parts you especially want your child to notice—or scrawl notes in the margins. Feeding a child's interest communicates, "I understand you *big time.*"

# # 453 Like-Minded

Support your children's interests by facilitating encounters with others who share their interests. Invite people to your home, or get out and do things with these people who are passionate about the same things your son or daughter enjoys. When one of our children became interested in art, we attended the annual local art fair with his high school art teacher. Show them you see what's important to them and that you're doing all you can to support their interest. Be on their side, creatively.

# # 454 Customized Gift Giving

Giving gifts is nearly always a positive action, but take it to its ultimate potential for building relationship by customizing the gift to fit the child. Choose or create something that's meaningful to your child, not something that's meaningful to you or that you think your child needs. Tailor a gift to your child's specific interests or idiosyncrasies, and you tell that child he's special, that he's worth your time to think about and search out just the right gift. You're honoring his unique personality, which is better than the gift.

# # 455 Just Because

Giving a thoughtfully chosen gift at unexpected times demonstrates your empathy. Instead of waiting for a special occasion, *declare* a special occasion. Choose a gift that speaks to one of your child's interests or that meets a current need. When I noticed that my son Peter, then a sophomore in college, was talking about a special kind of shirt he liked—but not even asking for it—I asked him to go along to run errands with me. When we got to the store, I told him that the "errand" was actually to buy him those shirts. I could have waited a couple of weeks until Christmas, but I wanted him to see that I enjoy surprising him and that I can't wait to meet his needs.

# # 456 Empathetic Home Run

Hit a home run with your kids by a gift or act of service that shows you understand right where they're at. One family's children ate lunch very early at school, so they were always famished by the time they got home. Their wise mother knew it and never failed to leave some treat in the fridge for her kids, labeled with their names and a quick note. Believe me, those kids were grateful. Empathy isn't just feeling the need—it's knowing what will meet it.

# # 457 Guess Who's Coming to Dinner?

Tell your child that you're expecting an important dinner guest. Elicit her help in making it a real big deal. Clean the house, get out the good dishes, create some delicious food—the whole shebang. Then just before dinner, inform your child that she is the guest! Treat your daughter with deference and courtesy throughout the meal, as you would an honored guest.

# # 458 Servant Leadership

A thoughtful act of service, especially one that touches a child's point of desire or need, shows your love. Base it on the best way for your child to receive your love, not the easiest way for you to show it. Maybe you'd like to show your son you love him by dusting his room—when what he'd really prefer is for you to bring home an Arnold Schwarzenegger movie for him to watch. Serve your child, unselfishly.

# # 459 The Best Luxury

I hear many people exhort parents to "lavish praise" on children, but it's even better to lavish *understanding*. Work hard to understand your kids. Give their underlying motives the benefit of the doubt; lie awake nights thinking about your kids until you understand them well. Why? It's an essential human need, but even more: as Emerson wrote, "It is a luxury to be understood."

# # 460 Fluent in Many Languages

Gary Chapman writes about how important it is to be able to put to use "language" (time together, touch, gifts, and so on) that speaks most clearly to each of your children (*The Five Love Languages*, Northfield, 1995). The wise parent will become fluent in *all* the languages Chapman mentions—and even more. You show your love to your children in numerous "languages"—when you forgive them, defend them, warn them, touch them, encourage them, spend time with them. Discover every road to empathy—and journey on them all.

# 12

## Powersharing

## # 461 Let Freedom Ring

Think "freedom" first—before you think "control." The highest delight in relationship comes with liberty, choices, mutuality. The point is not to restrain your kids but to free them to become what's best. The apostle Paul wrote, "It is for *freedom* that Christ has set us free" (Gal. 5:1, emphasis added). Let freedom ring.

## # 462 Attitudes versus Rules

It's easy for parents to become quasi-drill sergeants, really married to "the plan": an orderly household, clear guidelines, firm house rules. But this black-and-white orientation toward rules leaves parents *managing* their children, not leading them. The "rules" illusion, while tidy, is guaranteed to damage the bond you're hoping to build with your child. Real parental leadership is better exercised in your attitudes, which give shape to your conflict resolution, your discipline techniques, your empathy. Great parenting comes from a set of attitudes, not just a set of rules.

## # 463 Why Not?

There are always a million reasons to say no, but break out of this stranglehold approach to parenting with the best question you can ask yourself: *Why not? Can he roll in the mud outside? Why not? Can she spread her project on her bed and sleep on the floor tonight? Why not?* Why not, indeed. Many of the thousands of no's a child hears in his first eighteen years have no really good reason behind them. Should you drop most of these deadly no's? Uh...why not?

# # 464 Connect by Letting Go

"Letting go" isn't reserved for young adults who are moving out of the house. Letting go can also mean giving your kids breathing space to be individuals, room to make decisions (even if they're small ones for younger children), or opportunity for each voice to be heard. Don't hang on so tightly that you choke off that individual's chance to grow.

# # 465 Hold On Loosely

If you hold a tiny animal too tightly, you can smother it. So it is with love. Don't hang on to your kids too tightly. Control is an illusion anyway. The only worthwhile relationships are the ones that are freely chosen.

# # 466 Partners

In the best organizations today, leadership is abandoning the practice of categorizing staffers as hired help, subordinates, or even as employees. To maximize potential in all, they focus on workers as *partners* working toward the same goal. This respectful approach communicates, "We're in this together. We don't own you. We don't think for you. You bring a lot of value to what we're doing." Try this with your family organization. You'll find it won't diminish your authority with your kids; rather it will merely redefine it and will spur your young people on to achieve their maximum potential.

# # 467 The Golden Rule

In powersharing (see my leadership book *Balance of Power,* AMACOM Books, 1998) within your family, the Golden Rule is a perfect guide. How will believing that you should do unto others as you would have them do to you lead you in the parental issues of power and authority? A good question to ask yourself is, *Would I want my boss to treat me the way I'm handling my children? Would I want my spouse to treat me this way?* Brainstorm, perhaps on paper, what you'd most appreciate in those in authority over you. You'll create an outline of parenting positives you'll want to apply with your children.

# # 468 The Wheels of Justice

"Those who deny freedom to others deserve it not for themselves," said Abraham Lincoln, "and, under a just God, cannot long retain it." If this is so, then parents who misuse (or overuse or abuse) their leadership position with their children will somehow, in the long run, find themselves on the wrong side of an authority who does the same to them.

# # 469 Defining Power

One effective way to think about power is to call it "the ability to get something done." Constructive power does what's good; destructive power does what's bad. If your goal as a parent is to add value to your life and relationships, keep the perspective that everyone in the family brings power—an ability to get something done—to the mix. What can be accomplished by the team is for the family, its relationships and its individual members. Power is just a tool for family development, not a treasure to be hoarded by the grown-ups.

# # 470 Friends, Not Servants

In order to have deep connection and friendship, two people must perceive themselves to be of equal value, even if their position is not necessarily equal. Jesus told his disciples, "I no longer call you servants.... Instead, I have called you friends" (John 15:15). Friendship with your children doesn't mean you spill your guts about every burden you're carrying or that you don't deal with misbehavior. You each still maintain your different positions in the family. But you do have an equality before God that allows you to respect your children and meet them person-to-person in an I'm-glad-we're-buddies kind of way.

# # 471 Your Own Best Judgment

The policy manual of the Nordstrom department stores is cleverly simple: "In all situations, use your own best judgment. There are no other rules." Unfortunately, it's human nature to be reluctant to trust the judgment of other people, including our children. Responsibility is earned, not born. So if you can't trust your children's judgment, consider whether you've given them freedom to make decisions, which is training for making good judgments. The goal is to develop adults—men and women who stand on their own two feet and use their own best, long-nurtured judgment.

# # 472 Amazing Things

"Amazing things happen when you dignify their suggestions and their ideas ... when you show your respect for them by allowing them to exercise their own wisdom and judgment and discretion," writes Southwest Airlines CEO Herb Kelleher about working with employees. See what amazing things transpire when you dignify your children's suggestions and ideas. One of those things is likely to be devotion.

# # 473 Not Too Big, Not Too Little

As you share power in your family, keep each child's maturity level in mind so that you don't give very small children too wide a choice or force freedom when they're not yet ready. At the opposite end of the spectrum, don't frustrate older children with too little choice and/or forced boundaries when they're ready for freedom. Stay close to your kids, so you'll sense how to act wisely.

# # 474 Delegating versus Dumping

Powersharing doesn't mean abdicating your own authority or responsibility. Your children aren't there to pick up the slack for you when you haven't managed priorities well. Provide them power over carefully chosen decisions and projects that fit their level of responsibility and ability. Delegating builds relationship, while dumping wipes it out.

# # 475 Supervision versus Micromanagement

Effective leaders stay in control of the project and its intended outcome, but they willingly delegate the details of getting the job done to the middle managers. They know it's counterproductive to hang over the middle manager's shoulders, doing his job for him. Effective parents can help the family reach agreement on the overarching objective—say, to get all the chores done by dinnertime—but then delegate some of the decision making on methods and details to individual family members. An older child then has some ownership over when she'll start her chores, what order she'll do them in, and how best to get each job done. Provide input when necessary, but don't micromanage the issue. Let your children exercise their power (in this case, to get chores done) until dinnertime.

# # 476 Running from Rules

If your parenting is dominated by rules, your children will either be crushed by the rules or they'll run from them once they're old enough. If, in their perception, you and the rules are one and the same, they'll reject relationship with you at the same time. Parenting by the rules, while neatly black and white, can be deadly. God parents his children by relationship; the Christian's godly choices grow out of a thankful desire to serve God, who's convinced her of his love. Parent by relationship and not just by the rules. Mirror God's parenting to your children.

# # 477 Improving Judgment

U.S. General George Patton used to say, "Never tell people how to do things. Tell them what you want them to achieve, and they will surprise you with their ingenuity." This is excellent parenting advice. Agree on goals with your children, but leave the how-to up to them. This encourages their innate creativity to blossom into maturity.

# # 478 Inner Voice versus Outer Voices

Many parents complain that their kids have stopped listening to them and listen only to their peers. This may be partly their own fault. Parents who continually direct their children, question everything they do, and show no confidence in their children's judgment reinforce their children's dependence on an "outside" voice. For a while, the outside direction comes from the parents; later it shifts to peers. Ideally, parents should focus on helping kids learn to think and decide for themselves, based on well-developed value systems—no matter what their peers are saying.

# # 479 Exclusive Invitation

The best-loved parents are those who respect the "domain" of their children. These parents recognize that their children have their own souls and thoughts and feelings and space. That little world belongs to the children, and parents wait to be invited into it.

# # 480 Mutual Respect and Trust

The key to powersharing is mutual respect and trust. Do you trust your children? Why or why not? What would they have to do to prove themselves trustworthy? What would you need to change in order to be more comfortable trusting? In your relationship, a certain amount of trust has to be earned, but another amount has to be *granted.*

# # 481 No More Watchdog

Doublecheck to make sure you haven't structured your whole parent-child relationship on a system of "watching"—constantly looking over your kids' shoulders, nipping here, tucking there, fine-tuning, making sure they don't "mess up." You know what? It isn't your job to make sure they don't make any mistakes, that they do everything the "one best way." That kind of watching uses up a tremendous amount of energy and is almost guaranteed to produce alienation. Responsibility and accountability is preferred to a system of watchers and watchees.

# # 482 What Is Accountability?

Freedom without accountability is anarchy. You don't want your kids to feel so "free" that they lose their sense of what's right. But you can't build accountability with lectures on being responsible or doing the right thing. You establish *conditions* to go with their freedom. "Yes, you can go out to play in the rain—if you agree that when you come in you will take off your wet clothes, take them to the laundry room, and clean up any puddles." "Yes, you and your friends can have a party here if you agree to clean up the house afterward and replace anything that gets broken." Get agreement in advance, and let them know that if they don't follow through, they'll have created a no to their next request.

# # 483 Loss of Privileges

Accountability is built when children's irresponsibility results in a "loss" to them. If you clearly establish a house rule that their toys and other "stuff" have to be put away at bedtime or they forfeit the stray items for one week, you won't have to lecture them all day. You've made their mess their responsibility, and they're accountable if their stuff gets confiscated. Agree on conditions ahead of time: If you bring back the car without refueling, no car privileges for two days. This system precludes the need for nagging and lectures on your part—both of which are unattractive behaviors that hurt relationship—and puts the accountability on your increasingly responsible child.

# # 484 Don't Sap Their Power

When you do for your children what they can do for themselves, you're "disempowering" them at a fundamental level. In effect, you reduce your relationship to that of a servant to a master. To build a strong, mutually respectful relationship, let them do what they can do, even when you could do it better or more quickly.

# # 485 I Can Do It Myself

When your child says to you, "Daddy, I can do it myself!" celebrate that growth in ability and confidence in him. Be thrilled as you watch him learn how to stand on his own two feet—and kneel on his own two knees.

# # 486 Terrible Twos?

Those "terrible twos" don't have to be so terrible. Sometimes a small child continues to act immaturely because his parents seem to expect that of him. So don't categorize your child as deep into those terrible twos. Resist that label. Instead look at that particular child and ask, *What can I trust this young child to do?* A preschooler is ready for some responsibility and for simple choices. Share a bit of power with her, and you may find those tantrums fading away.

# # 487 Power Tools

To powershare with your kids without causing them frustration, you've got to provide the power tools as well. These are the skills, the learning, the resources, and the authority to confidently use the power (make some things happen). You can't just say, "You're old enough now to buy your own clothes" without providing an understanding of where to shop, how to compare prices, and how to budget. The goal is creative competence, not frustrated failure.

# # 488 Three Levels to Decisions

When your children are about to enter a whole new area of decision making, like choosing elective courses in middle school or high school, you can encourage their decision-making skills by leading them through a three-level approach:

1. Research. Encourage them to think about it, read about it, and talk to other students who have taken the classes. They could take notes and even give you a "report."

2. Practice. Have them try a simulation, a dry run, and somehow make a preliminary decision that they can review with you. You can give your input, and they can work on it some more.

3. Implement. They put their plan to work. Once the decision's made, they take the action to move forward and you're still there for them if they need advice. A perfect combination.

# # 489 The Choice to Need

Once you've freed your children to do what they can do for themselves, you've handed them the power to choose to need you. Perhaps you no longer fix your daughter's hair; she's old enough to do it herself, and you've shown her how. Yet she may come to you and say, "Could you do it for me today? I want it to look really special." This isn't taking away her power—it's connecting, because it's her choice.

# # 490 The Path to Creativity

Building relationships is essentially a creative exercise—one that requires the originality of both you and your children. But creativity flourishes only where there is freedom. "Un-inhibition or freedom is one of the elements of the creative nature," Anna Marie Bourdess, an artist friend of mine, once told me. Let your kids approach your relationship with their own finesse and flair. You work together to build an "us" that's a creative masterpiece.

## # 491 Don't Major on the Minor

If you're not careful, you can reduce your whole relationship to a long series of nagging interchanges: "Pick up your toys. Watch what you're doing. Don't spill your milk. Your clothes don't match. Eat your peas." This focus on largely meaningless details saps the life right out of your relationship. So don't major on the minors. Major on the majors: building a tight, healthy bond and a big-thinking adult.

## # 492 Structured Choices

A great place to start with powersharing is by giving your children structured choices—choices within boundaries, rather than simply yes and no. It is just too easy to parent by saying no. Provide safe boundaries, and instruct them in responsible decision making, then get started. Instead of dictating, "Put on your coat!" (which sounds a lot like "Do it or else!"), try "Would you like to wear your green coat or your blue coat?" That puts some power in your child's hands.

## # 493 Your Day, Your Way

When your kids have a day off school, try letting them call the shots: "How do you want to spend your day?" See where they go with it. And go along with their plan, if at all possible. Pizza for breakfast . . . ?

## # 494 Providing Alternatives

To prevent a constant stream of "No, not that way!" try saying, "Yes, that's one way. Let me show you another way," says my friend Maryl Janson, quoting a Montessori teaching method. You're not characterizing your suggestion as better, you're affirming your child's ability to make intelligent choices.

## # 495 Sharing Responsibility

Instead of granting (or not granting) a child permission to do something from your lofty position of powerful parent, try sharing the responsibility: "You've decided to redecorate your room? I'm pretty good at wallpapering. Let's do this together."

# # 496 Let Them Lead

Sometimes it's effective powersharing to get in the backseat and let your children "drive" a project or decision-making process. Letting them try their wings and learn from their own mistakes while we're following them demonstrates that we trust them. While they're learning about leadership, they'll grow in respect for you, an adult who is humble enough—and willing—to be a follower. They'll probably use you as a resource the rest of your life.

# # 497 Food Choices

One of the areas where you can give your young children some decision-making practice is the area of what to eat. With your guidance and with structured boundaries, you can let them choose pears or applesauce, peanut butter and jelly or ham and cheese. Or let them choose the restaurant once in a while when you're eating out as a family. But make sure the options are new and different and that you are expanding their field of vision.

# # 498 Menu Planning

Let older children take over the meal planning for a week, even attempting some of the recipes themselves. Bringing them into the shopping and buying decisions is good practice in pricing analysis. Let them choose who to invite for dinner guests one evening that week.

# # 499 Party Powersharing

It won't be hard to persuade a child to take on the challenge of planning a party. A small child could coordinate a tea party, taking the lead on how things will be done and what will be sipped and sampled. Let older children plan a holiday event or a small dinner party. But turn it over to them, with budget constraints and a few other considerations. Then really leave it to them, no strings attached. They hold the party; you hold your tongue.

# # 500 Household Powersharing

There's enough to do around the house to allow your children some freedom in choosing household tasks. You've probably got dishes duty and bathroom cleaning on a regular rotation. But try making a list of other tasks that need attention and say, "Here's the list. Tag the three you're most interested in doing, or at least willing to do, this weekend." Even better, you might hand the list over to all your children and encourage them to negotiate for themselves how they'll divvy up the chores. Be sure to identify a few tasks that you'll powershare completely, working together on the same job as a team (say, cleaning out the attic or garage). Your children should come away realizing that they have a voice, that the family needs their contribution, and that the job distribution has been fair.

# # 501 Powersharing Clothes

Clothes can become a tough parent-child battleground. Parents despair: "Why do they always want to dress inappropriately—for the weather, for the occasion, and even for being seen in public?" My advice to you is, for the most part, let the clothes issue go. As long as the clothes are appropriately modest, does it really matter? Even if you hate it that your kids want to dress just like their peers, keep your emphasis on helping them be unique individuals on the inside, where it counts and where it has eternal significance. When you give your kids some room, they'll appreciate you for your gracious attitude.

# # 502 Powersharing Entertainment

Let your kids have a say—sometimes even the only say—on some family entertainment issues. From a list of acceptable titles, let them choose the video. Put a few choices for a Saturday afternoon before them (zoo, picnic, theme park) and let them come to an agreement. On a night when you're all playing board games, let them choose. The goal is to model and enjoy mutuality.

# # 503 Seating Shuffle

Why should family members always sit in the same place at the dinner table or in the car or at the movies? Once a week or month, let one of the children set the seating arrangements. It gives them a sense of control, and it might bring a new physical closeness to the family.

# # 504 I Did It My Way

Their own room is their turf. Why not let them decorate and arrange it themselves? If they do a great job, let them help "design" one of the other, more jointly used, rooms in the house. With advice and guidance from you, it will end up good interior (not inferior) design. Their inclusion in the decorating plan tells your children, "This is your house—your opinion counts—I want this room to express who you are."

# # 505 Powersharing Vacations

From a list of vacation spots you can afford, let your children choose where the family will vacation. Then bring them into the trip planning. Provide necessary guidelines and the bottom-line budget, and point them toward the Internet or the library to do the research. You might prepare your kids for this kind of responsibility by letting them plan a "daycation"—a one-day excursion—when they're younger.

# # 506 Powersharing Money

Many adults don't know how to manage money because they were never given an opportunity to practice with it. "We have $50 left over in the charitable giving part of our family budget. What should we do with it?" Or "We can spend $200 to make the family room look better. How should we do it?" Or "We have $175 that we could spend on one of these four things. Which one should it be?"

# # 507 Let Them Make Mistakes

Mistakes are make-or-break points in your relationship. When you give them some room to make their own mistakes, even if you let them flounder a bit, you're respecting their free will, and you're helping them hone their judgment. This "makes" relationship by increasing trust between you. Sometimes their self-inflicted troubles can even show them that they can depend on you.

# # 508 Two-Way Respect

There's no way for children to love us if they don't respect us. "I also learned that it's not enough to love and respect your children—you must also ask for respect back," said Dr. Benjamin Spock shortly before his death. In "The Best Ways to Raise Loving Children," Bruce Raskin wrote, "It's through mutual respect that a healthy relationship grows.... That means they [parents] have to be firm about the limits they set.... Children sense this conviction and, as a result, respect those boundaries—and their parents" (*Parenting* magazine, May 1998).

# # 509 Health and Safety

Any decision-making area that relates to the health and safety (physical or otherwise) of your children is an area where parents have to retain authority—for the good of the children. Obviously, you can't let children play in a busy street no matter how much they want to. But don't overdo the health and safety category. It shouldn't include having to clean their

plates at every single meal or never eating candy (surely there'll be
chocolate in heaven) or never being permitted to climb a tree. Health and
safety issues can become the Trojan horse of control, smothering rather
than mothering or fathering your children.

# # 510 Discipline Defined

Discipline is most definitely *not* the same thing as punishment, although
many people use the terms interchangeably. Discipline is the process of
making a *disciple,* a person who learns how to live an effective life. If
handled well, it can bring you and your children closer. It consists of
developing your children—exposing them to real life and letting them
learn some lessons in the "school of hard knocks." It includes allowing
them to make some mistakes—like leaving their favorite toy out to be
ruined in the rain or joining a "rip-off" record club. And it includes not
covering up for them: He doesn't do his homework before bedtime, so he
has to get up early to do it or give an explanation to the teacher with no
note from you.

# # 511 Punishment

Punishment is correction for sinful behavior. But you want to do it God's
way: "He punishes everyone he accepts as a son" (Heb. 12:6)—not out of
rage or frustration or because their sin reminds you of your own. God
shapes his kids' behavior for their good because he loves them so much.
Punishment takes steps to stop sinful behavior. Discerning sin means, for
example, seeing consistent refusal to follow through on what you've
asked them to do as rebellion. Then you follow up by making the
punishment fit the "crime" (not too much and not too little) and
continuing the punishment until there is an attitude change, real
repentance, and a plan for restitution (like selling a favorite possession to
get money to replace something that was broken in anger). We must
"discipline [our children] consistently when they need to be trained and
punish them carefully when they need to be stopped" (*Walking through
the Fire,* Broadman & Holman, 1996).

# # 512 Family Council

When a major issue arises—a job change, a move, a vacation
destination—call a family council to access the wisdom of the group.
Think of yourself as a meeting chairperson or team facilitator, and make
sure everyone gets an opportunity to be heard.

# # 513 Treasure Space

Violating the privacy of another is a fundamental relationship breaker. You don't want your kids to go through your possessions, and you can afford them the same respect. "Everyone has treasures," says Dallas Willard in his book *The Divine Conspiracy: Rediscovering Our Hidden Life in God* (HarperCollins, 1998). "This is an essential part of what it is to be human.... Merely to pry into what one's treasures are is a severe intrusion.... No one has a right to know what our treasures are.... It is, for example, very important for parents to respect the 'treasure space' of children. It lies right at the center of the child's soul, and great harm can be done if it is not respected and even fostered." This includes internal treasures as well—relationship doesn't mean you have a right to know everything about the other person.

# # 514 No Parental Police

When a police officer's lights flash in your rearview mirror and the officer walks up to your window, don't you feel uneasy and uncomfortable? While police play an important role in your community, they aren't the model you want to follow in your parenting. You don't carry a gun, a club, or pepper spray. And you don't need to be constantly investigating, checking out, questioning, and even arresting and jailing. Be less like the police—and more like God, our loving Father.

# Learners Together

## # 515 Continuous Learners Forever

Help your child to see that education doesn't end with sixteen or so years in school and college but that you're committed to lifelong learning. Even better, make a pact with your child that you'll both be continuous learners together—for the long haul. It isn't fair to approach your relationship with an attitude of "You've got the questions; I've got the answers." It isn't even true! Challenge each other: "Wow! There's so much in the world to know about and understand. Let's get busy!"

## # 516 Never Let Schooling Interfere

"I never let schooling interfere with my education," said American writer Mark Twain. Help your child see "schooling" as only part of the bigger goal of "learning." If you see a chance for a terrific, one-of-a-kind learning experience, don't hesitate to pull your kids out of school for a day and go for it. This shows your children that you're willing to use parental power on their behalf in order to teach them something special.

## # 517 The Power of Example

Nothing can make your child love learning more than your own example. When they see you reading, studying, taking a class, doing homework, they understand that education is important. It binds you together through growth. Ultimately, children follow what you *are*, not what you *say* (see *Proactive Parenting*, Harvest House, 1993).

# # 518 Study Together

Instead of parking in front of the television while your kids do their homework, why not do your studying together? Working side by side is always more enjoyable and gives you a chance to trade ideas and frustrations. Even if you're all up to your ears in subjects that aren't your favorites, misery loves company, and you can share the pain.

# # 519 Sound Effects

One way to make reading out loud more of an interactive joint venture is to let one of your children mime the story or provide sound effects while you read. The whole family will probably find this hilarious. And they'll laugh even harder when you reverse the roles, having one of them read while you handle the fun stuff.

# # 520 Class Action

Take a course, workshop, or seminar together with your child. There are local colleges, parks and recreation workshops, or music lessons to choose from. And don't sweat it if your child gets a better grade than you do; you can always gain their sympathy!

# # 521 Research Assistants

When you're deep into a project or a problem you're trying to solve, enlist the help of your children as research assistants: "Could you look this up for me in the dictionary? Do you think you could find something on the Internet on this? Would you help me organize this information?" University professors always employ the help of assistants; why shouldn't you?

# # 522 Cultivating the Buds

When children first hear an idea or start to learn something, they'll sometimes offer it up to us as an unformed gift. How you react is crucial. Don't come down hard with, "No, that's not right" or "Where did you hear that?" Early passion is fragile—and so is your relationship. So tend to both! "Creativity is so delicate a flower that praise tends to make it bloom, while discouragement often nips it in the bud," writes Alex F. Osborn (as quoted in *Peter's Quotations*, William Morrow, 1977).

# # 523 Training and Learning

Consider the difference between training and learning. Dogs are trained, which involves building in a habit. But people can learn—through observation, analysis, questioning, testing, and synthesizing new concepts. So don't just pass along habits and information to your kids. Help them learn through immersion.

# # 524 Learn to Live

As you're emphasizing learning in your family, don't forget to include wisdom—seeing the world from God's perspective. It's always more important for a human being to know how to live well than it is for him to have a wealth of knowledge. Better to be a decent illiterate than an articulate fool. "For the Lord gives wisdom, and from his mouth come knowledge and understanding" (Prov. 2:6). Call it "spiritual intelligence."

# # 525 Social Observation

Make a pact with your children to become astute observers of social life. Dig into interactions at school: "What did you see at school today that was unfair? What was the strangest thing? the funniest thing? the most useless thing? the newest thing?" Watch people in restaurants and stores and airports. "Why are those people together but not talking? Why is one of them talking and the other is sagging in the chair?"

# # 526 Three Approaches to Homework

There are three ways to share in the homework life of your child, the first two being the most commonly employed methods and the third being the best. The first is a hands-off approach: "This is your responsibility. Just do it!" This method will cause distance in your relationship. The second is the takeover approach: "I'm so involved, I'll think up the ideas and really be the one to do the work." This approach will alienate your child as you imply distrust of his abilities and assume control. Try a third approach of being there to help whenever your child needs you but assuring him you know the difference between help and taking over. This communicates, "I care, so I'll help, but I care, so I won't help *too much.*"

# # 527 In Trouble at School

Years ago if a child got in trouble at school, he usually also got in trouble at home. These days when a child gets in trouble at school, he is likely to be defended by a parent, who blames other kids, the teacher, or the administration. Neither approach is correct. The right thing to do is to discover what really went on and to help your child learn from the experience. You can help your child handle the consequences of being in trouble and improve his ability to work with teachers and administrators.

# # 528 It's Not Fair

If they don't know it already, your children will certainly learn that life is often unjust while they're at school. The playground is often an education in injustice, and so are some of the actions of teachers and administrators (sometimes the whole class gets punished for the misdeeds of one child). When their school life just isn't fair, don't hurry to fix the situation with lectures or intervention. It's better to help them gain increased understanding about injustices in the world, explaining that righting injustice can take a lot of wisdom and energy and that unfair situations are sometimes simply beyond their control. When you're in it with them, you'll bond as a team dealing with the madness of humanity.

# # 529 Performance Consultant

Organizations often employ performance consultants to come in and analyze the company's current knowledge, future needs, and the gap between the two. Then they recommend methods for closing the gap. When it comes to the homework issue, parental performance consultants would say, "I know this is a tough area of study for you right now, but it's important for you to get everything you can out of the class. You'll need it to pursue (various interests of that child). Here are a couple of ideas that might help and an article I found on the same topic. Let me know if I can help you any further."

# # 530 Fun with Learning

Your kids will love it whenever you can make learning a game. When my daughter Bethany and I are reading or talking and come across a word that the other doesn't know and can't define, she races off to the dictionary (I keep a big one handy) to find out what it means so she can "educate" Dad. For added incentive, dangle the carrot of a prize in front of them: "The first person who can find the answer to this problem gets a double-chocolate sundae at Tastee-Cream!" Schools don't typically make fun a top educational priority, but you can.

# # 531 Stay Up Late

Most kids love to be extended the privilege of staying up late. Once in a while, allow your kids to stay up late *if* they choose to read or study with you. One of my favorite stories is about Thomas Jefferson, who, as an older man, would sit around the fire with his grandchildren, all of them reading quietly. If someone made a noise, they would look at Jefferson, who would indicate that they should go back to their reading—but they could also see a smile. Use your kids' pleasure in delaying bedtime for their improvement—and for the fun of being together.

# # 532 Stay Up Late Again

You could also make staying up late to do something with you an incentive for accomplishing some major learning mission—memorizing a long passage of Scripture or poetry, finishing the complete *Moby Dick*, writing an exceptional report, essay, or short story. This gives you a chance to wallow together in success.

# # 533 The Same Space

Life can be lonely enough. That's what makes studying together in the same room or at the same table so pleasurable, even if you and your child are quietly studying vastly separate subjects. Bethany and I recently shared some space: While she worked on a project with maps in my office, I worked on a book. Occupying the same space, where there is no need for words, can be a serene bonding experience.

# # 534 Go Gaga

Make the time to peruse their papers from school. If you start when they're young enough, the habit may become so ingrained that they'll still be letting you in on what they're doing in medical school! Go gaga over their progress. Discuss and praise content, whenever appropriate. Notice, but don't focus on the mistakes. In a future conversation, recall one of their papers. Or let excellent work on a certain topic give you an idea for some joint research you could do (maybe even checking out whether you can refute something the school presented as fact but that you consider dubious). Teachers give grades, but you can give glory.

# # 535 Write a Silly Story

Help your child write down stories—short stories, essays, funny stories, family histories. If you do the writing or typing while she brainstorms the story line, you can prompt her creativity with questions and comments. Then read the story to the rest of the family or close friends. When Peter was little, we once wrote a story together about "hayfaloes"—imaginary animals that look like cylindrical bales of hay.

# # 536 Write Plays

Make up a play together—something funny or dramatic—to be acted out by people or stuffed animals or action figures. Let them perform the play.

You can be an actor, too, or a stagehand. David and Bethany and I wrote a play called *The Great Gum Escapade* and filled up my office with all the stuffed animals who were auditioning for parts.

# # 537 Necessary Junk

Learning might require a very full house—or at least a room where junk can be collected—dress-up clothes, art supplies, props. "To invent," said Thomas Edison, "you need a good imagination and a pile of junk."

# # 538 Let Them Teach

There's no better way for children to learn something than to teach it, no better way for you to show humility than to be the student, and no better way to grow like-minded than to share a "classroom" experience. Laura has taught me about literature and nutrition. Peter has taught me a lot about computers, music, and art. David has taught me about computers, VCRs, and poetry. Bethany has taught me about U.S. geography and the benefits of early rising. Find something they can teach you, and make sure you're not late for class.

# # 539 Problems Not Answers

Often children need to know how to find answers even more than they need the answers. "Too often we give children answers to remember rather than problems to solve," says Roger Lewin (quoted in *Peter's Quotations,* William Morrow, 1977). Show them how to get information—at the library, on the Internet, in a string of phone calls that will help them find the person who has all the information and is willing to be interviewed.

# # 540 Help Me

Enlist the help of your children to keep you on the cutting edge. It'll keep you from becoming some out-of-touch old fogy. They can help you stay fresh and stay motivated by the excitement of learning. Peter helped me pick out a car, steering me away from the big sedans. I ended up with a fire-engine red convertible with real pow ... anyway, you get the idea. I paid for the car, but in a special way it was Peter's gift to me.

# # 541 Admit It

To paraphrase Confucius, "When you know something, say what you know. When you don't know something, say what you don't know. That is knowledge." And humility. And it makes for a very comfortable,

nonpretentious relationship. Don't be afraid to admit to your child that
you don't know the answer to his question. Build connection by finding
the answer together.

# # 542 Unlearn

"It's not what we don't know that hurts us," said American humorist Kin
Hubbard, "it's what we know that just ain't so." Be open to the idea that
you may be mistaken in some of your ideas. Mark Twain said that
"education consists mainly in what we have unlearned." Your kids may
be instrumental in helping you shed illusions and partial knowledge.

# # 543 Know It All

Pick a subject you think you've got down "cold" and have a contest to see,
within a certain time frame, who can come up with a question you can't
answer. Your kids will enjoy the challenge of teaching you something,
and they'll learn a lot while they're researching the topic. "It's what you
learn after you know it all that counts," said the great basketball coach
John Wooden.

# # 544 Size Matters

Sharing a buffet dinner is really fun. So many different choices can leave
your eyes wide and your waistlines bulging. (Instead of "All you can eat,"
they should call them "All you *should* eat"!) Share a buffet of all the
knowledge that's out there. Explore the possibilities, the widely disparate
fields of knowledge that can touch and cross each other. My son David
once told me, "I want to study everything." I was so very pleased. "There
are more things in heaven and earth, Horatio, than are dreamt of in your
philosophy," wrote Shakespeare in *Hamlet*.

# # 545 Home Schooling

Every home is teaching something all the time. Everything your kids learn is
either learned at home, confirmed at home, or denied at home. So give your
home life a checkup. Ask yourself, *Is what they're learning here useful?
harmful? bonding? separating?* Make home a school of truth and love.

# 14

# Parenting
# toward Greatness

## # 546 The Music in Me

Every person has "music" in them—personal, God-bestowed gifts to be developed. As a parent, you're the one most closely attuned to each child's "song." You're the one who can sing it back to your children when they forget the music. You're the one who won't let their music be wasted or hidden, or let them die with their music still in them. Learn their songs, and help them sing for all the world to hear.

## # 547 A Ferocious Champion

Everyone needs what author Calvin Miller calls an "I believe in you" person. Every child needs someone who cares as much about his future as he does, who believes in her even when she can't find anything to cheer about. Your child needs a ferocious champion for his future hopes and dreams. Let it be you.

## # 548 Feed Your Child's Dreams

"Dreams are the touchstone of our character," said Henry David Thoreau. When your child has confided to you a piece of his dreams, do everything you can to nurture it. When our son Peter was very young, he purposed to blend two careers—one as the driver of an ice-cream truck and the other as a violin player performing for customers and neighbors. From the realistic vantage point of adulthood, I knew that specific fantasy would probably not come true. But I encouraged what I saw as the roots of this dream—a love of making people happy and a love of music. I affirmed those inclinations. We discussed the pros and cons. I didn't co-opt his dream and make it somehow my own, insisting he take this or that step to fulfill it. But today Peter is an accomplished musician—and he knows how to throw a good party.

# # 549 Saying Good-Bye to Dreams

You can't mold your children to fit your dreams and connect deeply with them as individuals at the same time. So let go of your dreams for their lives, and get ready to participate in their dreams. Sharing your ideas is great; listening to their ideas is greater.

# # 550 Smelling like Love

Although you shouldn't force your dreams to become theirs, you still hope that the best that's in you will live on in them to make an impact in the world. "Your child's life will carry the fragrance of you for years to come; just as your life has touched many, so will the life of your child," writes Judy Ford in *Wonderful Ways to Love a Child* (Conari Press, 1995). Nothing smells better than love.

# # 551 Separate but Connected

You have to separate your life from your children's if you're really going to be connected. That sounds like a contradiction, but it's a reality. And it's difficult to live out because a good parent remains right in the thick of what's going on in their children's lives. We're so close that we can really louse things up. But you can respect their need to make their own decisions. You separate your success from theirs, your career mistakes from their career choices. Parents are uniquely qualified to help their children find their way, but a wise parent will be careful to remain an assistant or encourager and not become a meddler.

# # 552 Never Give Up

No matter what you try to do in life, there will be naysayers telling you that you can't, that you're kidding yourself. Take the opposite approach and encourage your kids. Remember Churchill's famous but brief speech? It consisted of only twenty-nine words: "Never give in, never give in, never, never, never, never—in nothing, great or small, large or petty—never give in except to convictions of honor and good sense." You can be your child's ally in a way no one else can be. You can be the friend who exhorts them not to give up.

# # 553 So Small, So Big

Many children struggle to believe their dreams are possible because of a keen sense of their insignificance. "I'm so little; can I really do this?"

Teenagers can feel overwhelmed by feelings of insignificance. But your children are amazing, astonishing facets of God's creation. Remind them of this—regularly and with conviction. "I am only one, but still I am one. I cannot do everything, but still I can do something," said Edward Everett Hale, nineteenth-century American clergyman and writer. Convince your kids of their magnificent potential.

# # 554 Create a Life

"People talk about 'finding' their lives. In reality, your life is not something you find—it's something you create," says David Phillips (as quoted in *Whatever It Takes*, Compendium Publishing, 1995). Teach your children that they can't sit back and wait for life to come to them or just magically appear. But with God's help, and your encouragement, they *can* create a life for themselves.

# # 555 Tell Them Yes

Your kids may need experience to be given a chance, but how do they get the chance without experience? "Whenever you are asked if you can do a job, tell 'em, 'Certainly, I can!' Then get busy and find out how to do it" (U.S. President Teddy Roosevelt). As much as possible, "try out" your kids on new ventures and new skills. Help them gain experience in a safe environment.

# # 556 Full-Time Ministry

Minimize the distinction between what people call "full-time Christian work" (meaning ministry such as missionary or pastor) and other occupations, such as doctor, graphic designer, or entrepreneur. When your children find the work God has designed them for, and they pursue it for righteous reasons, their work *is* full-time Christian work as well. Help them find the work they're called to do.

# # 557 Uncover the Possibilities

Children are as smart as you are, but they lack information and experience, perspective and framework. They have a swirl of ideas but no grid for sorting them out. That's where you come in. Expose them to many ideas and occupations. As their friend, help them see life's bigger picture and the possibilities for making a difference in the world.

# # 558 Heart's Desires

Because you love your children, you can try to discern the desires of their heart. You can help them identify who they are and what they want to be and do. When some inner truth bubbles to the surface, take note of it and write up "wish lists." This gets both of you out of the "what is" and into the "what could be." "We are not sent into this world to do anything into which we cannot put our hearts," wrote English critic and essayist John Ruskin (quoted in *12,000 Religious Quotations,* Baker Books, 1989).

# # 559 The Big Question

Don't be the person who puts a child's dream in a box, or his hopes in a straitjacket. You should be the voice that reminds him that all things are possible. When a fresh passion strikes your child and he wants to try it out, you be the one to say, "Why not?" As Mason Cooley wrote, "'Why not?' is a slogan for an interesting life," (quoted in *Whatever It Takes,* Compendium Publishing, 1995).

# # 560 A Chosen Cause

Ask key questions to bring out the crusader in your children, to get their hearts out on the table. "Is there a cause you would like to champion? If money weren't an issue, what would you like to spend most of your time on? What things are you going to regret at age eighty if you don't do them along the way?" But don't push for answers. Just open that new avenue of thinking for your children.

# # 561 Mighty Purpose

You can't give your children's lives purpose, but you can help them recognize it: "We are God's workmanship, created in Christ Jesus to do good works, which God prepared in advance for us to do" (Eph. 2:10). "This is the true joy of life, the being used for a purpose recognized by you as a mighty one," said playwright George Bernard Shaw.

# # 562 Opportunity of a Lifetime

Schools work with a large number of children in each classroom. Few schools are able to provide opportunities for students to experiment with individual interests or explore specific wishes and dreams. But you can provide those experiences. See if you can arrange a daylong visit to a professional in the field in which your daughter is interested. See if you can get an artisan or craftsman to take on your artistic son as apprentice for a weekend or a summer. Be the one to help them put flesh to their dreams.

# # 563 Career Paths

Do you remember how you felt as a teen or a college student, sorting through the zillion possible directions your life could take? Your children's passions and vision can easily get sidetracked or lost in the shuffle. As the years pass, you can keep a file or notes on possible career paths for each child, based on the clues you've picked up from them. It may become one more indispensable tool to help your children plan a life.

# # 564 Big Decisions

If you want to be part of your child's life journey, continue to be deeply involved in all of his big decisions. You achieve this, not by force or manipulation, but by being there as an asset during the process. From the early days when the invitation list for his birthday party is a "big" decision, you want him to feel that having you alongside in the planning process is *normal.* You'll be included because he can't imagine it any other way.

# # 565 Support Patience

Don't rush your kids. It's easy to be so much in a rush to get on with life that you get on with the wrong one. Let your kids know there is no prescribed pace or timetable for getting through college or finding a satisfying career. It's a savvy business practice to postpone any decisions that don't have to be made immediately—because more time often brings better perspective. Encourage some career testing or travel. Let them talk with a lot of people—and read and think. This level of understanding is irresistibly endearing.

# # 566 Along the Way

It's not just zealous parents who misdirect young people. There are all sorts of red herrings—people who have a plan of their own for your children's lives. Talk to your kids about this possibility, and remind them that it's fine to listen to—and also fine to ignore—other people's plans for them, especially those that suggest manipulation. "Just remember that you don't have to be what they want you to be," said boxing legend Muhammad Ali.

# # 567 Public Image and Private Calling

Help your children prepare for the possibility that no matter what choices they make—even when they're convinced that God's hand has led them or that a particular occupation is a good fit for them—some

won't "get it" and may criticize them or try to dissuade them from their
calling. Encourage your children that no matter who else misunderstands
them, they'll get understanding from you.

# # 568  Change of Mind

Your children will very likely change their minds about their interests
and desires as they mature and explore. If you respond by saying, "But
last week you were going into marine biology!" you can shut down their
willingness to think out loud with you about their dreams. Change is
the only constant; so be ready to accept these changes of mind or heart.
If you're receptive to them, they'll keep you up-to-date as the changes
come.

# # 569  More Can Be Better

Studies show that the more talents, interests, and values a person is able
to use in their lives, the more satisfied they will be. I enjoy writing,
speaking, coaching, and consulting. What a blessing—to be able to enjoy
them all! "A man can do nothing better than to ... find satisfaction in his
work" (Eccles. 2:24). Help your kids find the multifaceted path.

# # 570  Sort Out the Options

I love the fact that God has created a world that offers people so many
possibilities. The problem, of course, is trying to pick what's right from
among those options, like trying to pick the perfect toothpaste when there
are fifty choices in front of you on the shelf. Sweat it out with your kids;
pray with them and support them through the decision making, and
avoid throwing in quick answers. Sorting is *very* hard to do well.

# # 571  The Best

Once your son or daughter has identified what are probably bad alternatives,
he or she will still be faced with weeding out good options that still aren't the
best—the most well suited—to the gifts and passions and uniqueness God
has given them. "To comprehend a man's life," said British statesman
William Gladstone, "it is necessary to know not merely what he does but also
what he purposely leaves undone. ... He is a wise man who wastes no energy
on pursuits for which he is not fitted; and he is still wiser who, from among
the things that he can do well, chooses and resolutely follows the best." Help
your children discern these categories, and give them the confidence to say
both no and yes.

# # 572 Shoulder of a Giant

"If I have seen further it is by standing on the shoulders of giants," said Isaac Newton. You want your children to see further—not less, not the same, but *more*. Love demands it. It may even mean stopping some climbing of your own to do the lifting that helps them "see further."

# # 573 Take-Alongs

Take your children along, now and then, into the world of work, vocation, and avocation. When I was meeting with a programmer I had hired to develop an intricate data base, I invited David (who was then fourteen and interested in computers) along to the meeting. He wore a tie, looked sharp, and took notes. Whether he followed everything or not is immaterial; I wanted him to get the *feel* of that work encounter more than I wanted him to grasp the details.

# # 574 Bring Them into Business

No matter what field of work you're in, there's probably something your children can do to help you, to join in your work. Take them in, try them out. Insist that their efforts be their best work and professional. Pay them—even give them a business card, if you like. Over the years, my son Peter, who is now the president of Barrett Graphics, has designed my business logos, brochures, and stationery and has done computer and calligraphy work for me as well. When your children are helping you, treat their efforts as "real" work—because the efforts *are* real.

# # 575 No Black Sheep

Don't label a child a "black sheep" because his interests are off the beaten track. Whatever his passions are, make room for them, *celebrate* them. Sincerely say, "I just can't believe how terrific it is that you're interested in that."

# # 576 Double Enthusiasm

"If you can give your son or daughter only one gift, let it be enthusiasm," said advertising executive and politician Bruce Barton. Give them a double gift—freedom to pursue their enthusiasm and your enthusiasm for their enthusiasm.

# # 577 Male and Female

You'll need to avoid gender stereotyping if you want to help your children find their destiny, God's calling for their life. Not because it's politically correct, but because it is wise and brilliant and the right thing to do. They are male or female, but not first and primarily. First and foremost, they're unique creations of God with irreplaceable souls. Then they're human beings with all the glory and challenge that encompasses. At this level, there is no "male nor female" (Gal. 3:28).

# # 578 Pros versus Cons

A two-column chart for contrasting pros and cons is a simple, time-tested tool for making decisions. Listing all those positive and negative criteria brings clarity to the big picture. Help your children write up the list; then encourage them to leave it alone for a bit and come back later. That can bring clarity to the emotions represented in both columns of the chart.

# # 579 Competing with Self

If you want the best for your kids, discourage internal competition—with their siblings, with other family members or friends, with your past career and achievements. Urge them to adopt the motto of the Apollo 13 moon mission: "Ruthlessly compete with your own best self." In place of competition, create an atmosphere of cooperation and complementary efforts.

# # 580 Planning

Children don't come into life with an ability to plan it. You can serve as the coach, teaching them how to set goals, prioritize, and develop plans of action. Few friends are as valuable as one who helps bring order out of chaos and meaning out of the fog. "What could be more important than helping to shape and mold others' lives?" asked Guy Rice Doud, author of *Molder of Dreams.*

# # 581 Practice Goal Setting

Every year, I set goals (not "resolutions") for myself and ask each of my children to do the same. We set five to seven goals related to the spiritual area, the number of books to read, financial targets, etc. Then we discuss those goals during the year and review how we did at the end in a low-key, often humorous way ("I think I meant *gain* ten pounds"). This gets each of us used to setting goals in a supportive context with some "safe" accountability.

# # 582 Late Nights

Be alert; be ready for the late-night conversations that can be so intricately a part of guiding their steps. I remember conversations with Laura about her choice of schools to attend, and then later to teach at, with Peter about general coursework and ways to earn income while in school. Pizza and ice cream have been crucial ingredients in these late-night powwows. These all-nighters are more important than the ones I pulled in college and a lot more rewarding.

# # 583 Staying Home

Many parents want their children out of the home as soon as possible. After being around some children, I understand this feeling completely. But if you and your kids are respecting each other and combining your efforts to help them find the path God has for them, there may be no reason for them to leave until they form a new home of their own (and that's an *additional* home, not a *replacement* home). For this to work, of course, both you and your children will have to keep reinventing the relationship as you go. Share power and grant freedom with responsibility. "Independence" becomes necessary only when a home has imposed injustice and oppression. Without these "uglies," interdependence is a glorious path.

# # 584 The Road

An old American proverb reminds us that "the road to the head lies through the heart." Regardless of what you or your children think, chart a course together that runs first through your hearts. God says, "I know the plans I have for you" (Jer. 29:11). Parents who connect with their kids give them the secure place from which they can launch their search for God's plans for them.

# Part 3

# *People Who Need People:*

## Friends

## Who Create

## Connection

*Your* relationship with your children takes place within a wider context. Others who touch your lives, for good or for bad, can affect the bond you share with your children.

Your kids' friends will enter the equation—and peers are a hotbed of potential for either disaster or for increased connection. Your extended-family's role is complex; sometimes members are helpful, sometimes not. Even your peers can affect your relationship. And your church—a sort of larger family context—will be a major influence as your connection grows.

Don't let anyone damage or ruin your relationship with your kids. Draw out the best contributions that others can make, and leave the rest of it in the dust.

# 15

# Peer Pressures and Pleasures

# # 585 Barometer

Few decisions your children make tell you more about them than the friends they choose—or who choose them. It's too easy to scrutinize their friends in order to classify them as good or bad without asking the first and possibly most critical question: *What does this friendship tell me about who my children are and what they think is important?* Use their cast of friends as a diagnostic tool for getting to the heart of your kids.

# # 586 Patching Potholes

A child's friends can direct your attention toward something that might be missing in your relationship with your child. Is this "girl-crazy" mode he's in related to a need for a mother's closeness or affection? When she hangs with girls who are totally focused on her outward appearance, is that a clue that mom or dad have complimented external qualities at the expense of internal ones? Some problems grow out of your child's own individuality, and some are peer-related, but look for the possibility of holes you've left unfilled. It's never too late to get started on repairing that road.

# # 587 Substitute Yourself

Sometimes when parents recognize that a child is looking to meet some need through a dangerous friendship, they focus on "the enemy." They nag about that friend, attack the friend, forbid the friend. These tactics lead to a surefire disaster, failing to get rid of the friend and serving to put a chasm between parents and child. The difficult but more rewarding path is for parents to find clever and caring ways to meet the need. When you see your son responding to a friend's compliment ("Man, you don't take anything off of anybody"), you can take that in a different direction: "That's really cool that you had the courage to stand up for yourself without getting angry." This subtle approach is the way to relational connection.

# # 588 Down or Up

Keep a lookout for big steps up or down in the choices of friends a child is making. If suddenly she's hanging out with kids who are not ambitious, not courteous, not humble, and not doing well in school, she may perceive herself as not very worthwhile. If he's suddenly hanging out with kids who are a big step up—a lot more focused, better achievers with many more friends—it *could* be good, since spending time with high-quality people could improve him. But it could also mean he's reaching for something in attaching himself to these friends. Maybe he's made a friend who makes him feel alive, or maybe the friend is using your child to feel better about himself. Ask yourself what those giant steps up or down really mean and how you can incorporate what you learn into your relationship.

# # 589 You Pick Them

When children are little, they have neither the discernment nor the experience to pick friends well. It's all right for you to do it without feeling awkward or apologetic. If you think that little girl down the street is a negative influence on your child, turn down those play dates. If you discover playing with a certain older boy introduces your son to ideas he's not yet ready for, supervise or limit their interaction. If your child is struggling socially, directing him toward someone a little younger or less mature (but not problematical) could be just the thing he needs to boost his confidence. Choosing their early friendships is a terrific gift to your much-loved children.

# # 590 Pick Activities

An indirect way to influence your children's friendships is by directing them to certain activities where they're more likely to interact with other children who share your family's core values. If your children have a hard time making friends, being involved in an activity with those who share the same interest can be just what's needed. Discuss this with your kids. If possible, come to agreement on the best activities to help them develop first-class friendships.

# # 591 Deep and Wide

It's great for your kids to encounter a wide range of people so they learn to discern points of connection and discover kindred spirits. But when they do meet one of those kindred spirits, you want them to go deep in that friendship. These friendships matter. Even experts miss it here: "I don't think the quantity or quality of young children's friendships is necessarily a concern," writes pediatric psychologist Dr. William Coleman in "Best Buddies" (*Parenting* magazine, April 1998). Is it really possible that we are not affected by those we spend time with? If they don't cast the net widely, your children could become isolated or dependent on whomever comes along for friendship. If they spread their net too widely, your children might become social butterflies who don't discover the kinds of deep friendships that strengthen their souls. Help your children navigate these decisions and use you as a trusted advisory board as they become excellent fishers of friends.

# # 592 Develop Them

Taking time to show your children's friends what your values are, teaching them about right choices, and correcting them when they're out of line is a double gift, to them and to your children who are spending time with them. Do you need to do this? Yes. Do you have a right to do this? Yes, because you are your "brother's keeper," and every child is or can be part of the family of God.

# # 593 Different Is Good

Avoid the "that's not the way we do things around here" approach with your kids' friends. Go ahead and take your stand on matters of critical principles: "We don't use those words; we don't hit; we don't watch that kind of stuff on television." But make room for differences, and adopt the good ones. Maybe one of your kids' friends has a family tradition of eating the meal together at the table and dessert while watching TV. There's nothing to keep you from trying that sometime. Maybe another family develops raucous debates over dinner—that could make for a fun change of pace at your house. If you're not dead, it's not too late to try something new.

# # 594 Running Wild

It's uneven parenting for families to be overly restrictive about family issues (how much television can be watched, which movies can be attended, and what foods cannot be eaten) but then allow their children to "run all over the neighborhood." These kids are allowed to go far beyond parental range, where they can spend time with anyone and pick up the grossest of ideas and values—and then their parents later wonder what's happened to their kids. Don't worry more about your kids picking up a flu bug than about them picking up a terminal character flaw. Just one evil and commanding friend can do vast, virtually irreparable damage. Find creative alternatives—other friends, more family time, more one-on-one time with you, whatever it takes.

# # 595 Too Private

Children need quiet and privacy, but you don't want them to develop so secret a life that they never expand their social horizons or get involved or make meaningful friendships. Stay a vital part of their friendship life by talking with them and encouraging and just being there, so you can avoid the pitfall of a secret life.

# # 596 Start Young

The earlier we are intertwined with the developing social life of our children, the easier it will be to continue doing it. It is so easy to stay on the sidelines when small children are playing together and then figure we'll get involved when their friends are older. But that day never comes. Get an early start in helping your kids develop their social skills, building good habits in interactive play. Play fort with them. Join the tea party. Work one of the puppets in their play—not always, but often. Set the stage early for your continued interaction.

# # 597 Still a Kid

In my work I meet a lot of top-level executives, and I've found I enjoy people who are movers and shakers, who are going somewhere. I also thoroughly enjoy being part of a group of kids, of any age. I've found there's that same kind of dynamic energy with kids; they're going somewhere, too. Don't be too "mature" to get down on the rug to play with Matchbox cars or to get soaked in an outdoor water war. Playing with your kids and their friends is important in staying connected with them.

# # 598 My Place, Not Yours

Do your best to make your house the "friend center." Encourage your kids to invite their friends over—for the afternoon, for events, for supper, for overnights. This lets you be part of those friendships, where you can enjoy the fun or become aware of red-flag warnings. Get the game on your turf.

# # 599 Cool

To get into the inner world of your children and their friends, be cool. I don't mean you should talk or dress or act like them. But do try to relate to them by caring about and knowing what interests them. It can be illuminating, even surprising. I've had very interesting conversations with young boys about their pets and video games—and stuffed animals. I've talked with older boys about their computers and sports—and gourmet desserts. With young girls, I've discussed American Girl Collection dolls and favorite colors—and sledding on death-defying hills. I've met older girls who were passionate about their music and fashions—and self-defense courses. Here's the secret: You're cool when you're interested in them as people, in the details. And if one of her friends tells your child, "Your dad's cool," she might even believe it, too.

# # 600 Build on the Interests

Once you discover what your kid's friends are interested in, dive right in. Get more information on the topic. Clip an article to pass along. Invite your kid's specific friend to activities that interest him or her. To encourage that friendship for your child, serve the friend's needs and preferences. Stock up on the Doritos he likes best, or rent a video that will appeal to her. Show these friends that their individuality is important to you.

# # 601 Have Parties

Parties, from a practical perspective, are expensive and a pain in the neck. But you gotta have 'em—and not just for special occasions, like birthdays. The party itself needs to be the special occasion. For an observant parent, a party becomes a learning lab where the parent studies youth culture and ways of relating. The other big reason to have them is that parties are fun, too. The family that prays *and* plays together, stays together.

# # 602 The Cutting Edge

You can bring something that they don't already have to these young people who are your children's friends. Even at your "advanced" age, there's something about you—some skill, interest, achievement, computer system, sports memorabilia, whatever—that can dazzle these kids. Enthusiasm and passion for life are contagious. May you never be so old as to outlive your enthusiasm.

# # 603 The Right Direction

There are two ways to connect with your kids and their friends "where they're at." One is by following or copying them (picking up on and adopting their fashion or language trends, watching the videos they think are cool). But the better way is by setting the stage for them to want to get to your level, to follow you, to aspire to something beyond where they are now. When you interest them in what you have to offer, you're setting the standard.

# # 604 Generation Gap

A simple thought about generation gaps: Refuse to accept them. Generation gaps are really only relationship gaps—you've allowed a divide to develop between you. Communication doesn't dry up because you're older; it dries up when you haven't watered it.

# # 605 Not a Nuisance

Children—people—can be very annoying. But discipline yourself not to think of these extra kids who are hanging around your house as a nuisance. Rather, see these friends as an avenue into your children's hearts. There is a price you pay by having their friends around, but it can provide an excellent return. And the cost of not having them around is so much higher.

# # 606 Try a Little Kindness

You reinforce your connection with your kids every time you're kind to their friends. It is the right thing to do and shows greatness. "If a man be gracious and courteous to strangers, he shows he is a citizen of the world," wrote Francis Bacon.

# # 607 Accept First

Approach your children's friends with an attitude of "innocent until proven guilty." Leave yourself open to explore who they are and how they connect to you and how you can connect with them. Your kids will sense and rebel against any premature guilty verdicts. Accept first; there's plenty of time later to evaluate.

# # 608 Adopt-a-Kid

There are certain friends (especially the ones who pass the "Are they barbarians?" test) whom you'll want to make unofficial members of the family. Treat them with respect and everyday welcome. Praise them and celebrate their successes just as you do with your own kids. This "adoption" tells your kids you respect and affirm their people choices.

# # 609 Wanna Come Along?

When your family plans an outing, consider taking your kids' friends along. Everybody likes to go places and do things. Make room in some of your family's activities, daycations, vacations, and even family reunions. You'll discover a million ways to connect with your children through those closely involved friends.

# # 610 Get Busy Together

Occasionally, get into a project with your child and his friend, whether it's planned or spontaneous. Bake something—the bigger the mess, the better. Build something. Plant something. And keep talking while you do it, crawling inside two hearts.

# # 611 Hug 'Em

Although some children have been mistreated physically, nobody ever got too many good hugs. When you've reached a familiar level with your kids' friends, go ahead and give them a little hug or pat on the back. Be careful, of course, but not so careful you miss a connection with someone important to your kids or miss filling up another heart just a little.

# # 612 Speak Up and Ask

In a straightforward manner, ask their friends questions that will broaden your perspective on your child. "What three things do you like most about my child? What three things do you think are the best about yourself? What will you do if the two of you disagree? How will you react if someone says bad things about him? In what ways can you encourage each other? What will you do if you see her making a mistake? How will you react if you hear him saying something bad about other people?" Take it seriously, making the conversation real and deep. Tighten up that three-cord knot.

# # 613 Nicknames and Secrets

Keep your sweet and silly pet names for your kids sacrosanct to family time; try *not* to use those nicknames in front of their friends. And be sure not to spill your child's "secrets" (he still needs a night-light, she has a small bladder, they like liverwurst sandwiches). Even if the detail seems trivial to you, it can feel like betrayal to your child.

# # 614 Kid Talk

Even as you get close to your children's friends, don't horn in on their nicknames for each other or any new words they invent in a language all their own. Every relationship has its own form of dialogue, and you can and should respect this.

# # 615 Praise Limits

There's a time and place for everything. Watch out for praising and affirming your children a great deal either to their friends or in front of their friends. Your kids may feel awkward, and you could inadvertently introduce jealousy or resentment into their friendship. Guard the praise, and try to affirm your children's friends in equal measure.

# # 616 Correction Limits

If you want to hang onto your children's respect and love, never, ever, under any circumstances criticize or correct them in front of their friends. It will feel like emotional violation, regardless of how justified your words are. Even if they're wrong, even if they're driving you crazy, wait.

# # 617 Analyze Them

Analyze together what factors appeal to your kids about their friends. Approach this very openly and nonjudgmentally. Don't "load" your questions: "What do you think about the rough language she uses?" It's fun to analyze why you've chosen some of the more surprising friends you have, and it's just as interesting for your kids to explore their friendships and motivations for having them.

# # 618 Dissect Their Ideas

With great care, wade into the subjects your kids' friends are talking about. There are certain "parent-unfriendly" topics—like sex, cheating, stealing—that many children are reluctant to bring to the surface. So don't sound suspicious and skeptical. Broach these subjects matter-of-factly, with a light touch and perhaps a little humor, and you might be able to work yourself into their dialogue. It's a great way to bring difficult and confusing questions up for discussion in a safe environment, and before any damage is done.

# # 619 Rebuffs

Sooner or later your kids will be insulted, betrayed, ostracized, or mistreated. When this happens, it's an opportunity to enhance your relationship. Every problem has the seed of something positive in it. Stay away from I-told-you-so lectures ("I always knew she was no good") and blasting away ("I hate him for doing that to you"), which could backfire if they're fine friends again by Tuesday. Sympathize, empathize, and remind them just by being there that they're not alone, that they're worthy people to know and love. You be their refuge in the storm.

# # 620 Assuming Potential

Assume that every child who befriends yours might become a lifelong friend. Assume that every friend of the opposite sex could someday be your in-law (the best marriages usually start out as good friendships). Most of these relationships will fade, but some will carry on, and it's hard to know which are which. Don't push certain friendships or critique heavily and withhold welcome from other friends. Just make your kids' friends, and the friendships themselves, comfortable.

# # 621 Making and Losing

Benefit your kids by regularly discussing, often and deeply, how to make and keep friends. What works? What doesn't? Why did that friendship take off and that one collapse? Take on the opposite topic, too: How can they "lose" a friend who's harmful, who tears them down, who makes everything negative?

# # 622 Grieve a Loss

When a friendship ends—either by fading away or breaking off when someone moves away or conflict divides them—how can you help your kids accept and deal with that change? One way is to explain that life is something like a play with some main characters (like you) who are on stage with each other all of the time. Other people come on stage during the performance, stay for a while, finish their part, and leave. It doesn't mean you didn't love each other or that these people weren't important. It's just the ebb and flow of life. If the friend was dear to you, nearly a member of the family, draw your child close and grieve the loss together.

# # 623 Glad to Have a Friend like You

Redouble your efforts to foster an excellent, respectful, productive, encouraging relationship with your kids because the friendship patterns and qualities they learn from you become what they're looking for in others. If what you offer is positive and fulfilling, you increase the possibilities that they will search out and develop great friendships with their peers. Offer something worth imitating.

## Get By with a Little Help from Your Friends

### # 624 Ask for Help

It is important to realize that you're not the only one who can help your children develop into whole, caring beings. Help is there, in your good friends who care about your family life, and you need only to ask for it and assure them that you really want it. The best helpers tend to be the productive, busy people, so you may need to grovel and beg (or even "bribe" them: "If you help my boy, I'll do your grocery shopping next week"). The other good relationships in your life can enrich your relationship with your children

### # 625 Wear You Out

Kids wear out everything—clothes, shoes, upholstery, books, and parents. And parenting is especially draining. There's no way you can do it, with excellence, all by yourself. Family is a typical source of help, but family may not be available or may be inadequate (or worse). So turn, with honesty and vulnerability, to your chosen friends. When you're worn out, look to your friends for comfort, understanding, and help.

### # 626 Swap Time

Years ago our family cared for severely disabled or sick children in order to give their parents a much-needed evening or weekend off. But any parent would find such time off invigorating. Ask your friends to give you a retreat, while they spend quality relationship time with your children. Absence does make the heart grow fonder; there is connection in separation. Then offer to do the same for them.

# # 627 Someone to Look Up To

Children need mentors, and who better than your friends to amplify what you're doing with your children? Sometimes a friend can mentor in a certain area of your children's interests—say, a musician friend could take them to concerts. These folks share your values and broaden your kids' experience by bringing a fresh perspective. It binds your kids to you, since they'll understand you better by knowing your friends.

# # 628 Career Day

A terrific matchup of your friend to your child is based on career possibilities. Find out what your children are interested in becoming, and set them up with the friend whose chosen work is closest to it. Ask your friend to blend in some commentary or discussion about you.

# # 629 Unvarnished Truth

Only close friends can tell you the truth about the failures they see in your parenting. Be courageous enough to ask for their advice. Convince them that they can deliver their insights openly and honestly without harm to your relationship.

# # 630 Another Perspective

Encourage your friends to tell your children why you're friends—what it is they like about you. This can give your children a whole new perspective on you and increase your apparent "value" at the same time.

# # 631 Grown-Up Talk

Don't separate conversations into categories: adult, family, children. Instead, draw your children into adult conversations, and then steer those discussions toward relational issues. Children need to hear these topics explored and debated so that they can see their size and scope.

# # 632 Rap Session

Plan a dinner or outing that includes a few of your friends and your children. Include invigorating, diverse people, and give them advance warning if there's a certain topic you'd like to discuss. Ask questions of your children, too, to elicit their opinions. This can build a multilayered bond, based on a shared experience. Perhaps this goes without saying: Don't put your kids at a separate table. Your rap session could show your kids how big life and its issues really are.

# # 633 Topical Dinner

Invite an intimate friend to join you and your child at a restaurant for a meal. Let both of them know before you go what the main topic of conversation will be. It could be friendship, what you've both learned about friendship, or levels of friendship (like acquaintance, friend, close friend, intimate friend). Talk openly with the adult friend about why you're close. Your child probably can't help but be drawn into the subject.

# # 634 Shared Vision

No doubt you have friends who share your important interests, and some of those interests coincide with your children's. So get together to share those interests, attending related activities, trading articles and books, working on projects. Much of relationship is built on shared vision.

# # 635 Give Them the Scoop

Explain your friendships to your kids. What do you like about Phyllis? What would you change about your relationship with the neighbor across the street? What brought you together with certain friends? When you talk about your friendships, you're talking about yourself—and your kids will be connecting with you.

# # 636 Teachers As Friends

Considering the time and attention they afford your kids, their teachers are powerful forces in their lives. They're a great source of extra care for your kids, extra insight for you, and they're usually really caring. But they're also very busy, typically without sufficient help to do what they need to get done. So offer to help, give them encouragement, attend field trips, invite the teacher to your home, find out what they're interested in and support that interest. The parent-teacher-child friendship triangle is a great connector.

# # 637 Questions for Teachers

Help your child get to know her teachers better by first getting to know them yourself. Ask questions! What are the biggest interests you see in my child? Would you describe in detail how she relates to other children in her class? How do you picture him at twenty-one? What kind of person would make a good friend for her? How do you cultivate mutual respect in the classroom? How do you handle misbehavior? Is it OK with you if he confides personal problems? What do you like best and least about her? Where do your interests and his coincide?

# # 638 Adventures in Baby-Sitters

Sooner or later someone is going to watch the children while you're out. But "watch" is a really low form of relationship. Try to find sitters who share interests, temperaments—and of course values—with you and your child. It's too important to leave to a business transaction. A baby-sitter can be a wonderful addition to the relational circle—or a tremendously negative influence. Be discerning, and find the great ones (they're out there), and don't settle for anything less.

# # 639 Questions for Baby-Sitters

Of course you'll have to leave *instructions* for baby-sitters. But do more— draw them into conversation with questions: What will you do if he disobeys you or if she complains? What will you do if they fight? What will you do to get to know who he really is? What could you do to make your time memorable? What would you want the children to say about you tomorrow? How will you handle emergencies? Dialogue beats instructions ten to one on the relational scale.

# # 640 Uncles and Aunts

As your friends get close to your child, make them honorary aunts and uncles. They can fill that place of caring relatives and trusted role models, and they'll help you bond with your child by providing their own insights or passing along what they hear about you from your kids. Especially if you're a single parent or if your spouse is emotionally distant, these better-than-relatives relationships bring benefit to your kids and you.

# # 641 Brothers and Sisters

If your friends have children, you might be able to match your kids up with an adopted "big sister" or "big brother." Make sure your friends' kids share the same values as you and their parents since occasionally parents and their kids can be miles apart. Then bring in that older child and broaden both your child's relationship experience and your perspective on your child.

# # 642 Parent Switch

Try switching kids with a close friend for a day. The goal is to talk about the other child's parent in a fresh way and, of course, to have some fun, too. At the end of the day you'll either feel better about how you're doing or have some new goals for your parenting and relationship with your child.

# # 643 Joint Activities

Consider doing joint activities with your family and your friend's. Plan an outing, daycation, or vacation (if there is a really close connection). Talk with your friend in advance about the topics and angles you want to discuss, so that you can dig in deep and have memories of conversations to fall back on when you're home.

# # 644 Their Sibling, My Friend

As your older children mature, they make excellent advisors to the younger children. Ask for their input. Not only will it help you with parenting the younger ones, but you'll also enhance your relationship with the older child as you trust and confide in him.

# # 645 Dear Abby

Do the unexpected, and ask your children for their advice on one of your adult friendships. It shows trust in them, which they'll appreciate. Beyond that, they'll develop better concepts of friendship by thinking and talking with you.

# Family Ties: Strong Bonds versus Strangleholds

## # 646 Your Way

There is no way you can implement every parenting idea that your extended family members come up with—not if you're aiming at a solid relationship with your kids and a relatively sane version of parenting. "I don't know the key to success," says comedian Bill Cosby, "but the key to failure is trying to please everybody."

## # 647 When Your Mommy or Daddy Was Little

Get your folks and even your grandparents, if they're living, to pass along meaningful true tales about your childhood to your kids. As they consider you as a young boy or girl, you'll seem more human and accessible—and more valuable. Pick a topic, find some time, and then point the conversation in the direction you want it to go: "Mom, why don't you tell the kids about that time we were all so scared of that storm that we spent the night in the basement?" Ask questions that help your parent provide details about your feelings and reactions.

## # 648 Magic That Takes Time

There are some parents who are decent but superficial, some that are manipulative or coercive, and some that are downright rotten and nasty. If your parents fall into these categories, be careful to structure the time they spend with your kids and monitor what goes on in those relationships. Don't fool yourself that these same people who confused or harmed you as child won't repeat these mistakes with your kids. But perhaps your folks are some of the "good guys"—in which case your parents can provide an incredibly rich experience for your kids through generational bonding. Your parents will support your values and not contradict your parenting decisions. So give them a lot of time to work their magic, even if it means higher long-distance phone bills.

# # 649 They're My Grandkids

Some grandparents will pressure parents to do things a certain way with their grandkids or try to force invitations to visit. If this happens, resist their attempts to manipulate you with the "They're my grandchildren" approach. This demeans your kids by turning them into bargaining chips. It shows that the grandparents are focusing on their own rights instead of on building a relationship with the grandchildren. Your kids are people, not possessions. No false guilt here.

# # 650 The Underhanded End-Around

Some grandparents will go around the parents to persuade the grandchildren of their own ideas or to undermine the parents' authority with the children. Some may even try to get your children to relate to them more closely than they do to you. Others might say things that cause your children to lose respect for you. This is deadly relational ground. If your children have been spending time with a grandparent who tends to say harmful things, talk with them as soon as possible so that you can analyze what was said and try to make sense of it together.

# # 651 Honor Thy Father and Mother

Some parents feel they can't limit the grandparents' access, in time or influence, because they've been commanded to "honor" their parents. But "honoring" doesn't mean you ignore their deficiencies, allow them to wreak havoc, or pretend they're loving when they're not. You do carry a measure of duty toward your parents, but not a duty to sacrifice your children's well-being. So structure involvement with parents to maximize the positive—the joy, happiness, and value—and minimize the negative.

# # 652 Parent in the Present, Not the Past

Whether you're ready to admit it or not, your parents remain a dominant force in determining aspects of your life—including your parenting style. If you're going to build something great with your own kids, you'll have to avoid whatever parenting pitfalls your parents fell into, especially actions that were harsh or abusive. You'll find you'll have to work hard not to duplicate those problems or get on a "pendulum"—giving nasty punishment and then hating it so much that you let your kids get away with murder the next time. So sit down and think through the past, without wallowing in the problems, and move forward into intelligent and passionate parenting. Of course, if your parents were fabulously gentle and relational parents, you won't have as many problem areas to look out for—and you can thank God that every day you're reaping the benefits of their godly behavior.

# # 653 The Positive Teaching Tool

Be sure to direct your children's attention toward the great personality traits you discover in their grandparents. This can improve their bond with their grandparents and make them proud to be in a family that has a history of "greatness." Their grandparents' positive character is one more mentor model of how adults should behave and achieve.

# # 654 The Negative Teaching Tool

When they're old enough to understand it, you can talk with your kids about the harder aspects of your relationship with your parents. Be open and honest about your relationship. For instance, if your mother manipulates you to call her and visit her and change your plans to suit her, talk about this with your kids (eventually they'll notice it on their own). While still modeling love and respect for your mother, you can help your children learn from a negative character trait or from a pattern you don't want to duplicate in your relationship with them. You're modeling love for your mother even while seeing her clearly, and you increase your child's empathy for you.

# # 655 Abusive Family Members

If you were abused as a child—whether verbally, emotionally, physically, or sexually—sometimes those abusive patterns carry into your adult life, where they can continue to do harm. If your relationship with a family member has been troubled by his or her abuse, don't hesitate to protect your children from contact (or from unsupervised contact) with that person. And if your children see you being harshly attacked or even subtly attacked, they can be enormously confused and unsettled. The abusive behavior may extend to include them.

# # 656 Control versus Bonding

Some parents' idea of developing a bond with their children is more about control than a loving relationship: "You'll do what I say because I'm your mother and I love you," or "You owe me respect because I'm your father." That's connection by chain instead of connection by choice—it's definitely not true bonding. If your parents (or one of them) are controllers, face the fact and reject that manipulation. Then keep a healthy emotional distance between your kids and the controllers.

# # 657 Great Relatives

Thank goodness most families have at least one or two relatives who would make wonderful friends and mentors for your children and who'll benefit the connection you're developing with your kids. Bend over backward to find ways to bring these loved ones together with your children, working to make time they can spend together one-on-one so they can bond. Family parties and reunions can be great, but only individual time leads to an unbreakable bond. Your love for your children will have a longer reach as you love them through this one you love.

# # 658 The Storytellers

Let your really great relatives "explain" you to your children, divulging stories about you from the past when you were a kid so that your children can truly know you as a child during their childhood. These relatives bring to your kids a new perspective on you—a fresh angle with which your kids can connect.

# # 659 Vice Versa

If your much-appreciated relatives have children of their own, you can play the same role in their home. You spin the stories of when their parents were young—the adventures you had, how character developed, how they behaved, and why you loved them so much. In this way, you serve to build the bond between those children and their parents. If your children are there when you do it, so much the better. They'll see you building a relationship and understand how it's done—and they'll love you for it.

# # 660 Just Say No

If you've got rotten relatives—real "nasties"—just say no to time with them, at least to unsupervised time. Don't inflict their personalities or their influence on your children. You don't need to put your head in a sewer to know that it stinks. Go where kindness is liberally given.

# # 661 Unintentional Damage

You probably have relatives who seem fairly harmless, but they just aren't careful. Look out—they can do a lot of damage with their words. Perhaps they'll trivialize your children's character by giving lots of skin-deep praise: "You're so cute. You're the prettiest little girl in the family. You're even better looking than your father." Or they'll deliberately make a cutting comment, such as telling a father of three daughters, "Too bad you never got your boy!" while speaking right in front of the girls.

# # 662 Extreme Relatives

It's OK for you to limit or avoid spending time with your "extreme" relatives. I don't mean "extremists" who are holed up in the mountains with dried food and guns (although they would make excellent candidates for avoidance). I mean relatives who are rigidly strict or lavishly overindulgent. You don't want your kids spending time with adult relatives who say yes to everything the kids think of doing or say no automatically without even hearing. These approaches contradict the person-to-person interdependence and accountability you're trying to build with your child.

# # 663 Developing Discernment

To help your kids develop discernment in making wise decisions about whom to spend time with and how much time, involve them in decisions about extended family: "Which family members do you like being around? Which ones make you uncomfortable? Why?" It's amazing how even very young children can clearly differentiate among the good, the bad, and the ugly.

# # 664 Don't Overreact

When, suddenly, one of your kids does something to remind you of one of your less-than-desirable relatives, don't panic or overreact. Give yourself time to think about how to handle your child's behavior pattern. Maybe it's a one-time coincidence. Maybe the traits really are being passed along, and you'll have to limit your child's contact with Uncle Bill, who is loose in language and morals. There is time to shape your child's behavior, so don't treat your child as if he's Uncle Bill! It's assumptions and unthinking reactions that can take a big toll on your relationship.

# # 665  Who's Got the Victory?

Some people make it into old age with their positive attitude, their
enthusiasm, and even their idealism still intact. They have spent a
lifetime becoming a bastion of joy. They'll attract you and your children
like bees to honey. Warm relationships are built in the glow of ancient
fires. My mother's brother Jack is such a person. Even in the midst of a
long recuperation from back surgery, he offered no complaints. When we
visit him, he's positive and funny and *encouraging*. I love feeling that
thread of connection winding its way through our times together. Spend
time with those who, even in a small way, have victory.

# # 666  No False Fear

If you have family members whose lives rise and fall around their fears,
keep your kids a safe distance from them. Sure, the world has always
been a tough place, but there's no need to go through life with a "siege"
mentality, withdrawing or isolating yourself in protective retreat. Relating
out of false fear leads to a false bond; relating out of real fear leads to a
dysfunctional bond. Drive fear out of your heart and home.

# # 667  Family Traits

Talk with your kids about your family's traits as a collective group: "One
thing our family does is . . ." Once, when my son Peter and I were talking
about my brothers and sister, he told me, "In this family, we always take
responsibility and get the job done." As he noted this, he was personally
encouraged to become this kind of person himself. But along with that,
he felt connected to the whole family—and closer to me.

# # 668  Time Drainers

Some family members can take up a lot of your time for no good reason.
Don't hesitate to cut their time short in order to gain more time with your
kids. Connection is more important than duty.

# # 669  The Fight for Privacy

Some family members may be constantly on the phone, dropping by,
planning events—just *there*. They may be well intentioned, but they
simply interrupt. Your family needs regular times of solitude. And you
need private time with just your children if you're going to build that
beautiful bond. So set a few boundaries (and get caller I.D.)!

# # 670 Hit the Road, Jack!

Take charge of your family's visits with extended family, setting the necessary limits. You may have to limit *who:* Which cousins will work best in combination with your kids for this afternoon or outing? How will that smart aleck's behavior affect my child's attitude? And you'll definitely have to limit *how long:* Is this profitable for a whole afternoon or just for an hour? An old Portuguese proverb teaches that "visits always give pleasure—if not the arrival, the departure."

# # 671 The Gracious No

Connect by empowering your kids to say no if they need to. "Hey, when Grandpa starts tickling you so hard, just tell him, 'Grandpa, I know you don't mean to, but that hurts—please stop.' When Uncle John pushes you to ride on his motorcycle, you can say, 'I like you, Uncle John, but that thing scares me to death—so I think I'll pass.' When Aunt Jennifer starts putting more food on your plate, it's OK to tell her, 'Aunt Jennifer, I love your cooking, but if I eat any more, I won't be able to love it as much.'" Authorize them to say no, and show them how to do it graciously.

# # 672 Rescue the Little Ones

Siblings often criticize one another, especially older children who try to be little parents to their younger siblings. They often do it badly, even tyrannically. When you overhear such criticism, come to the rescue: Defend and champion your criticized child. That will build your bond. Don't ignore the situation, and don't add your critique to the one he's just received from the older child. This is what God does for us: "Reassure me; let me hear you say, 'I'll save you.' . . . You put the down-and-out on their feet and protect the unprotected from bullies!" (Psalm 35, *The Message*).

# # 673 The Dinnertime Derby

Dinnertime can be a terrific bonding time, and it can also become a demolition derby. Some children will dominate the conversation, argue, and put others down when they speak. So create house rules that allow freedom of speech. Maybe you can decree, "No arguing at dinner—it's a safe place. If you start an argument at the table, your dinner is over." Practice having meals where each person gets to speak without interruption, correction, or questions—just listening.

# # 674 Relational Math

When discussing family members, or even your own behavior, talk about the mathematics of relationship with your children:

- Multipliers are people who build something new into your relationship. Back and forth in synergy, both of you encourage growth and confidence.
- Adders are positive people who add to your life. Time spent with them is pleasant, with occasional contributions to growth.
- Subtracters are people who gradually eat away at your souls, exhibiting little criticisms, put-down tones and body language, and no thought for who you are.
- Dividers cause great harm by delighting in being nasty or degrading. These are the bullies, gossips, slanderers, and meddlers.

When you look at the "score" for your family, do all you can to add to your relationship and multiply love.

# 18

## A Chosen Church Family

### # 675 Other People's Kids

Several years before my first child was born, I served as a youth pastor for a fairly large youth group. I wanted to serve and I really loved the teens, but I was also interested in investigating how children raised in "decent" homes turned out and why. I was stunned. Many parents who really wanted the best for their children simply failed. Sometimes their kids even ended up in trouble of some kind. The only common denominator I could find among most of the cases where things went wrong was the absence of real relationship. Volunteer to get involved with other people's children, so you can learn how to love your own.

### # 676 In the Church Nursery

Sharing common experiences is a building block of relationship. Churches typically provide separate classes for different age groups. This is often useful, of course, but not necessarily great for building relationships. So see what you can do to get where your kids are—even in the church nursery. When your child is in the nursery, take your turn as a nursery worker—just so you can be with your child. Bonds are built in those early years, so take advantage of those shared church nursery experiences. If Jesus were in your church, where would he be?

### # 677 Everybody Ought to Go to Sunday School

The Sunday school hour is another time when families are divided into classes by age for Bible teaching. Once again, see what you can do to get into your child's department from time to time. Visit your son's class. Substitute for the teacher in your daughter's class. Have the Sunday school class to your home for a party. Invite them all out for pizza. Use the church to unite you with your child, not to create a gap.

# # 678 Youth Group

"Our church has a terrific youth group—the kids are really kept busy. And it gives us a break!" So many parents feel this way and then wonder why their kids feel more in touch with their peers than their parents. Your children's teen years are a great time for them to find their place in the whole church—beyond just the youth group and kids their age. Include them in your adult ministry opportunities. Get your teens to fill in when ushers don't show up. Make your teens your assistant teachers in the preschool department. Take them with you to sit in on your committee meeting. Let your teens participate in wedding and baby showers. During those teen years you can join in youth activities as well—agreeing to drive to activities or chaperone some overnight adventure or a longer missions trip. Keep your relationship alive.

# # 679 Do Something Together

Most churches have more tasks to accomplish and ministries to staff than there are volunteers, so there will be no shortage of things to do when you and your child get interested in serving together. When you're choosing among service opportunities—teaching, cooking, maintenance, business, cleaning, outreach—select projects that could include both you and your child, at least part of the time. Paint a classroom together, deliver food to the needy together, participate in a youth-group car wash together. Be selective. Make sure a portion of the things you sign up for lead to closer relationship with your kids.

# # 680 Potluck Musical Chairs

Potluck dinners are appropriately named in many cases—you're lucky if you come away having had a balanced (or edible) meal. At church meals be careful not to banish the kids to a "kids' table" so adults can eat alone together. When this happens, I always try to go sit with the kids for at least part of the meal (sometimes the conversation is more honest, and they usually know more about the desserts). It's good to mix things up a bit to create opportunities for your children to interact with other adults, too. Go ahead and let your kids sit apart from you—as long as it's not always with peers only.

# # 681 Church Friends

Friendship cliques can develop in churches just like they do anyplace
else. If one child or group of kids is absorbing all of your child's time and
attention, his youth-group activities may have become more liability than
asset. "That love for one from which there doth not spring wide love for
all is but a worthless thing," wrote poet and essayist James Russell Lowell.

# # 682 Adopt the Youth Group

When I was a youth pastor, I pushed for parents to host our meetings in
their homes, knowing how important it was for kids to be exposed to
more people and varying lifestyles. If you want to understand your older
child, adopt the youth group. Have them in your home. Sponsor activities.
Talk to them. Have *lots* of food. You'll get a lot of insights from watching
how kids relate to other kids. How could your kids not relate to you, a
parent who is interested in young people?

# # 683 Adopt the Pastor

Get your pastor or some member of the pastoral staff involved with your
family. Invite that person to dinner or out for a good time together. Get his
insights on your family and your relationship with your child. Don't
assume that he even knows who your children are. In many churches,
unfortunately, only adults are counted and treated as members of the
church family.

# # 684 God's Family

The people at your church are supposed to be God's family. Like all
families, your church family probably has kindly "grandparent" types,
"aunts" and "uncles," good guys and bad guys, saints and nuts. The
connections made there will affect your children and your relationship
with your children. Select those connection points carefully. Maximize
the ones that build your relationship, and run like the wind from the
others.

# # 685 Older Pals

Our church has a program that matches up children, even from
two-parent homes, with adults who are interested in spending time with
them. Try to find an adult "pal" for your child, but make sure that person
will reinforce your relationship with your child and not tear it down or
usurp your role.

# # 686 First Fridays

Our family has planned "First Fridays," a monthly night when we'd invite some interesting mix of people from church to our home for a dinner party. We tried to invite people who would be interesting to our children. Fellow church members who show you and your children respect and care can help to unite you in the midst of a most interesting evening.

# # 687 Casual Fellowship

It's too easy to want someone to watch your children while you chat with adults before or after worship services. Why not draw your kids into that informal conversation? It'll build your connection and ignite their interest to be included in lively chats about spiritual issues.

# # 688 Skip It

Church is supposed to be about relationship—with God and with other people. So when you get loaded up with too many activities, even good ones, it's time to just say no. Take time off from a committee. Get a friend to teach your Sunday school class. Trim back the things that keep you from your priorities of honoring God and connecting with your family.

# # 689 Career Counseling

Let your kids provide input on what areas of ministry activity you should be involved in at church. This shows them you trust their opinions. It can also benefit your connection with them because their ideas about where you could participate are usually somewhere pretty close to where they are. A long time ago I enjoyed playing the piano, sometimes for church services. In a rough time in my life, I dropped my music. Years later, when I was in the midst of many busy and interesting things, Peter—who played guitar on the worship team—worked it out for me to substitute for the vacationing pianist. He gave me back my music, and I'm so very, very grateful.

# # 690 Questions about Sunday School

Avoid the don't-ask-don't-tell pattern connected with dropping kids off at Sunday school. Find out what's going on in their classes so you can connect. Ask, "What do you like about your teacher? Which kid in the class do you sit with? Which kids do you think are the most genuine? Do you think the kids in your class are really here to learn more about God?" Even at an early age they can learn to discern.

# # 691 Youth Pastors

I've had a wonderfully varied and exciting career life, but few things I've done were more exhilarating or rewarding than serving as a youth pastor. Adopt the youth pastor at your church (it doesn't matter how old he is in actual years—he has to be young to do this job) and get him into your home. Buy needed resources or just-for-fun gifts. Get him tickets to a concert. Feed him. Send Christmas and birthday cards, with money in them. Love him hard. Your children are probably already connected to him, and as you build this bond with this young shepherd, you build their bond with you.

# # 692 Questions for Youth Pastors

To get to know your youth pastor, draw him into discussion. Ask, "What are the main principles that help you guide the youth group? Will you be comfortable talking with me if you sense my child has a problem with me? Who are the kids to whom you'd like to see my child relating? What can we do to encourage these relationships? What will you do if you see my child developing negative relationships? How will you handle group members who have no interest in God or healthy relationships? Will you befriend my child? Will you help me get inside her heart?"

# # 693 Befriend the Youth Pastor

Most parents have hopes for the youth pastor or expectations for the youth pastor. Be the friend who goes deeper to *love* the youth pastor—in actions and in truth. Help him, volunteer, run errands, send notes of encouragement—draw him in, and build a three-cord knot.

# # 694 Theologians Together

You and your kids can dissect sermons and Sunday school lessons and anything else that's being taught at church—together. Your friendship will deepen as you talk about these ultimately important topics related to your spirit, your faith. That's the core of who you all are as human beings. Agree, disagree, challenge, wrestle—whatever it takes to keep digging into God's character and truth with the same shovel.

# # 695 Only Two Religions

It is really easy to get sidetracked onto bogus religious issues that distract and don't enlighten or bond you with each other or God. There are really only two religions—God's and all the others. You can get engrossed in talking about cults, end-times prophecies, or religion-by-rules and miss a relationship with God entirely. Your faith is all about connection—with God and with others, like your children. Talk with your children about what true religion looks like.

# # 696 True Spirituality

Don't confuse formal church with spirituality. Much of spirituality isn't covered by Sunday-morning activities; neither is everything that goes on in church actually spiritual. Discuss true spirituality versus fake religion in the context of your church and your relationships with those who claim to be of like mind. As you sift out the chaff to get to the truth, you'll connect with each other.

# # 697 Inquirers

Every soul is on a spiritual journey. One of the exciting things about parenting is that you get to journey with your children. Be spiritually inquisitive together—digging for the truth, asking questions, probing, not confusing faith with taking things at face value.

# # 698 The Wreckers

Because Christians are just a group of forgiven sinners, every church has some share of wreckers—wolves, haters, judgers, condemners, gossips, slanderers, meddlers, nuts, losers. The worst wreckers are those who do their damage in the name of God: "Anyone who kills you will think he is offering a service to God" (John 16:2). I once knew a woman who felt she held responsibility for "the purity of the church" and used that "mission" to justify being hateful, nasty, raging, and awful. Avoid the wreckers like the plague that they are, and focus on those who affirm your values, broaden your perspective, and build your important relationships.

# # 699 Believing God

Believing together in God's goodness and presence is a wonderful tool of connection. If you can look into the sky and see behind it the one who made it and talk about your great God in the most intimate of terms, you become more aware of your connection with that invisible realm.

# # 700 Asking God

Few parents pray for real, detailed, actual needs with their children, even if they encourage a token prayer of blessing for others or regularly give thanks before eating. Don't be afraid to pray about the "hard areas" of your lives. Pray in a specific, believing way about school, career, jobs, friends, or activities.

# # 701 Someone's Watching

Let your children see the quiet spiritual side of you (if you don't have one of those, it's not too late to develop one). Let them see you praying, reading Scripture, poring over spiritual books, singing in worship services, crying over a good sermon point. The real you comes through these spiritual connections with God—the part of you that's eternal. Let your children know and love the real you.

# # 702 Bless You

A pastor named Phil Ellsworth encourages parents in his church to place their hands on their children and repeat a blessing after him. It might be as simple as "I love you. I am glad God gave you to me. You're a special blessing to me." It might be more or different. But it's an exceptional practice, and it's something you could suggest to your pastor or try on your own. You will reap big blessings when you bless your child.

# # 703 Leave Out the Hammer

All good parents are concerned with the moral and religious training of their children. But if you translate that into hammering your children with certain Scriptures, such as "Children, obey your parents" (Eph. 6:1), you're sure to push them away from you *and* God. Love raises up, but hammers flatten.

# # 704 The Rest of the Story

It's too easy to focus on Scripture applications that pertain to your kid's end of your relationship (like the need for children to obey their parents) without introducing your kids to the fact that the Bible has something to say to you parents as well. How about "Do not exasperate your children" (Eph. 6:4) or "Do not embitter your children" (Col. 3:21)? If you want connection—if you want *obedience*—start with the Scriptures that apply to you.

# # 705 Service

Joint service to a church can be a wonderful bonder. When someone tells you, "You two are like a pillar to this church," you have received a reward and a connection that money can't buy. Serve as one.

# # 706 Be Wise—Internalize

Religious training that makes sure children are controlled, that they act properly in public, that their clothes are "appropriate," that their hair is the "right" length, and that they learn Scripture and Sunday school lessons and catechism can be superficial or worse. It's like washing "the outside of the cup and dish" (Matt. 23:25). All that fakery between you and your kids separates you from your children and creates resentment. Real spiritual training is messy, feisty, open, and honest. It expresses doubts and disagrees. It's the stuff of true spirituality and the raw material for real relationship.

# # 707 Home Is Part of Church

A Chinese proverb says, "Better do a good deed near at home than go far away to burn incense." Live out those "one another" commands by loving your nearest neighbors—the people who live at your house. Cultivate your spiritual life at home first.

# Part 4

# *Hard Times:*

## How Problems

## Create

## Connection

*Life* can be hard. You and your children will encounter fear—and pain and mistakes and hurdles. These challenges take your relationship with your children to the edge. But God can turn bad into good. Heartache can become joy, mourning can yield to dancing, giant errors can become the seeds of something magnificent. God is the God of second chances, and your relationship can benefit from this great heavenly principle.

Can fear and pain become allies in building your relationship with your kids? Yes. Can your children's mistakes and other relational obstacles be turned to advantage, yours and theirs? Yes. Can your relationship really bounce back when you, as the parent, have really messed up? Absolutely yes! Nothing can separate you—unless you let it.

# 19
## Triumphing through Tears

# # 708  A Refuge
Life is tough. With so many challenges along the way, both you and your kids need a place to hide and rest, or you'd just give up in despair. Your first place of refuge is God. But you can also find refuge in a human heart. Relate to your children in such a way that no matter what terrors come their way, they know where they can find refuge.

# # 709  Watch Them with Your Heart
Stay sensitive to when your children are oppressed by some unnamed fear or pain. Most parents find it easy to notice physical sicknesses—fevers, rashes, stomachaches. Seek to be just as sensitive to those internal sicknesses that can cripple your children's souls—maybe even a struggle they simply can't yet articulate or make sense of. Be there, gently paying attention, helping them to find comfort and a peace that's beyond understanding.

# # 710  Home Base
When playing tag, there is usually a "base"—a place where you can go and no one can tag you. Your home becomes "home base" for your kids when they feel secure in connection with you. Help them know that they don't need to worry about getting chastised for a slight misstep, that they can "think out loud" without having to perfect their words, that they can challenge your silly and idiotic ideas in a respectful way and you'll listen. They need a place that's safe, and that's home.

# # 711 Adversity's Bond

Few things bond us like adversity. People who haven't spoken to each other in years will often join together in prayer in a hospital room, their priorities readjusted by the trouble they're facing. You can hope that adversity won't come, but be ready when it does. Don't let it crush your relationship. Instead, build the strength of your connection. It takes a lot of intense heat to make the best steel.

# # 712 Don't Be Afraid

Parents sometimes mistakenly think their mission is to make life as easy as possible for their children. But if you want the best out of them *and* your relationship, you can't be afraid to challenge them to live a courageous life. "Leaders who offer blood, toil, tears, and sweat always get more out of their followers than those who offer safety and a good time. When it comes to the pinch, human beings are heroic," wrote George Orwell (quoted in *The Ultimate Book of Business Quotations,* AMACOM Books, 1998).

# # 713 Nothing to Worry About?

When your children are afraid of the dark or terrified of thunderstorms, you might tell them that there is "nothing to worry about." But the truth about life is that there is plenty to worry about—it's just not useful to do it. Instead of responding to their fears and pain by trying to pretend there's nothing to worry about, take advantage of a marvelous opportunity for connection. Say, "That thunder really *is* scary. I used to feel exactly the same way; I know it can't hurt us, and I bet you do too, but our feelings are sometimes stronger than our heads. Let's cuddle up here till the storm's over." You take the lead in dealing with the worry by letting them depend on you. They'll love and trust you more than ever. Remember that no one is designed to face the storms alone.

# # 714 Communication

Fear and pain enhance the senses and open doors to deeper communication. If you keep your wits about you, you'll use fearful or painful times to probe subjects that are typically off-limits during "normal" times. Provide assurances and comfort, but talk to each other, too. The important and caring words you share during the stinging moments can last a lifetime.

# # 715 Memories of War

"Remember that what is hard to endure will be sweet to recall," wrote Tote Yamada (as quoted in *Whatever It Takes,* Compendium Publishing, 1995). When you and your kids endure together in the right spirit, the sweetest of all war memories will be the "buddies" you fought alongside.

# # 716 Bully for You

Life is chock full of bullies. At least those playground bullies were out in the open and not hidden. Older bullies are more adept at subtle forms of manipulation or force. When someone is trying to dominate and control your child, he or she needs your wisdom, strength, and support. You don't need to solve the problem for your child, but you need to help him believe he can solve the problem and win.

# # 717 Powerful Enemies

Use the power of enemies to bind you together. It could be a common enemy—say, someone at church who doesn't like your family—or an enemy facing just your child or you. The second kind becomes a common enemy by virtue of the bond you share. Few things can bring you closer than the threat of a common foe. Handle the challenge properly, with love, but handle it together.

# # 718 Beware the Wolf Pack

You may think wolves can't harm you if you're loving God the Shepherd and doing good to people. But wolves—those who take perverse pleasure in devouring others, sometimes even telling themselves they're doing it for God—go where the sheep are. They attend church, go to meetings, attend showers and dinners, volunteer for service projects. And they travel in packs. I have watched one wolf pack eat its way through four churches. When wolves inflict their damage, draw in close to your children and face the wolves in the power of your love. Expose the wolves among the sheep, and let them see that they can't hurt you unless they can get you alone.

# # 719 Let Them Help

Allow your children to "help" you work through a fear. "Sometimes we walk deep into the woods," my friend Anna Bourdess told me. "I pretend to be lost and allow my children to encourage me and lead me back home. Even though this is a 'setup,' it builds a foundation for understanding fear, the freedom to be afraid, how to work through it, and that we can do it together." Share your real fears, and let them lead you through them.

# # 720 Don't Hide

When you have a great pain or loss, you may be tempted to hide it—and yourself—from your children. After I finished writing this very chapter, I went back to make a few corrections. The manuscript was gone—from the hard drive, from the disk. This had never happened to me before, through the writing of eight other books. Peter and David walked in, and I told them (with great grief) what had happened. They gave me much encouragement. We went out to lunch. Peter sealed it when he said, "It will probably be better the second time than it was before. Besides, if you don't calm down, you won't finish the book, and it will be called *825 Ways to Connect with Your Kids*. So I considered it pure joy....

# # 721 Their Sick Days

Sickness isn't just a difficult time to get through with your kids. It's a perfect opportunity to talk and get closer in the midst of the pain. Their physical discomfort slows your kids down and allows time for their hearts to open. Don't miss it.

# # 722 Your Sick Days

When you're physically ill—and so miserable that dying starts to sound like an improvement—let yourself need your kids. Be helpless. Be grateful for anything they're willing to do. Talk to them. Use the time of physical vulnerability as a time of relationship vulnerability as well.

# # 723 Pain As an Ally

Whatever the pain, it can be used as an ally to bring understanding to your hearts and closeness to your relationship. Even as you try to "fix" it, you can accept the chance to drain the truth and learning out of the experience. The key question to ask yourself is, *How can this pain be turned to our advantage?* Bad things turn into good things under the onslaught of a pursuing love (Rom. 8:28).

# # 724 The Heartache of Misunderstanding

When your children are misunderstood, you can offer them a place of understanding. When no one else "gets" them, they can't help but love the one who does. We're like this with God—we feel closer when we get understanding from him. Showing your understanding and support is especially important when your kids are taking a beating for standing up for truth or a good cause. You can be there to say, "I get it. Don't stop." You can say with Ralph Waldo Emerson, "To be great is to be misunderstood."

# # 725 The Lost Cause

Politicians remember it long afterward and are the most grateful for the help when someone sticks with them on a losing campaign. Everyone knows it's over, but that staunch friend dukes it out to the end. Be that staunch to-the-finish support for your kids. When your children have no chance to finish that project, complete that assignment, or meet that deadline, get in there and help anyway, even when it means "losing" together. Like the politicians who don't forget, neither will your kids.

# # 726 Bye-Bye Love

Whenever your child has lost a relationship—a friend moves away or betrays him, that "love of a lifetime" turns out to be a "love of a semester," or shared interests dissipate—you're gaining the opportunity to draw your child close and help fill the void. Don't say, "I told you so!" or, "Now don't take any more risks." Don't say, "All you need is me." Just say, "Let me hug you and make it a little bit better."

# # 727 Sick Friends

When one of their friends gets really sick or hurt, go all out along with your children in bringing the friend comfort. It's a double bond—you're bonded in service, and you're showing them their friends are really important to you.

# # 728 Sick Family Member

When a family member—either from your immediate family or your extended family—becomes seriously injured or ill, the world can turn upside down. The longer it lasts, the more the uncertainty, chaos, and fear. Get together with your child to wage an all-out love and care assault on this enemy of health and life. Turn your fear and pain into action, conversation, and connection with the sick loved one and with each other.

# # 729 Last Good-Bye

Death is a defining moment for those who are left behind. When a relative dies, avoid getting completely absorbed with funeral details, getting reacquainted with people you wouldn't see any other time, or with your own grief. Don't miss the rare opening for deep conversation and heart-melding with your kids. Focus on it, and you'll find you've gained a great good out of a very tough moment.

# # 730 Death of a Friend

When I was in first grade, Larry, one of my best friends, was killed by a drunk teenager in a car accident. It stopped me in my tracks. I was all ears, but no one was talking. Everyone was busy feeling bad and trying to "cheer" me up. But I didn't need cheering as much as I needed understanding, perspective, and some deep-soul intensive care. No matter how old your children are, when they've lost a friend, they have a burning hole you can help to fill.

# # 731 Sick Pets

I remember when David's first hamster (he has twenty-two as of this writing) got very sick. We took her to the veterinarian and spent about $1.5 million on her care (OK, that's a slight exaggeration). But really, it was a terrific investment. When a beloved pet gets sick, show your connection to your child's heart and go all out. Stay up together through the night. Treat the wounds. Cry and pray. Spend the money. It's the *journey* that has the meaning.

# # 732 Grieving a Pet

When a much-loved pet dies, you feel as if a piece of you has died along with it. So go ahead and grieve. Have a burial. You can make a big deal because God cares about animals. Use this loss of life as a jumping-off place for discussing death, what it means, how it feels. And talk about how glad you are to have each other to walk through the pain arm in arm.

# # 733 Physical Imperfections

Imperfection is part of life—it *is* life—but it can feel like such a burden, especially to children. Show your kids your minor physical deformities, since your imperfections put theirs in perspective. Tell them how you dealt with them, conquered them, learned to accept them as marks of uniqueness.

# # 734 Character Flaws

Confess, too, your character flaws, since your children will surely be dealing with disappointment in themselves now and then. Tell them how you've depended on God to do better, how others have helped or encouraged you, how you've handled your disappointment over how hard it is to mend these imperfections. It makes you human, and real, and approachable.

# # 735 A Bad Substitute

"Duty first" can be a bad policy. If you see your role as a parent as only to raise a responsible, orderly person, you'll insist on obedience and compliance without regard for your child's emotional state. With this approach, you actually train the child to go through the motions no matter what they're feeling, and that can deaden their souls. Yes, responsibility is important. But what about your responsibility to nurture and mend a heart? There are times to cancel appointments, skip the chores, and go off together in a joyous fit of "spontaneity."

# # 736 Discipline and Punishment from Others

When your children are facing the pain of discipline and punishment from others, be there to offer empathy and comfort when it is unfair or undeserved, and understanding and advice if they brought it on themselves. While not agreeing with mistakes or sins, you can still connect deeply during these tumultuous times.

# # 737 Make a Disciple

The word *discipline* is derived from the root word *disciple*—a follower of the way. Do you see discipline as the process of making your child a disciple? Making disciples consists of teaching them, redirecting their thinking, gently correcting their errors, and testing them to see if they are "getting it." It includes allowing them to make mistakes so they can learn some effective lessons in the school of life. You discipline your children because they need to be educated. If you make disciples through natural consequences and not lecture ("parenting by annoyance"), discipline won't get in the way of your relationship.

# # 738 Wiser, Deeper, Stronger

The German philosopher Nietzsche wrote, "Anything that does not kill me makes me stronger." This is true, but only if you come through it wiser and deeper and more closely related to the world around you. Evaluate, and help your children evaluate, whether or not pain is making you stronger. If it isn't, what can you change to make it so?

# # 739 Count Your Blessings

When the pain comes, you have an antidote close at hand: "Reflect upon your present blessings, of which every man has many; not on your past misfortunes, of which all men have some," wrote Charles Dickens. Talk about the blessings, count the blessings, list the blessings, make blessing flowcharts—help your child get out of the "Woe is me" category, and back into knowing and believing that life, indeed, is good.

# # 740 Happy Warrior

As you and your child go through the pain together, remember that "when you grow old or ill, the most important things to you will be who and what you've loved" (June Martin, as quoted in *Whatever It Takes*, Compendium Publishing, 1995). Live with humility, knowing that at the end, it is just your kids and you and what you've done together that will matter. Love them through the pains of their lives, and they will join you in the pains of yours, into the future, right to the end.

# 20

# Winning on the Obstacle Course

# # 741 The Real Goal of Parenting

The goal of parenting is not to make perfect children—the most attractive, smartest, most socially adept, ambitious and goal-driven, spiritually mature, and possibly sinless kids. This is not only a fantasy, it's a distraction from the real goal of parenting: to show your kids how to live well as an imperfect being in an imperfect world, with an imperfect you.

# # 742 Show Some Restraint

A big part of parenting involves restraint—not saying something when it could be said, not punishing harshly in the face of a grievous fault. "God strikes with his finger, and not with all his arm," said the seventeenth-century poet George Herbert. Follow God's lead.

# # 743 Merits of Mercy

When your kids deserve chastening and you don't give it, you build their understanding of merciful love and redemption—and their bond with you. Justice is crucial. You can't and shouldn't ignore sin and failure. But once in a while when you don't give them what they deserve, you remind them that mercy has its merits. You wouldn't want to get what you deserve in your relationship with God. Because if he treated us as *our* sins deserve, well ... Consider how much his repeated forgiveness means to you.

# # 744 A Merciful Servant

It's really easy to be tougher on your kids than you'd want others— including God—to be on you. When your kids are procrastinating with their homework and turning it in late, try to remember when you did the same with your homework or a project at work or with paying your bills. In addition to remembering the "Golden Rule" in these situations, it's also helpful to recall that there is justice in the universe. The way you treat others (your children) may, in the long run, be how judgment is meted out to you.

# # 745 Getting Away with It?

There does seem to be a fine line between receiving mercy and developing a pattern of "getting away with it." The problem is that you might show mercy, but your children receive it in the wrong spirit and "benefit" by missing some consequences and continuing the behavior. They may be taking advantage of your goodness; it will certainly feel that way. So teach your kids what mercy is and that the goal of mercy is to produce change, not more bad behavior. We may need to let the consequences come in ever-increasing intensity. But their behavior can never put them beyond the reach of your love. Help them know that's true with God as well: "Lord, if you kept a record of our sins, who, O Lord, could ever survive?" (Ps. 130:3, NLT).

# # 746 Taking Off the Lid

Kids are absolute experts in taking off your "lid." They can do things that drive you totally bonkers. But when the lid comes off and your reaction comes spilling out, that's when relational trouble kicks in. You might say terrible things that wound and damage and cripple, making huge emotional withdrawals from the relationship. You can—and should—ask for forgiveness, but you can never recapture those words or completely erase their effects. Each word counts. Do your best to use only good ones, and leave the rest unsaid.

# # 747 I'm Sorry

Say "I'm sorry" a lot. Believe me, it still won't cover it all.

# # 748 Holding Off

Most of the time your first reaction is not your best reaction. In the heat of the moment, you'll tend to magnify offenses. "I don't want to eat that vegetable" becomes a threat to your parental authority. In addition, other stuff going on in your life—a bad day at work, a nasty comment from a coworker, a tyrannical boss, running out of money before the end of the month—can get built in to your emotional reaction. Generally, your child's wrongdoing won't require an immediate reaction. An old Jewish proverb reminds us, "A fool shows his annoyance at once" (Prov. 12:16). Wait. The better you will come out later, given a little time.

# # 749 Wild and Woolly

What a great and marvelous concept God had when he opted to create us out of glorious, freedom-loving, wild-and-woolly raw material. Try to appreciate how wonderful it is that your children can choose to think, act, and change—and that they can even fail—spectacularly. Because the same freedom of choice allows them to say "I love you" and to spit in the face of tyrants. You can say: "Wow! I didn't have any idea what you were capable of, how much you could accomplish, how deeply you could love. I only caught a glimmer. But you're the most amazing thing I ever saw or heard of. I'm with you on the journey. If you go off the road, holler, and I'll come with a tow truck." Enjoy the whole rough ride.

# # 750 Good from Bad

It would be nice if your children could just hear your wonderful parental advice, based on years of hard-earned experience, and automatically follow it. Sure, and it would be nice if I could lose ten pounds without giving up chocolate. Learning doesn't come just from listening; it comes from doing and trying and failing. Your children have to make some bad decisions to learn how to make good ones. So cut them some slack. See the positive potential, not just the negative result. If you do, they'll love you for the freedom, the vision, and the compassion.

# # 751 Anticipation

There are times when you're able to see that your child is headed straight into a problem. Don't ignore the threat; get ready for impact. Acknowledge that your child is headed for disaster (perhaps through their choices in friends or their approach toward schoolwork), and prepare your thoughts and actions in advance to help guide them. A one-size-fits-all emotional panic reaction is completely unhelpful. A proactive plan not only guarantees that you'll be helpful, but it also builds your relationship.

# # 752 Drop that Shield

Parental love can lead you to shield your children from mistakes and the results of failure. But the same parental love can help you drop the shield, step back, and be ready when they come to you to help them deal with the fallout. If you want them to be great, not merely protected, you'll let them meet a few disasters head-on. In the end, they'll love you for it.

# #753 Loving Confrontation

No great relationship is built by avoiding necessary conflict: *As long as I stay away from tense confrontations, they're sure to love me.* Loving confrontation is a crucial component of a great relationship because if either of you fails to confront, you may end up resenting the other. Every time you see or think about the conflict, it will come back to life, and resentment will flourish. At first glance, confrontation appears to be the path to relational death when, in fact, it can give it a brand-new life.

# #754 Fight the Right War

You may see a glitch, say, a behavior problem in your children, and focus on it. They're not doing their chores, and you're just not going to put up with such irresponsibility. That's why they've got parents! Hold everything. Doublecheck what's going on in your children's life. Maybe they're not doing their chores because they can't concentrate on anything but the stress of dealing with the nasty bullies who are tormenting them at school. Is it really going to help if you start tormenting them at home? If you insist on rigid performance and obedience even in the face of emotional pain, you're telling your kids to "scrap your feelings and grow up!" But do you really want a relationship with people who have died to their own feelings. Fight the right battle (you can do it without excusing irresponsibility). Help your children solve that school problem, and you can make home a demilitarized zone. And *that's* why they've got parents.

# #755 Understanding in Context

Nothing in life really makes sense unless it's understood in context. You walk into a room just in time to see one child hit another, and you leap into action. There's no way to know that the other child started it and the hit you saw was merely self-defense. Life and the facts can get muddled. Maybe your daughter receives a disappointing grade in a subjectively graded course. Do you ground her on the spot, or do you take the time to discover that she received that poor grade because she stood up for her beliefs—*your* beliefs—in the face of derision from a teacher? Beware the quick analysis. Uncover context.

# #756 Behavior Is a Symptom

Because we are complex beings, the source of our outward actions lies deep within. So in the final analysis, behavior is only a symptom of ignorance, or malice, or some unresolved grievance. You can keep dealing with and addressing the surface symptoms of a problem behavior, but it won't go away until you've dealt with the cause. In the long run, battling at the surface will shred your relationship. Let the outward behavior lead you to the root cause.

# # 757 Drop It

It's hard to let offenses go—little ones (they keep chewing their food with their mouths open), middle-sized ones (they resist doing their chores or homework), and big ones (they take great delight in insulting their siblings). You work to correct these deficiencies—and correct, and correct, and correct. It's pretty hard not to sound like a tape on continuous play. Once you've confronted your child on a certain offense, drop it for a while and give it a rest. You don't want that offense to become the center of your relationship.

# # 758 Bust the Myth

Parents start out with a pretty clear idea of how their parenting will go—how the kids will turn out. Then the kids fool you when they're babies, convincing you that they're so helpless and needy. When you put them somewhere, they're still there when you get back. But order and control are illusions, and sooner or later most parents have to deal with their child's individuality and will. "Why does my child keep *doing* that?" parents ask me at my parenting seminars and workshops. Why? Because they're kids. Because they're human. Because they are trying to figure out who they are and where they are going. Because they can. It might be more peaceful and orderly at your house, and less aggravating for you, if your children conformed to your every expectation. But where's the relationship in that? You'll relate to your kids as you dare to understand and guide instead of trying to control and regulate. You just might live longer too.

# # 759 Punish the Crime, Love the Child

When your child goes over the line on a really serious offense—lying, cheating, stealing, hitting, insulting—you must deal with it. You love him too much to let him be a fool. But be careful to punish the *crime*, not the child. When your child is expecting to be crucified and is instead given loving correction, he can't help but respond with a deep connection to you.

# # 760 When They Stray

When your kids are really fouling up, remember that God is an expert on straying children. Ask yourself how you would like to be treated when you miss the mark in the same way. Then do the same with your children. Your gratitude to God will be mirrored in their gratitude to you.

# # 761 Unfailing Love

The mantra today in almost all circles is "unconditional" love, but of course there are some conditions that accompany love in all relationships. It's principled love to say, "I'm with you through thick and thin, regardless of any mistake or sin you might commit." But saying "There are no conditions (such as mutual respect or honesty) that you must meet to keep receiving my love," is not real love. That attitude creates the possibility that your children will take advantage of you, and resentment will begin to grow. Your love should be unfailing ("I'm here for you when you come back to your senses") but not without conditions.

# # 762 Friendly Management

Business executives often wonder, *Why don't my employees show more initiative? Why don't they bring me great ideas? Why do they cover up their problems instead of fixing them?* It's possible that these managers are off the mark by looking for the source of the problem *out there* when the problem lies *in here*—with the management. Perhaps the managers have created an environment where it isn't safe to try out ideas, take risks, or admit mistakes. If you want an open culture in your home, where mistakes can be easily admitted, you'll have to create a truth-friendly, risk-friendly, and mistake-friendly environment. Don't "beat them up" when they miss the mark. Truth grows in loving ground.

# # 763 Flop Party

When your children fail in exactly the same way that you've failed in the past, acknowledge it and mark the occasion. They tried to bluff their way through an assignment at school and got a lousy grade, just like you tried to bluff your way through an assignment at work and got told off by your boss. Have a "flop" party. Go out for dinner. Laugh about your deluded plans. Celebrate your humanity. Reinforce your connection.

# # 764 The Good Try

When your child tries something new and fails, celebrate anyway. This goes against the grain of only wanting her to be "successful," which misses the point that bigger and greater success is usually built out of learning from mistakes. Maybe she chooses an elective in school— computers, industrial technology, a foreign language, biology, or history—because she thinks it might be interesting. But she bombs; she has no aptitude in that area at all. She's looking back and wondering, *What was I thinking?* Meanwhile you can celebrate her good try, her courage in stepping out of her comfort zone, the milestone of figuring out which direction not to go. If you allow your child to keep beating herself up, she'll shrivel—and you'll lose some part of who she is.

## # 765 The Next One's Coming to You

They say that hall-of-fame quarterback Joe Montana never let another player stay stuck on a mistake. If a receiver dropped a catchable ball, Montana would send another pass right back to him: "The next one's coming to you." This told his fellow team members that a mistake didn't diminish his respect for them or confidence in them. It communicated that mistakes aren't fatal. So when your daughter dribbles the milk the first time she tries to pour it on her own, don't come back with, "I guess you're not ready to do that." Instead, hand her another carton. When your son is trying to become a good driver but has a fender bender, give him the keys to the other car. Milk and cars are nothing compared to the self-worth and deep connection that comes from hearing the soul-reviving words, "The next one's coming to you."

## # 766 Poor Baby

To help your children learn to acknowledge their mistakes and move on (a nice alternative to criticizing them), try a silly phrase we use at our house. When one of us blows it—spills something, breaks something, messes up a project he's been working on—I say, "One, two, three," and everyone says in unison, "Poor baby!" Everybody laughs, and life goes on. I tried it recently in a meeting with a high-powered group of professionals and leaders when a woman spilled her drink. The executives all laughed, and when someone else spilled something later on, they did it on their own. Dismiss the embarrassment.

## # 767 Silver Linings

When most parents see a report card with, say, all A's and B's and just one C or D, where does the focus go? Train yourself to look first and primarily at your child's efforts that are getting good results. Stay open to the possibility that he's working just as hard to get the C in one course as he is to get an A in another. Are you equally good at everything? Even a lack of effort may be more related to a lack of interest than a lack of care. Encourage your child to see that C as an opportunity to work together, to learn a different way to approach the subject, to get a deeper understanding about your values and interests: "This can be exciting. What are you going to get out of this?"

# # 768 The Ennobling Question

In the midst of a child's failure, there is a wonderful, ennobling question you can ask: "Do you realize the great knowledge and experience you've gained from this situation?" Disconnected parents focus on the fire; connected parents focus on the phoenix that can arise from the ashes.

# # 769 What Do You Think?

When your kids have really messed up and finally crossed your "baloney" threshold, you could charge in like the marines to take charge and pound the enemy into submission. But do you really want to think of your children as the "enemy"? To move forward (instead of annihilating your relationship), put the burden of solution on *both* of your shoulders: "What do *you* think we should do to help you do better in this area?" Capitalize on a moment to be creative, and grow something good out of something ugly.

# # 770 Down but Not Out

"You're not finished when you're defeated; you're finished when you give up" (U.S. President Richard Nixon). The difference between being defeated and being finished is the difference between experiencing a failure and being a failure. Parents who make every failure feel like a demolition wreck their children's chances for success and push them away from their relationship. Parents who communicate the truth ("You're still standing, babe. It can't take you down. You're bigger than anything that can happen to you. You will win") help to create human dynamos and love that "never fails" (1 Cor. 13:8).

# # 771 Don't Make an Issue

You compound mistakes and demolish your relationship when you make an issue out of events that have bruised your children's hearts. One young man was involved in a relationship with a young woman, and in spite of the needs it met, he could see it wouldn't work. There were problems in the relationship, and each one had some personal issues to resolve. She wanted to get married, but he said no; and she later moved away. The young man told his father that he was thinking about visiting her. It was a perfect opportunity for the father to remind, lecture, and resist. Instead, he offered to buy his son an airline ticket. The battle over whether to please the father or to do what he wanted was over before it started. The young man felt free to make his own decision without pressure. He decided not to go, and the bond with his father grew a little bit stronger.

# # 772 That Figures

When your children make their inevitable mistakes, don't berate them for their naïveté by emphasizing your own wisdom or longsightedness: "Well, that figures. I thought it would turn out this way. I told you this would happen." This makes them feel *less* competent and *more* likely to repeat their mistakes. They feel less connected to you as well, as shame tends to create distance. Remember this: *You get better results with empathy:* "I know what you're feeling. I know it feels really bad. I feel the same way in these situations." Let the consequences do the talking; you do the "bleeding" with your child.

# # 773 Let the Past Go

Parents deeply discourage children when, confronted by some new mistake, they bring up all the "priors" that seem even remotely similar. Those mistakes should be dealt with at the time, if necessary, then let go. It takes a fine mind to be able to forget the past, a strong will to choose to let it die, and a good heart to be glad of it.

# # 774 Don't Imagine a Horrible Future

Sometimes parents extrapolate a current problem into a massively ugly future. The kids' rooms are an ongoing mess. So we bring out the heavy artillery: "How will you ever succeed in life with this kind of sloppiness? How will you ever hold down a job?" This hardly solves the room-cleaning problem, and it could immobilize a child. It could even push a child to become obsessive about neatness and order. Any way you look at it, this kind of gloomy future prediction disconnects you from your kids.

# # 775 Don't Take It Out on Them

Parents can easily think they're parenting when in reality they're working out other problems or issues that aren't related to the kids. Maybe you've got problems with your spouse, your boss, another friendship, discouragement about your own failures, an illness, or disappointment in the way life is turning out for you. That's too much weight to bring into your parenting. If you find yourself responding to a child's minor infraction with rage or other intense emotion, double-check to make sure you're not working out other unrelated issues while you're parenting.

# # 776 Be a Guide

When your children fail, they don't so much need you to give them the answers as they need you to help them find the answers for themselves. It takes real love to let them flounder, while control masquerading as love simply tells them what to do. Help them come up with their own solutions. Respect them enough to let their solutions be different from yours. Use the power of questions: "What do you think you should do? What's the best way out of this?" Give them time, which gives them dignity and gives you their love.

# # 777 Be an Inspiration

When things are going badly for your children, and they feel incapable of doing anything right, what they really need to hear is not some version of "You're going down in flames!" but rather "This ship can be saved. You can turn this around!" Conflagration, trumped by inspiration.

# # 778 Saving Face

The great Chinese thinker Sun-Tsu advised against putting someone on "fatal terrain"—a place where they had no choice but to "kill or be killed." You can put your children in a position where they either have to accept feeling bad about themselves or build a wall of resistance against you. They want your respect just like you want theirs. Preserve their dignity and feelings. Let them save face, just as you would want to with a friend or coworker or fellow church member. You can use humor: "Goodness! Someone sneaked into your room and left pizza crusts under your bed!" You can be supportive rather than annoyed. Instead of saying, "I told you not to buy that piece of junk," say, "Let me help you fix that." Sometimes it's *not* saying what could be said that builds the bond.

# # 779 It's Only Natural

Some of the time you'll want to show mercy toward your children by freeing them from some of the consequences of a mistake. But most of the time these natural consequences act as very effective teachers, and they come with a bonus: They teach without damaging your relationship.

# # 780 Honesty

The goal of punishment is a change of direction. The goal is not to win, to prove your children wrong, to feel better about yourself by comparison, to feel like you're discharging some grave parental duty. The point is to help them become decent human beings. That means you need to help them work toward repentance. Speak honestly and clearly—no beating around the bush. "You lied to me. When I asked you if you lied, you lied again. How can I trust you? How can I believe you when you tell me something? What will you do to repair the damage to my trust?" Trust is at the core of your relationship; take care to dig into anything that can damage it.

# # 781 Restoring Relationship

Don't respond to false repentance—they're sorry because they got caught. You can't even accept "I'm sorry" at face value. In order to restore the relationship between you, there will have to be true repentance, a real change (see *Walking through the Fire*, Broadman & Holman, 1996). If you gloss over a wrong, the sore spot will fester, and the infection of resentment will keep your relationship in a sickbed. When wrongs have been done, openly work toward the restoration of your relationship.

# # 782 Wishy-Washy Love

Don't be quick to come up with a punishment; plan it carefully so that your action will carry the possibility of building your relationship. Most parents come up with a punishment, feeling, *I hope our relationship can survive this.* This can cause you to "waffle" on needed correction. But real love isn't vague and wishy-washy. Real love will confront bad attitudes and behavior without succumbing to emotional blackmail. "The Lord disciplines those he loves, and he punishes everyone he accepts as a son" (Heb. 12:6).

# # 783 The Complaints Department

Whining is an effective, slow-acting destroyer of relationship. Kids can, if left to themselves, become giant complaint-generating machines—they don't like the food, their room is stupid, they hate the school, they have too many chores, they're bored. Life stinks. It's really hard to love and be affectionate toward a negative, complaining person. At our house I cured the complaining with this simple formula: When you complain about it, you get more of what you don't want and less of what you do. You whine about your 8:00 bedtime? Now it's 7:45. Still complaining? Now it's 7:30. You don't have to like the spinach, but you want to complain about it? All right, now you get another spoonful, and we'll remove a serving of the potatoes you prefer. Still complaining? Let's see what a plate full of spinach looks like. Kids are smart. Watch the complaining disappear.

# # 784 Unfairness

When your kids' complaints reach the level of "Life is just unfair," it's time to intervene. Children can see everything as fair or unfair as it revolves around them. Help them broaden their scale for judging what's fair or unfair about life. While you can agree that many things in life are unfair, help them answer the question "Is your life really that bad?" Take them to visit those who have it much tougher—a children's cancer center, a home for severely disabled children, a rescue mission for the homeless. Ask, "Where are you on the unfairness scale?"

# # 785 I'm So Mad . . .

When people treat your kids unfairly, when obstacles not of their making are blocking their path, you can draw close to your kids and help them express their anger and frustration appropriately. Instead of "Life stinks," suggest, "That was crummy, but I will get past it." When you understand their feelings and give them an outlet for expressing them, your kids will feel better about themselves—and you.

# # 786 Save Your Own Face

Don't wrap your feelings of self-worth around your children's failures. When they fail, it's their failure, not yours. Analyze any part you may have played in it and correct it, but ease up. Chill out. It isn't you.

# # 787 Thousands

There are so many opportunities for your children to receive negative reviews. "It has been estimated that between first and twelfth grades, the average child has been criticized 16,000 times," says John Kildahl, Ph.D., in "Life Lessons in Living Happier" (*Bottom Line Personal,* December 1996). Maybe you could help cut that number in half. Or more. *Much* more.

# # 788 Eliminate the Traps

Some of your children's mistakes are avoidable if you'll lead with love rather than rules. Instead of warring over "breakables," move valuables out of reach. Instead of arguing over clothes on the floor, purchase a cool hamper or put in a laundry chute. Become a detective, searching out ways you can improve their ability to obey you. Ask: "Is there anything *I* can change to make this go away?"

# # 789 Errors in Judgment

You'll make errors in judgment as a parent now and then. Maybe you commit to something that turns out to be inconvenient or beyond your ability to deliver. Don't make excuses to your kids; certainly don't blame them. Admit your mistake: "I guess I'm only human. My enthusiasm got the better of me. Help me develop plan B." If at all possible, deliver on your commitment. When Peter was six, I foolishly promised him that he could stay up as late as he wanted on New Year's Eve, thinking surely the latest he could manage would be midnight. My last fuzzy memory is lying on the floor at about six o'clock in the morning with play money in my hand and Peter warning me of the dangers of landing on Boardwalk. And we played on. It was an error in judgment on my part, but it was a real vehicle for relationship improvement.

# # 790 The Sunny Side of the Street

Almost every negative trait in a child has a positive flip side. One child seems extreme, but he's wonderfully dramatic. She may seem overemotional, but she's terrifically passionate. He seems given to exaggerations, if not outright lies; be glad he's a fabulous storyteller. Her activity pace borders on hyperactive, but how wonderful to be so energetic! Stubbornness can also be shaped into determination. Don't attack their problems so hard that you throw the baby out with the bathwater. Look for the positive aspects of their annoying character traits.

# # 791 Extract What's Good

Say your kids are so mouthy you're starting to wonder if a muzzle couldn't be a useful parenting tool. Of course, it's important for your children not to be mouthing off all the time, but look for some strength that's represented in the problem. Instead of taking failures and conflicts at face value, you can often seek out a little good, something positive to bring up as you talk about the problem. Maybe mouthing off is just that they've taken some good things too far. Perhaps you've gone out of your way to teach them to have spunk, that you took great pains to give them a voice, that you've taken the lid off honest dialogue in your home. There's something good in the problem—extract it!

# # 792 Problem Exploration

Develop a process for exploring dilemmas. Try this one:

1. Acknowledge it: Talk about the problem honestly. Let's say the problem is that you're not showing each other respect.
2. Define it: Discuss the problem enough that you agree you've got one. Write it down if necessary: "We don't listen to each other when we're talking, and we don't try to understand the other person's position before we start saying what he ought to do."
3. Explore it: Divide up the problem to discover together what's causing it. You might discover, in the case of disrespect, that you've each got presuppositions that lead to wrong conclusions: "I assume you're taking your cues from your peers, while you assume that I don't trust you to make good decisions."

As you take the time, finding out what the problem really is can lead you together to a better relationship.

# # 793 Seeking Solutions

You can build your connection when problems arise. Here are some tips for ways to seek solutions together:

1. Brainstorm solutions: Maybe go out to dinner, and make solving a specific problem the topic of discussion. Focus on similar situations where you have had success.
2. Agree on a solution: Decide on a course, and commit to each other to do it. Go for the wow solution that adds other benefits to your relationship.
3. Develop a plan: Agree on the steps each of you will take to make sure the desired changes really get achieved.
4. Follow up: Keep talking until you're sure you've solved it. Reserve the privilege of saying, "Hey, this still isn't working as well as it should."

The alternative to finding a solid solution is to keep repeating the mistake until your relationship is in tatters.

# # 794 Rebound

There are times when life just takes its toll on your relationship. You've made mistakes; your kids have. Feeling despair at the break in your bond is understandable, but every low moment contains a seed for change and new life and growth. Seize on truth, and make the changes needed to rebuild your connection. Making a comeback is noble work.

# # 795 When Others Mislead

Ever heard this one: "But everybody's doing it!"? How about this one: "Yeah, but he told me to"? Nothing aggravates a parent more, and when you're annoyed, you're likely to respond with some exaggerated comment like, "Sure, and would you eat worms if everyone else was doing it?" (they might). When their friends seem to be able to sway them easily, especially toward stupid or wrong behaviors, it's time to revisit the development of their individual decision making. By using powersharing techniques and giving your children structured choices, you can build up their personal strength and purpose and help them be less easily persuaded. Use your heart for your child to help him use his own mind.

# # 796 When Others Fail

When you and your kids see the mistakes of others, respond ethically and compassionately. The teenager behind the counter at McDonald's forgets to charge you for one Happy Meal—and you go back with your child, wait in line again, and pay the money. This kind of behavior goes beyond mere honesty (a good reason on its own to do what's right). It communicates the character of your relationship: "This is who we are. We do the right thing, not the easy thing." I don't remember ever meeting a child who didn't respect and love an honorable and compassionate parent.

# # 797 Welcome Opposition

There are times when obstacles can lift you to greater effort, greater achievement, and a greater sense of unity in the fight. Welcome opposition. Maybe even create opposition by saying something like, "The committee didn't think we could get this done by the end of the month, but I think we can if we work together." Uniting in the face of the difficult or impossible can join you at the soul level. "Friendship, of itself a holy tie, is made more sacred by adversity," wrote John Dryden in *The Hind and the Panther.*

# # 798 Pity Party

There are times when both you and your children have recently experienced failure or disappointment. They're going down in flames in math class, while you just got denied a promotion. Throw a pity party. Count your tragedies, add them all up, be honest, no holds barred. Eventually, you'll be laughing. Exaggerate a bit: "I'll bet my boss and your math teach get together to plot out how to make us miserable. What do you think?" or "Can you be sent to prison for poor performance? Can you be tortured?" As you move from self-pity to being silly, you start putting things back in perspective—then you'll be able to move on to finding solutions.

# # 799 Your Neighbor and Your Self

A big mistake we can make as parents is to put our children first. The Bible's second great command (after "Love the Lord your God) is to "love your neighbor *as* yourself" (Lev. 19:18, emphasis added). It's interesting that the command isn't to love others before yourself or instead of yourself. In your positive determination to avoid selfishness, be careful that you don't ignore yourself or, worse, do yourself harm. Take a bit of time to develop your interests, to have some time to yourself. If you run yourself ragged to make your kids feel loved, you may end up exhausted and resentful. The most excellent businesses put employees, not customers, first, knowing that it is the cared-for employee who will best care for the needs of their important customers.

# # 800 Yuk It Up

Never shortchange the power of humor to help you through your mistakes, failures, and obstacles. I remember once I came under heavy-artillery criticism from a few judgmental people. I felt so discouraged. I was kicking myself for trusting those people; at the same time I was wondering, *What could I have done differently?* Just then Peter lightened up the whole conversation by hawking a pretend product, Fund-a-Matic: "It slices, it dices, it judges, it condemns." I couldn't help myself—I fell down laughing. With a joke, Peter reminded me that the problem was theirs and didn't have to affect me so deeply. Use humor to conquer despair, and build your bond with the kids who join you in your belly laugh.

# # 801 I'll Get You Back

A child's mistake isn't made better if you add one of your own. He makes a mouthy comment—and you snap right back. That's revenge of the worst kind. You do need to "get them back" though—get them back with gentleness. "Requite injury with kindness," said Chinese philosopher Lao-tzu.

# # 802 Help!

When you make a mistake, ask your children for help in correcting it. Ask for advice. It will teach them how to solve problems, how to admit weakness, how to humbly ask for another shoulder to carry the burden (be age-sensitive, of course). If you're like most parents, you'll have plenty of opportunities to apply this idea.

# # 803 See Past the Mistake

Once an episode of wrongdoing and restoration is behind you, treat your child as if he isn't ever going to make that mistake again. "Treat a person as he is, and he will remain as he is. Treat him as he could be, and he will become what he should be," says NFL coach Jimmy Johnson. He doesn't necessarily deserve your trust, but your faith in him will undoubtedly strengthen the bond between you. And that loving relationship will do a lot more to motivate him to live up to your good opinion.

# # 804 Each Other

When all else fails, when you have no answers, when you're too tired or beat to learn, when you're too numb to work at problem solving without giving it a bit of time—remember you still have each other. Talk about it: "I know we've had it tough. But we have each other and God. Nothing changes that. We'll make it. 'If God is for us, who can be against us? . . . [Nothing] will be able to separate us from the love of God' (Rom. 8:31, 39). God is bigger than this problem, and somehow we will beat it." That kind of relationship is Grand-Canyon deep.

# Comeback: Reconnecting When You've Been Disconnected

## # 805 It Is So

What could hurt more than the realization that you're no longer connected? Suddenly you find that you're just being tolerated—perhaps barely—by the child you once carried in your arms. As painful as it is, and though you want to deny it, give up illusions of connection with your child. Get ready for whatever hard work is going to be necessary to build on what's left between you. Honesty is the indispensable beginning of a better tomorrow.

## # 806 Blind Spots

Know yourself. Expose your own blind spots. You catch your kids lying but don't want to admit that they've heard you time and again tell lies over the phone to get out of meetings or responsibilities. And resist others around you who are offering blind spots to ease your conscience: "It's not your fault. It's just a stage. All kids are like that. It's hormones." Don't make excuses. Admit the problems—and create solutions.

## # 807 Do As I Do

Avoid giving your children detailed advice on character issues where you are failing, not just because of hypocrisy but because of the toll it will take on your bond. "He that gives good advice, builds with one hand; he that gives good counsel and example, builds with both; he that gives good admonition and bad example, builds with one hand and pulls down with another," wrote the English philosopher Francis Bacon.

# # 808 Plain As the Nose on Your Face

One of the hardest things to do as a parent is to assess attitudes correctly. When your children treat you disrespectfully, you may deal with those symptoms without ever facing the reality that they don't respect you. If they hate going to church, you may have laid down the law without ever acknowledging that this means they're getting nothing out of it (whether because of their own spiritual hard-heartedness or because of faults within the church). Reality is what it is. "It requires a very unusual mind to undertake the analysis of the obvious," wrote historian Alfred North Whitehead. Face reality. You can take it. It's the beginning of comeback.

# # 809 Cause and Effect

Every family is perfectly designed to get the results it is now getting. If you don't like the results, change the design. Look for the behaviors that are leading to disconnection. One of the first steps to a comeback is accepting that your family life created this problem.

# # 810 Own Up

When you're disconnected from your kids, it's time to ask yourself the hard questions, with determination to answer them honestly: *What did I do to cause this? I hate what I'm reaping; did I do the sowing?* When parents come to me with problems but can't answer these questions, I end the conversation. They can't be helped. They won't be helped until they can triumph over denial and illusions.

# # 811 It's Not All Your Fault

At the same time, there's no wisdom in falling into a "Woe is me—I caused it all!" despair. Rarely is a relationship broken without contributions from both parties. False guilt and self-flagellation offer no way out. Accept that you're causing at least part of the problem, perhaps the bigger part. This leads to the healthy conclusion that as you make changes, you'll have power to change at least part of the disconnection.

# # 812 Nix the Nagging

Most of the time relationships aren't broken over gargantuan events. Usually, relationships crumble one molecule at a time. A little nagging, every day, over and over, eats away at the core of your friendship with your children. You become the reminder of faults, annoying them until they can't love you. No one was ever nagged into heaven, or even into being good. Give it up, now and forever.

# # 813 Control or Connect

Parents can feel so desperate to make sure things turn out "right." Our children seem so little, so ... well ... ignorant. "Kids are stupid, Marv," one of the bad guys advised the other in the film *Home Alone*. And parents buy into the myth that kids need them to decide everything. The need to control can be compounded by family history (if your own parents were controlling) or by personal insecurities (if you just can't feel comfortable if you're not in charge). But your children need the respect of being allowed a voice and a choice. You choose—control or connect. Control is stupid, Marv.

# # 814 Powerful Anger

Anger murders relationship. If you're often angry, don't hesitate to uncover why. It may be issues from the past or from your current stresses, not your children, that are driving your volatile emotions. Don't underestimate the power of anger, rage, and contempt to destroy any hope of relationship. Find out why, and give it up. Jesus said, "I tell you that anyone who is angry with his brother will be subject to judgment" (Matt. 5:22). A demolished relationship is a fearsome judgment.

# # 815 Put Out the Fire

In ancient times certain people sacrificed their children to the gods by burning. Appalling? Yes. But you may also be burning your kids: "Consider what a great forest is set on fire by a small spark. The tongue also is a fire" (James 3:5-6). Degrading comments ("You're not very good at that. What's the matter with you? I can't believe you're that dumb.") rip the heart out of a child and your relationship. Forget the "I didn't mean it" routine, because "out of the overflow of [your] heart [your] mouth speaks" (Luke 6:45). Your kids will know that your words express who you really are. Their provocation didn't make you this way. It just highlighted it. Forget trying to control your child; controlling the tongue is a full-time job.

# # 816 Respect Boundaries

Your kids can't love you if you don't respect their boundaries. Many parents don't respect their children's privacy in the bedroom or bathroom. They snoop through their children's rooms and possessions. They open their children's mail. They tell embarrassing stories about their children to those outside the family ("He's still wetting the bed" or, "She's just started her cycle"). Healthy boundaries are good additions to a family. Broken boundaries will break their spirit and at long last will break your heart.

# # 817 Don't Send Them to Boot Camp

Some parents take a boot-camp approach to training children. They think that small children are such blank slates or are so stupid that they'll need a supremely controlled environment with rigid rules and restrictions enforced by a tough-as-nails drill instructor. These parents figure that they can "loosen up" as their kids mature. There are several problems with this approach. First, children are complex beings who need to develop self-control, not depend totally on the drill instructor to set limits. Second, nobody loves the drill instructor. Third, controlling others is a habit. I have yet to see a leader in an organization or a parent in a family start out as a serious controller and give it up over time. Healthy guidelines, with lots of freedom between them, is the way to have powerful children and relationships. Boot camp produces soldiers who follow orders and die in wars.

# # 818 Are You Violent?

It's easy to identify physical violence, which includes beating or molestation. But there are other violences that you may never have looked for in your parenting. Emotional abuse pounds your children's hearts into submission. Mental abuse fills their thoughts with prejudice and condemnation and religious lunacies. Volitional abuse allows children no room to make even small decisions and leaves them vulnerable to ugly relational dictators. Environmental violence allows tempers to flare and war to rage around or among children. Violence or abuse destroys any hope of healthy connection. Abandon it in all its forms.

# # 819 Center of the Universe

It's the most usual thing in the world to make that darling new baby the center of your universe. Even if you don't intend to, a baby seems to insist. He wants to be treated well and on his own schedule, thank you very much. But if you cater to his demands as he grows, planning your life around him and giving up your own dreams and plans, you'll almost certainly produce a demanding child at the least and a Napoleon at the worst. He can't love you if he is, like Narcissus, in love with himself.

# # 820 Stop the Pendulum

When you swing back and forth in your leadership at home, you keep your children off balance and at a distance. First you're tough—set the rules, enforce them, punish, take no prisoners. Then, you start to feel guilty or just plain bad; you get soft—cancel some of the rules, slack off on others, apologize for delivering legitimate punishment, burn down the prison. Strike a balance, a middle ground between these extremes—because it's hard to bond with a moving target.

## # 821 The Fix-It Mentality

There are a zillion books out there on how to train and sort and fix your kids. But keep in mind that your home isn't a laboratory and your children aren't mice. Much of what's out there approaches parenting mechanically in a "do this, get that" mode. Mechanical parenting systems are too small and, worse, have no room in them for learning to create connection.

## # 822 The Bigger Offense

If your son draws pictures—with markers—on the new wallpaper and you respond by screaming at him, slapping him, and throwing away the markers, who committed the bigger offense? The child—maybe a Rembrandt in training pants—writing on a wall or the parent demolishing his spirit for doing it? Sometimes your righteousness won't hold up to scrutiny. "From the one who has been entrusted with much, much more will be asked," said Jesus (Luke 12:48). Own up to your failures. The bigger portion often belongs to us parents.

## # 823 Drivel

In some homes every day is just a long rough edge. Nothing quite suits, everything is a nuisance, the hubbub of life takes precedence over living. Make the big decision to let most of the little stuff go. Overlook it. Put a blanket over it. Don't shrivel over drivel.

## # 824 The Right Tool for the Task

An old proverb says, "If the only tool you have is a hammer, every problem looks like a nail." The same "solution"—like time-out—offered for many different problems is a formula for failed parenting and relationships. And tools can be applied at the wrong time. Even if you use spanking, for example, it is certain that you are spanking your way into relational oblivion with children over age three or four (and probably not dealing with the problem, either). Be creative in devising punishments that fit the crimes.

# # 825 What's Driving Your Parenting?

Be careful that your parenting doesn't become driven by your own insecurities or pain or fears. Look backward to move forward: *What bogus things about my childhood and past life were big enough to affect my parenting approach? Where am I feeling particularly sensitive? What would my top five fears be? How are these things directing me?* Your reaction to past relational mistakes can *be* a relational mistake.

# # 826 When the Time Is Right

Timing and degree are so critical to successful parenting, including relationship. "Anyone can become angry," said Aristotle. "That is easy. But to be angry with the right person, to the right degree, at the right time, for the right purpose and in the right way—that is not easy." You may have a good point, but if you make it at the wrong time, it may serve to open a deep wound. Pay attention to timing as you work to connect with your children, and own up to when you've said too much, too soon.

# # 827 No Mini-Therapists

Make sure you aren't trying to solve your deep personal problems with your children or through them. They aren't equipped to be counselors through their growing years. They've got a big enough job just being kids. And you shouldn't use them as "emissaries"—for example, have them talk to your parents about the problems you're having with them. Your kids might try to fill these roles for you because they want to help and please you, but the toll on them and on your relationship will be too high.

# # 828 They're Driving Me Crazy

Children are excellent vehicles for bringing your failures and flaws to the surface. "I've never hollered at anyone in my life until now," a mother told me. And I believe it. But "there's no use in saying, 'My kids are driving me crazy,'" says Maryl Janson of the Relationship Development Center. "We can't use their effectiveness in highlighting our weaknesses as an excuse to go crazy." Your failure is not their fault.

# # 829 You Go First

When an argument or other problem has separated you from your kids, who's responsible for taking that first step—especially when they've been really horrible? Jesus answers this question: If they offended you, go to them and sort it out (Matt. 18:15). If you offended them, go to them and sort it out (Matt. 5:23-24). You first.

# # 830  The Victim

When things go wrong between you and your children, don't fall back on whining, "But I did the best I could." The answer to the question "But what could I have done?" is, "Something different." You're not a victim, helpless and disempowered. If you want to recover your relationship—or build one that was never there—give up the victim role and get creative.

# # 831  No Scapegoating

I have seen parents refuse to accept the devastation they have created in their families and relationships. They didn't do anything wrong. It's their spouses. It's their churches. It's the schools. It's the society. It's their peers. This is victimization with a nasty edge. The only solution is to stop looking for the cause "out there" and start looking in the mirror instead. Just fess up. The best words for the long journey to recovery are "It's my fault."

# # 832  Stop the Bickering

No one was ever argued back into a decent relationship. It doesn't work, except to destroy what little affection you might still have for one another. Abandon arguments. Period.

# # 833  Shift It to the Back Burner

When a discussion about problems and fault starts heating up, have the wisdom to move it to the back burner. Agree to table the issue until you're both ready to talk again in a calm manner. Your relationship requires more light than heat. You need to keep talking out a problem until you can see at least the outline of a solution, but you may have to do it over weeks or months and many conversations.

# # 834  Below the Surface

When kids on the playground say, "You're mother is ugly," they probably don't even know your mother. The real antagonism lies below the words. When you have a surface argument with your children, reflect long and hard over what really triggered it. Often, the first "rational" reason that comes to your mind will have nothing to do with what seemed to be the reasons behind the argument. Maybe you're arguing over their chores, but what's really driving your antagonism is their lack of respect for you, or the way they treat their siblings. Once you know why you're arguing, you'll be able to stop doing it.

# # 835 Get Some Help
When a relationship reaches the warfare stage, it is very difficult to bring
it back to any semblance of peace without some outside intervention—
advice from a trusted counselor or even mediation. The possibility of
reconnection is worth the embarrassment. The alternative is a slow
dance of death for a love that was once as fresh as a newborn baby.

# # 836 An Act of the Will
If you want relationship badly enough, you can make a decision to
change yourself. In spite of regret, shame, hurt, or anger, you can
choose to change. It is an act of the will: *I will bite my tongue. I will respect
them to make their own decisions. I will stop smothering. The past is dead.
I will build a better future.* "What people say you cannot do, you try
and find that you can," said Henry David Thoreau.

# # 837 The Power of Sincerity
The power of sincerity, of a genuine admission of fault and desire to reunite,
should not be underestimated. When combined with patience, enough time, and
gentle persistence, sincerity can win the day—and the hearts of your children.

# # 838 Small Steps
Most relationships are damaged an inch at a time, moment by moment.
You don't have to—probably can't—get it all back at once. Be prepared to
recover a relationship the same way it was lost. A little note on the bed,
with no details, that says, "Just wanted you to know I miss the way we
used to be," or "Sorry we lost what we had—I want to find it." Lots of little
things, piled high enough, can reach all the way to the heart.

# # 839 The Whole Truth
What if they lie to us? What if we can't tell if they're telling the truth or
not? What if they don't seem open or sincere? Lying is a serious problem.
If their behavior comes from the darkness of rebellion, you'll need to
confront that sin, gently, and work toward change in them. But if your
kids are being insincere because you've made it too hard to tell the truth,
the problem is at least partly yours. Create a safe environment, so you can
earn the right to ask for the whole truth.

# # 840 Whose Faith?
"They're not just running away from me; they're running away from the
faith." I've heard this statement of grief many times. It's quite possible

that you've presented scriptural truths accurately and have modeled a godly life. But it's also possible that your children are fleeing from your version of the faith (and you along with it). Maybe it's certain interpretations, rigidities, rules, or hypocrisy that have turned off your kids and not really Christianity at all. Some soul-searching—and doctrine-searching—might reveal at least a partial key to your child's rejection of your beliefs.

# # 841 Taking Some of the Blame

All parents cause some amount of damage to their children. You can't help it because you're not perfect. So when your children experience significant, serious life failures, you probably have contributed to their downfall in some way—perhaps even significantly. Your kids know this too. So you may as well face it and admit it and own up to the percentage of the problem derived from your actions or inaction. It will help you to stitch the wound. And always round your percentage up.

# # 842 The Big Three

If your child has pushed you away, all sorts of factors may be part of the scenario. One is heredity: Your child is part of a long line of people and ways of living and relating, some good and some bad. Another is environment: Your home has been run by principles and rules, some good and some bad. And a third is choice—yours and theirs, acting and reacting, some good and some bad. By making a healthy and productive review into all of these to find the causes of problems, you will find seeds of hope.

# # 843 Devastating Behaviors

Sometimes children can do terrible, horrible things to others—and it's completely devastating to you as a parent. Even in your anger and shock, deep down you wonder, *Where did this behavior come from—from me?* Psychiatrist Karl Menninger said, "What is done to children, they will do to society." This carries a seed of truth. Without excusing their actions or making it all your fault, you have to admit that your children came from somewhere and that you must have contributed to the person they've become. Do this not to beat yourself up with shame but so that you can pursue a real solution and be part of it.

# # 844 The Role of Others

As you try to rescue your relationship with your children, look around to see who's holding out a life preserver and who is offering a cement block on a rope. Siblings can be an asset to recovery or a part of the problem. Your own parents can give you perfect advice or perfect nonsense. Other relatives and friends can help or hurt. It is important to group people into two camps: If they're not *for* you, they're *against* you. Draw the helpers into the thick of the fight for restoration, and send the cement blocks packing.

# # 845 But I <u>Really</u> Blew It

One of the most crippling feelings for a parent is despair: "I have *totally* messed up this relationship. I don't even know where to start repairing this relationship with my child." That can become self-fulfilling, and we stop trying. But you do have a choice today. With the help of God and others who care, and with patience and determination on your part, you can begin to build a better relationship with your child. You can't change the past, but you can begin today to build connection for the future. It's never too late to start.

# # 846 Go Public

If you've blown it in a public way with your children, you'll need to "go public" with your efforts at restoration. If you've insulted them in front of seven people, round up the same seven and apologize to your child in front of them. You might feel mortified and worry that the witnesses' respect for you will diminish—but not if they're people worth knowing. Besides, it's your child's love that's most important to cultivate.

# # 847 Second Chances

God is the God of second chances. If he could redeem you, if he could redeem me, then he can redeem the situation you find yourself in with your children. Remind yourself of past times of connection. Think of the "I love you's"—not to dwell in the past but to spur you on in the future. When your heart is clear, ask your kids for a second chance. You might receive the gift of relational resurrection.

# # 848 What to Abandon

To renew your relationship with your children, abandon the use of force ("You owe me respect") and manipulation ("Look at all I've done for you"). Neither course is right, and neither works. Be real—listen honestly, ask heartfelt questions, avoid playing cover-up, quietly admit where you lost it. Authenticity is messy, and it takes a while to be believable. But over the long haul, the genuine have a shot at redemption.

# # 849 No Blackmail

While you're admitting your failure, guard against a subtle backlash. Perhaps you sense that your children will let you get close only if you'll admit that the break in your relationship was all your fault. Perhaps you were too harsh or abusive. Perhaps you didn't understand them. If they accuse you ("Do you know how much you hurt us?") or give hurtful examples ("We got in with that crowd because you weren't there for us"), you'll discern that they've gone beyond assigning you true blame to blaming you for all the brokenness between you. Don't fall into the bigger hole of saying, "Sure, honey, you're right. It was *all* my fault." Instead of helping your children be authentic and deal with you honestly, you'll allow them to grow in smugness or even dismiss you as flawed. Make sure they don't have a knife before you put your heart out on the table.

# # 850 The Long Haul

Remember: It took years to break your relationship, and restoration may take a long time. Even if there comes a breakthrough moment of crying and hugging, there will still be many issues to work through. Don't expect too much too soon. It took me eight years to find a way to relate to my father after I left home. It seemed impossible, but we did it. You can do it too. Just keep working at it. Where there's life, there's hope.

# # 851 Think Again

If you've been failing for a long time, or if your relationship is just beginning to rally, be extremely cautious. Nothing in creation is more fragile than a damaged or recovering relationship. When your "love account" is low, you don't have anything to "spend" on the little disciplines and minor issues. Don't excuse wrongdoing or dodge important issues, but do keep them in perspective and see the scale clearly in your mind. Because your relationship is fragile, you may want to let the little things wait for a while.

# # 852 Keep Your Balance

As you navigate the rough waters to recovery, work to keep your balance. Resist arrogance: *I did the best I could. We did things basically right. He was a good kid. I don't know what happened.* And resist despair: *I'm a failure. I can't recover my child's love. We'll never be close again.* Neither of you— parent or child—is perfect, neither knew anything about the other. You got into parenting with no prior experience. Neither extreme reaction will help you in the good fight—and you've got to wrestle.

# # 853 Reaping
"Don't be misled.... You will always reap what you sow!" (Gal. 6:7, NLT). If you change what you're sowing, you'll change what you're reaping. It's a law of the universe. "Shallow men believe in luck.... Strong men believe in cause and effect," said Ralph Waldo Emerson.

# # 854 Become the Change
"We must become the change we want to see," said Mahatma Gandhi. Act as though you're already living the new relationship. Love them before they're able to love you back. Don't wait. Just do it.

# # 855 Strong in the Broken Places
They say that a bone that's been broken and healed is actually strongest at the point of the original break. What a word of hope that offers for relationships! When your friendship has been tested to the limit—when you yourself were the main cause of the whole awful test—and yet the relationship has survived and healed, you are very strong indeed. Work for that moment, see it in your eye, claim it for your own—for when you are once again connected at the heart, hell itself will be powerless to harm your love.

# Part 5

## *Special Connections:*

**Getting**

**a Little**

**Closer**

*Just when you think you're getting really close to your kids, you can take your relationship even further.*

*Positive, healthy touch can build your bond. You can explore ways to reach that son or daughter who couldn't be more different from you (even if you're nearly convinced there was a mix-up at the hospital!). There are special ways mothers relate specifically to sons and daughters, and fathers to daughters and sons (although I encourage you to read them all—there may be something there for you to adopt). And there are ways to keep the connection growing even when geographical distance keeps you away from your children.*

*Let your relationship thrive!*

# 22

## Reach Out and Touch

### # 856  Both Hands

If you can add a gentle touch to at least some of your praise and even to simple conversation, so much the better. "Hold a true friend with both your hands," says an old African proverb.

### # 857  Start Small

You can start showing your affection with touch as soon as you can get your hands on your children. Take opportunities to rock them to sleep, hold them on your lap, even change their diapers. The more we touch the easier it is to touch and to love.

### # 858  Ongoing Need

The need for touch is there from the get-go. Babies *demand* it. They make a big, big fuss until they get it. You pick them up, rock them, walk the floor with them, bundle them up, and hold them tight. Before they have words to ask for touch, they need it desperately and respond to it mightily. The inside scoop is that teenagers (and elderly people in nursing homes) need touch just as desperately and respond just as mightily. Parents who want connection believe it; while respecting boundaries, they let no "stage" or "phase" prevent them from fulfilling that need.

### # 859  Becoming Ours

A good salesperson knows that it's an effective sales technique to put an object to be sold into the buyer's hands. When you hold something, you feel a sense of ownership. It becomes yours. And if it works in the department store . . .

# # 860 Little Touches

Even small, routine touches can say so much. There is some kind of cumulative effect. Maybe a hundred little touches equals one big leap into each other's arms. A squeeze of the arm, a pat on the hand, a rub on a shoulder—passing wisps of touch, gathering love power.

# # 861 Soothing Anger

When someone is angry with you and you take his hand, the whole dynamic between you changes. When you don't know what to do or say, you can still touch. There is some anger that touch alone can soothe. There may be some breaches beyond touch, and you'll know by your children's reaction when this is so. But you'll discover that only by reaching, risking, touching.

# # 862 Soothing Fear

When you're afraid, you want to be near other people. Children get wakened by a thunderstorm, they're disoriented, they want to be held *right now*. This is a marvelous way to connect, to give close-up assurance when the fear is raging. But wise parents know that the need itself really never goes away; it just becomes a little less obvious. When they're afraid—like before their doctoral dissertation—hug 'em tight.

# # 863 Soothing Stress

Touch can lower stress levels, slow you down, quiet your hectic insides. "Not only is holding and stroking your baby a lovely soother, it may also help shape her ability to cope with stress later on.... This study suggests that the effects of loving care and stimulation can stay with you for a lifetime,'" reports psychiatry professor Paul Plotsky in "Cuddle Power" (*Parenting* magazine, June/July 1998).

# # 864 When Words Fail

Sometimes there just aren't any words of comfort. They all sound hollow, cheap. That's when you see the basic, fundamental, deep-river essence of touch. You can't talk, but you communicate—holding, clinging, not letting go for anything. Touch says, "I'm here; I understand. We're connected and going through this thing together." When words fail, touch fills the void.

# # 865 Those Tears Are Mine

Next time you see a tear, or stream of tears, flowing down a face you love, reach out and take that tear. Don't wipe it away; claim it. Take it in your fingers, and then move your fingers to your heart. Symbolically put your children's tears into your heart. They'll see it. And without words, they'll know what you are saying.

# # 866 Seeing with Your Fingers

Take their face in your hands and "outline" it with your fingers. Describe what you find there. Tell about the uniqueness, the fineness, the marks of beauty. Tell them what you like about them. You may be following in the tracks of the Maker who formed that face with his own hands.

# # 867 Premarital Touch

How many young people have gotten themselves into some really horrible relationships because they offered some desperately needed touch? Your kids need touch—they've got to have it; they can't live without it. If they can't get physical closeness from us, they'll start looking, yearning for that contact their soul is so much in need of. If you meet this need, giving truly and deeply, your children won't need to find loving touch with someone who offers it with way too many strings attached.

# # 868 It's Just Not Me

Some people seem to be natural touchers; others find it harder to get comfortable with touch. Fortunately, touch is a matter of choice. You can choose to touch, and even if it takes a long time for it to feel natural, the price you pay will buy you a mountain of treasure. My mother grew up in a home where no one touched and, as so often happens, raised us the same way. Now, in her seventies, she hugs everybody. She is living proof that it is a matter of choice. She told me, "I can't believe I never hugged anybody all those years, but I'm sure going to do it now." It may not come naturally, but it is a matter of choosing to love.

# # 869 Poor Excuse

"They know that I love them. All this touch stuff just isn't necessary" is worse than a poor excuse; it's a false one. In fact, a study by F. B. Dressler of the University of California, Los Angeles, in the 1960s found that children require at least ten meaningful, affectionate "touches" a day if they are to grow into healthy, well-adjusted adults. Touch and displayed affection are valuable beyond description. If you want connection with your kids, you'll act on this truth.

# # 870 Touch Journal

In one of my children's college classes, the instructor had everyone keep a "touch journal" for a week. They had to document any touch, any details, and how they felt about it. If touch isn't easy for you, or if you're not really using it to connect, this could be an excellent exercise. For a week or two, write down your thoughts and feelings about the touches you offer and receive. You'll begin to see the value of touch clearly and move ahead more confidently.

# # 871 Resistance

Resistance to closeness can come from many factors. If we're not connecting on any other front, touch won't mean much and can easily offend. But assuming there is some basic connection, different personalities at different times can struggle with physical closeness. One father approached his daughter this way: "Honey, I really love you and want to hug you. But when I try, you stiffen and pull back. I don't want to do something that bothers you. Touch can be uncomfortable, I know. But even dads can feel rejection. I've heard women say it really hurt when their dads stopped hugging them; I don't want that to happen to us. So now you know that I want to hug you and want you to hug me back. Whenever you're ready for the next one, you be the one to start the hug. I'll be ready." Get it out in the open, be vulnerable, and give your kids a sense that decisions about touch belong to them as well as you. By the way, the daughter approached him that same day to give him a quiet hug.

# # 872 Talk about Touch

Talking about touch can disarm the negative reactions. "What do you like? What are you comfortable with? What makes you a little uncomfortable but you want me to continue anyway? What makes you tense?" When you've collected this information, you can offer the gift of touch in a way it can be accepted.

# # 873 Skip It

I don't remember when I started it, but for years I have grabbed a smaller hand and started skipping—across a parking lot or down a sidewalk. Does it look silly? Probably. Have I had to modify my leg movements since I had knee surgery? You bet. Do I plan to retire from skipping someday? Nope. I hope I never get that... whatever.

# # 874 Dance

Touch and closeness with music can be a wonderful bond. "Indeed, bonding is a wonderful benefit of dancing with your baby, say experts. . . . Scientists and educators believe that early exposure to these elements of music may actually help children academically as well as musically later on" ("Born to Dance," *Parenting* magazine, August 1998). Let there be music and dancing.

# # 875 Good Touch, Bad Touch

Talk with your kids about good touch as opposed to inappropriate or bad touch. "What touching is good? What sends the right message? What is appropriate? What is out of bounds?" Be a safe haven where your kids can discuss and analyze the language of touch. Take the mystery and fear and confusion out of it. Touch is a gift, but like all gifts, it can be broken or misused.

# # 876 Four Loves

C. S. Lewis described four different kinds of love in *The Four Loves.* There is godlike love. Friendship love. Family love. And passionate love. Should you love your children as God loves and with his love? Of course. And should you love them as friends? The best. And shouldn't your family love resound with connection? Of course! And shouldn't you love them *passionately?* Isn't that how God loves us? Wild and passionate (and appropriate) love belongs to all who love. Pour it on.

# # 877 Three Languages

Other people understand you through your words, your tone, and your body language. Words are often the least important, while tone and body language speak volumes. You might squeak out an "I love you" (or more likely "luv ya'") while you're on the run, and that's OK—it's just not enough for every occasion. You change the transaction totally by slowing down, saying the words with a focused and meaningful tone, and putting a hand on a face or shoulder while you say it. With some desire and effort, you can become fluent in all three languages.

# # 878 Slap

Many debate the pros and cons of corporal punishment. Some too easily dismiss its value, and others too easily make it a mark of parental dedication. But whatever your thoughts on this, don't use your hands to deliver the spank. Don't let them associate your hands and fingers with pain. If you do this, use something inanimate that won't do any damage. Reserve your hands for love. Too many times I have seen a parent's hand reach toward a face and watched a child wince and pull away. You can slap or you can love, but it's hard to do both with the same tool.

# # 879 Trust and Touch

The freedom to give and receive touch comes from relational and physical trust. Trust provides the feeling that it is safe to reach out. Touch is an extrapolation and affirmation of the inner trust between you. Touch without that trust is meaningless at best and confusing and harmful at worst. Touch is no substitute for trust. Build it, and the touch will say so very much.

# # 880 Back Rubs

There must be a tension reservoir in our shoulders and backs. Because of that, few human beings can resist the pleasant and relaxing touch of a back rub. The back is a "safe" area for touch with most people. When you're watching television together, take that back into your hands and love it. Even when you're dead tired, do it. It's there for the loving.

# # 881 Back Scratch

An itch on the back is an invitation to connection—especially since you can't get to it by yourself. Back scratching becomes service and love rolled into one and feels so blasted good that it's really hard to turn down.

# # 882 Cuddly-Coze

To curl up on a couch with a loved one, a bunch of pillows and blankets, and a good game or movie can be one of life's great pleasures. But make the closeness and warmth, the coziness of the cuddling (or "cuddly-coze," as one family calls it) a central part of the time together.

# # 883 Tucking In

There is something really comforting about being tucked in. Maybe it's like going back into the womb, where your mother wouldn't let anyone harm you. Take every chance to tuck your children in, even as they get older. You may be in their room to do it only when they're hurt or sick, but what an opportunity!

# # 884 Where They Fall

Sometimes your children might fall asleep on a couch or on the floor. I used to get them up so they could go to bed, not get a stiff neck, etc. They usually mumbled and resisted and finally went. Now, I just find a blanket and cover them up where they've nodded off. And I might slip in a little kiss on the forehead or cheek. Will they know that I've done it? Somewhere in their souls, I believe the answer is yes.

# # 885  Leave a Note

Be there even when you're not there. Leave a note for your child to find in the morning, on his bed or on the floor by his door. As he climbs out of his sleep and dreams, your child will awaken to a little portion of love. And it's better for him than coffee.

# # 886  Swings

Nobody is too old to be pushed in a swing. Pushing each other on a swing is a wonderful, fresh way to have closeness. And you can slip a loving word or two in your child's ear on the backswing.

# # 887  Hugs and Wrestles

A little bit of playful hugging and wrestling can bring warmth and affection and some fun, too. One father plays "get-away" with his daughter: She tries to break out of a hug or the holding of an arm. He almost lets her, and then he pulls her back while she squeals in delight. Be careful not to let playful wrestling turn to roughhousing and possible injury; obviously, avoid creating any fear or discomfort. But done with love and humor, physical horsing around can create a feeling that touch is a good and enjoyable idea.

# # 888  The Laying On of Hands

Remember how Jesus touched the children? "Then little children were brought to Jesus for him to place his hands on them and pray for them" (Matt. 19:13). He couldn't keep his hands off them. He had made them out of dust, formed them in his hands, and he delighted in holding and caressing. You can lay your hands on your children to bless them and pray for them—even if it is a quick touch and a silent prayer.

# # 889  Towel Baby

One mother plays "towel baby" with her little boy. When he gets out of the bath and dries off, she wraps him tightly in several towels and then holds him tight. It's OK for a child to go back in time and be a baby for a few minutes now and then.

# # 890 Greetings

"Greet one another with a kiss of love," exhorts Peter (1 Pet. 5:14).
Greetings—in the morning, just after school or work, after a trip—are
built-in times to easily share a hug and kiss and pat on the cheek. Don't
waste any of them.

# # 891 Good-Byes

One of the few really terrific things about good-byes is that you can
affirm your closeness in a safe format. People who never touch at other
times find it hard not to hug someone going off to summer camp or on a
long trip. Plan it in advance—how you'll start the hug, what you'll whisper
in your child's ear. The touch can say, "No matter how far away or how
long, home is in these arms."

# # 892 Eye Contact

Touch your children with your eyes. Most parents use eye contact—a
deep form of touch—to show disapproval. That's like using your hands
just for spanking. "Studies have shown that most parents use eye contact
in primarily negative ways, either while reprimanding a child or giving
very explicit instructions," writes marriage and family specialist Gary
Chapman (*The Five Love Languages of Children,* Moody Press, 1997). Talk
to your children with your eyes. Search their souls and listen. Spirit can
talk with spirit, even when the mouths are closed.

# # 893 The Kiss of Peace

A simple gesture can say so much. Take their faces gently in your hands,
look into your children's eyes, pull their faces slowly forward, and kiss
them on the cheek or forehead. Then let them go with a pat on the cheek.

# # 894 Never Stop

Many have told me that the physical contact with their parents just sort
of "stopped" somewhere along the way. For some it was a sense of loss;
for others a sense of rejection. You'll need to vary the form and intensity
as your children grow and change, becoming teenagers and then young
adults. But touch never loses its value. Don't quit, no matter how old they
are, no matter how awkward either of you feels. Commit to yourself: This
will never stop. Never.

# 23 Connecting despite Differences

## # 895 Different from Day One

In one sense none of your children are "like you." So you've got to get started working to connect with these alien creatures right from birth. Don't postpone building the relationship because they're little. They're adults in process. If you think you can "train early, relate later," you're a dead duck. If possible, learn how to relate to your children's differences while you've got time to be confused by them and recover, because they don't know enough to know you're baffled.

## # 896 Not the Same

Many parents have boldly said, "I love each of my children the same." But this is simply impossible. How do you apply love to them? Differently for each one. What about intensity? Your intense feelings of love won't even be the same for each child over time. Likemindedness? You'll share more with this one, less with that one, more on this topic, less on that one. Interests? All over the landscape. Don't even start playing the "love each child the same" game. You can't win, and you'll just turn your children into people who measure your love for them compared to the others. It's a superficial distraction from connection, not a path to it. Over and over, meet them where they are, at this time, in this place.

## # 897 Rooms of Their Own

It's the *differences* that make each relationship unique. "I tell each of my children that I have a special room in my heart that only he or she can inhabit," Maryl Janson told me. "No one else can fill it, and it would be an empty and sad place without them. I've told them that even if they died, their rooms would always be there, waiting for them, until we were reunited in heaven." Kids don't really want to be loved like someone else; they want to be loved like *nobody* else.

# # 898 Honey, They're Playing Our Song

Even with small children, there can be a special "thing" that belongs to just the two of you. A game, a favorite restaurant, an unusual activity (jumping on a trampoline, doing projects for the needy), a certain private language, music, a hobby—something. Focus on developing a unique connection with each child, and stay out of the comparison-and-measurement game.

# # 899 Give Up the Image

When you start out as a parent, you may have an ideal image of what your child will be like, or *ought* to be like. And then this kid comes along who has little or no resemblance to the image. Where did she come from? She must take after the *other* side of the family! When your imperfect little angel spreads those wings and starts breaking glass, when your unrealistic image shatters, you may be thoroughly disappointed—and she won't miss it. You only add to the problem by trying to relate to a mythical someone who isn't there, by trying to mold her to fit the ideal. So give it up—and choose instead to love the incomprehensible being that God gave you instead of your ideal.

# # 900 Encourage Diversity

"As for conforming outwardly, and living your own life inwardly, I do not think much of that," wrote Henry David Thoreau. Encourage your children to be themselves—not you—outwardly, not just in appearance but in every way. Parents who insist that their children look and talk and act just like they do squeeze out the originality of a one-of-a-kind treasure, and reduce much of their connection to similarities that don't count for much. Accent their uniqueness. They'll love you for it.

# # 901 Respect the Difference

You can tell your children that it is OK—no, terrific—that they are different from you and from their siblings, from everyone on the whole blasted planet. They can think their own thoughts, feel their own feelings, choose their own paths. What an affirmation! And what a bond.

# # 902 Difference of Opinion

You are sure to have differences with all of your children, but one who is very different from you can have incredibly divergent opinions. On matters of principle or family policy, you'll have to put your parental foot down. But be gentle. In his military treatise *The Art of War*, written more than twenty-four hundred years ago, Sun Tzu wrote: "To fight and conquer in all your battles is not supreme excellence; supreme excellence consists in breaking the enemy's resistance without fighting." To persist, to gently break down your children's faulty thinking, to get them to cooperate without bloodshed. Now *that's* the way to parenting with connection.

# # 903 Individuating

When children are trying to firmly establish their own identities, they can challenge and bait parents, setting traps with their words. Don't fall for it. Don't "bite." If you find yourself in a conversational loop or arguing the same topic for the umpteenth time, get off the train—it's going to the wrong destination.

# # 904 Celebrate the Difference

When you see a difference, make a big deal out of it in a positive way. You're still happy with your quill pen—and your daughter shows amazing aptitude with computers. You can barely run straight, yet your child is Little League MVP. Brag on your kids, and listen to them (even if you have no idea what they're talking about), ask enthusiastic questions ("You mean a mother board has nothing to do with PTA?"), pick up magazines related to their interests, buy them computer stuff and athletic equipment, send them to seminars. Celebrate their differences. They'll know you really don't get it, but it won't stop the relationship rocket.

# # 905 Look at the Heart

Some children will be more responsive to you than others. Some jump right on your ideas and requests, and others come around *very* slowly. But keep on looking at their hearts. The children who seem less responsive may just need more time to align with you. "There was a man who had two sons. He went to the first and said, 'Son, go and work today in the vineyard.' 'I will not,' he answered, but later he changed his mind and went. Then the father went to the other son and said the same thing. He answered, 'I will, sir,' but he did not go" (Matt. 21:28-30). Which child really heard his father and did what he asked? Outward agreement and compliance can mean nothing. Give the resister a little time, and see if your "different" child comes around—and does it her way, of course.

# # 906 Reduce the Gap

Whatever gap there is between you and a child, it doesn't have to be a relationship gap or a communication gap or a gap between your hearts. You can't magically erase the gap entirely—at least in most cases. But you can certainly put a dent in it. Shrink the gap. Make the gap a bonding point. It's a matter of choice and a matter of time.

# # 907 No Excuses

Using the differences that exist between you as excuses not to be closer than you are is a cop-out. "Ninety-nine percent of failures come from people who have the habit of making excuses," said botanist George Washington Carver. No excuses. Unity is available, if you'll work toward it.

# # 908 Common Vision

Whole nations are built on the principle that millions of different people can unite around a common vision of life and the future. Can your family do any less? What is your "theme" as a family? Do you have a special purpose? Set out to determine what your family vision is, and invite all of those personality differences equally into the melee. You'll end up on a rich and complex journey with a destination different and more beautiful than any you'd have chosen by yourself.

# # 909 If You've Got the Time

When you and one of your children are really different, you're going to have to spend more time together to find a way to make things work. Obviously, this breaks the "equal time for each of my children" rule that some parents swear by. But it's necessary if you want to form a relationship with that unique child. If you've got the time, you've got the connection.

# # 910 Patience

It has been said that parents can learn many things from their children—how much patience the parents have, for example. It takes an extra measure of patience when one of your children is very different from you. How much patience do you have? By patience, I don't mean waiting for that child to "come around" to your way of doing and seeing things. I mean that while acknowledging you may never fully see eye to eye, you will still talk and work and pray and play and try until you make a pretty complex mosaic.

# # 911 Hokey Parenting

You've got to take some risks if you're going to relate to this very different personality. Risk being hokey ("Oh, Dad, come on. That just isn't you"). Risk being annoying ("No, I *can't* explain why I enjoy underwater basketweaving"). Get creative. Try a zillion things, and see what works. And though there are plenty of ways to be hokey, if just a few of them work...

# # 912 What's the Truth?

To love that different child, avoid intolerance. "Man is always inclined to be intolerant toward the thing, or person, he hasn't taken time adequately to understand," says Robert R. Brown (quoted in *12,000 Religious Quotations*, Baker Books, 1989). Instead of asking your child, "What's the matter with you?" a parent should ask, "What's the truth about you?"

# # 913 I Think I See

Though you may never fully understand the differences between you, you can pay close attention. You can earn the right to say, "I think I can see where you're coming from." Efforts at understanding are always bonding and even more so when the difference—and the effort—are so great.

# # 914 Ask Them

Bridge the gap of understanding by asking your children what the best ways of connecting with them are. I asked Bethany for a list of three ways to connect and three things to avoid. Connections for her: Ask her what happened when she was "little" (she was eleven when she gave me the list!); ask her what happened to her today; and ask where she went today. Things "not to do": Roll my eyes at her; interrupt her; or walk away when she is still talking. Sound advice all around. When you don't know what connects and disconnects, go right to the source.

# # 915 Be Impractical

If a child is really different from you, her ideas are often going to sound odd, funky, or impractical. They may just sound uninteresting. Just because you're a parent doesn't mean you're really interested in all of this stuff. But choose to get past the "odd" feeling. Be impractical. Try doing what doesn't really appeal to you at all—for the relationship, not for fun.

# # 916 Room for Rocks

If you're going to connect with the ones who are different, you've got to make room—sometimes physical room—for that difference. Maybe you love peace and quiet, and your daughter yearns for a parakeet. Or you like an orderly kitchen, and your son likes to mess it up while he does a little baking. Perhaps you dislike clutter around the house, and your kid brings home leaves and bugs and worms and rocks. What does connection mean? You make room for the rocks.

# # 917 Orientation

You'll discover many differences of basic orientation with your "different" child. One is pragmatism and dreaming. You want him to "get serious," and he's off in a different world. What's the matter with him? Maybe nothing. "I've come to the conclusion that the gift of fantasy has meant more to me than any talent for abstract, positive thinking." Strong words, since they come from Albert Einstein. Once in a while, join your child on that distant planet.

# # 918 Maverick

Few parents run their families without some rules. Some children may chafe under those rules, even if they are reasonable, but others seem always to be outside the lines. How can you respond? Tap into that energy. When the activities aren't blatantly rebellious or dangerous, join your child "outside the lines." Love is where you find your child—so go there. Relationships have been killed by inflexible rules.

# # 919 Who's the Parent?

Some children seem to be a bit confused about who the parents are. Or they aren't confused: They're convinced they're in charge. "My mother loved children," said comedian Groucho Marx. "She would have given anything if I had been one." The answer? Let them take the lead where possible and become great parents: "Anyone who becomes as humble as this little child is the greatest in the Kingdom of Heaven," said Jesus (Matt. 18:4, NLT). You don't have to be in control to be in authority—and can't always be in control if you want to be in love with your kids.

# # 920 Personality Profiles

While avoiding labeling, you might generate some useful dialogue by taking a personality profile together. Charting out your personality differences increases your mutual understanding and empathy. You'll note your areas of contrast and perhaps even learn how they can complement one another. And—glory be—you may even discover some similarities! Just finding out that you're not *completely* different can be a boost to your bond.

# # 921 Play with Me

Play is the great equalizer. "You can do anything with children if you only play with them," said—incredibly—Otto von Bismarck, Prime Minister of Prussia, who was known as the "Iron Chancellor." Get into their world, and erase the difference for a moment. Some of it will never come back.

# # 922 Always Leave Them Laughing

Use humor to lighten the load of difference. There must be something in this silly world that both of you can laugh at. Search it out. Even laughing over your differences can bring you together. "I can't believe you like to get up that early—I didn't even know five o'clock came twice a day!" Just be sure you don't share a laugh with an "edge," where you're subtly putting down their difference. Good laughing covers gaps and builds bridges.

# # 923 Music

If ever there was a surefire divide between the tastes of parent and child, it's in the area of music. How can they listen to that horrible stuff? (They are probably asking the same question.) Plan a listening session—where you each listen to a few of the other's favorite songs. Ground rules? No making faces or other reactions. And you both can talk only about the positive points—about what you liked. It's OK to laugh if the "positives" are funny ("It was really short"). Don't war over the language of the soul.

# # 924 Energy Cycles

Some people are "morning" people, while others are people of the night. Each person has his own pace and flow of life. Learning what that is—writing it down, plotting it out on a piece of paper—can bring a lot of understanding. You'll discover practical applications—like there's no point in discussing anything "heavy" between 10:00 A.M. and noon because he's starting to sag or between 7:00 A.M. and 8:30 A.M. because you haven't yet remembered you're human. Cycles, rhythms, and ebbs and flows can heighten your differences or become part of your deep understanding.

# # 925 Team Up

Even one child and one parent have the potential for conflict. But with more than one child, the chances go way up and increase with each additional child. You're each so different, but you're a family. How important is it that you overcome the differences to become a team? The great baseball player Babe Ruth once said, "The way a team plays as a whole determines its success. You may have the greatest bunch of individual stars in the world, but if they don't play together, the club won't be worth a dime." The family won't be either. I agree with the Babe.

# # 926 Acquisition

If you adopt or bring a new member into your family, you will have a built-in difference. Your "acquisition" will have a different "culture" and will understand many things differently from the way you do. Some differences may be obvious (foods, clothes, movies), and some may be more subtle (the person doesn't view "telling the truth" in the same way as everyone else in the family). But don't pretend these differences aren't there or that they aren't potentially crippling. When you long for deep connection so badly, it's easy to be tempted to put an illusory gloss over differences. But this will work to the harm of everyone. Differences are overcome by facing them honestly and with more than a touch of compassion.

# # 927 Merger

When organizations merge, cultures collide. Stephen Covey is one of the best-known writers on how to make collaborations work, and yet his own merger (of Covey Leadership Center with Franklin Quest) "is a textbook example of a merger gone awry.... 'It's been one tough baby,' says Covey" ("Gurus: Do as I Say, Not as I Do," *USA Today,* 7 December 1998). Blended families have colliding cultures and plenty of potential to hurt connections more than help them. Lots of open dialogue—such as a "committee of the whole," in small groups, or one-on-one with your spouse's children and your own—combined with a great sense of empathy for all the readjustment and discomfort is a good starting point. Squelched dissent, minimized concerns, and any sense of preferential consideration sound the death knell of closeness. Your merger can be done, but it's "one tough baby."

# # 928 Preference
"We all prefer certain kinds of personalities, and our kids are no different," wrote Barbara Rowley in *Parenting* magazine ("When You're Rejected," Dec/Jan 1999). It's painful but neccessary to accept the fact that some of your children may simply like you less or less easily. That's OK. Preference doesn't have to stop the love either way.

# # 929 Importance
Do your best to avoid the relationship-killing issues with your "different" child (the one who really gets beyond your frame of reference). He wants to wear a necklace? She intends to buy that fire-engine red convertible? He likes to stay up all night and sleep all day? She loves music that makes your skin crawl? There is one big, overriding question to ask in the face of these off-the-scale differences: Is this important enough to war over and risk severe damage to your relationship? Seldom—very seldom—will the answer be yes.

# # 930 Proud
The reality is that the one who is most different from you may leave you with the best feelings. "Likely as not, the child you can do the least with will do the most to make you proud," says writer and editor Mignon McLaughlin. Love your kids in their uniqueness, and love the magnificence that uniqueness can yield.

# 24

# Mothers and Fathers, Daughters and Sons

## *Mothers and Daughters*

### # 931 Origins

Tell your daughter the origins and meanings of her names. Explain why you chose them and why you think she can grow into the meaning. That name probably is so near and dear to your heart that you can't hear it said by others without feeling a potpourri of emotions and memories. Share them all with her. Take your little girl back to her birth, and before.

### # 932 Car Talk

After shopping, just stay in the car and talk. Pull into a drive-through and get a drink. Or park in your driveway. Face each other and curl up your legs. It's one of those rare combinations: total privacy and freedom from interruption, yet it happens on a fairly frequent basis. Another good reason to shop.

### # 933 Gingerbread

Bake a gingerbread house together. But don't stop there. Imagine a family living inside, and create a narrative to describe the good things that should happen in that house of sweets and the kinds of bad things that could happen. As you chat in a warm and playful way, you'll hear your child's views about family life. Gently allude to your own family's strengths and weaknesses. Then taste and see that the house is good.

### # 934 Dressing Mom

Ask your daughter's advice on your clothes—and then take it (this can be the hard part). Even if you'd like something else or feel a bit uncomfortable, try it out. When you follow her lead, you reinforce her confidence—and perhaps reinvent yourself. You may even like what you see.

# # 935 Hairdressing

Walk your daughter through the whole hair deal from the time she's tiny. Let her see you working with your hair or going to the salon; interact with her about the details and options and bad hair days (daze?). You'll help her see how important great-looking hair is (and isn't). Be there as she gets into it. Allow her to make her own choices about hairstyle, and listen to her opinions of the other girls' hairstyles. There's a lot of self-consciousness about physical appearance—and marvelous opportunities for comforting and helping and connecting.

# # 936 Surrogate Mothers

If you've got a little nurturer, or if you're extremely busy, avoid making your daughter into a surrogate mother to her younger siblings. She'll probably do it for you—perhaps even gladly if she is a certain personality—but it's too much for her, too much for her siblings (no one needs two mothers!), and too much for your relationship. It's inevitable that she will one day take charge when you don't want her to, go further than you intended, and argue with you over the best way to run the household. This will all take a toll on your relationship. Let her be what she is—a daughter. Hire a nanny, or bring in an adult to help if you're overloaded, but spare her.

# # 937 Pseudo-Counselor

You want to be your daughter's confidante, but don't make her yours. You can't tell her too much too soon or depend on her heavily as a sort of counselor, in the midst of troubles. It will take the innocence out of your relationship, force her to grow up too fast, and annoy you when she doesn't understand, agree, or support you.

# # 938 Women in Society

Talk openly with your daughter regarding criticisms you have about the role of women in society, whether you think those hang-ups are good or bad. Talk about limitations, how to break through them, and how to get a voice. Discuss how they can get a full vote in their own future and how to avoid oppression.

# # 939 Boys and Men

Let your daughter see how you relate to men—your husband, friends, men at work and church. Include her. Invite her along. Make her part of your conversations. Evaluate them with her—why you like this one, why you're keeping that one at a distance, why you're avoiding that one like the return of Charles Manson. The goal is not to praise men or disparage them but to understand them and relate well to them.

# # 940 The Fix

Moms find it tempting to intervene to keep their daughters out of bad relationships—or fix them. Especially if they see their daughters repeating some of their own mistakes. It brings on feelings of panic! But stepping in and taking over is not the answer. Such power plays become a source of annoyance and even destruction in your relationship. A better course is to help your daughters talk out the problems, think out loud, and consider optional paths or solutions. You can't protect them from themselves. Trying to do so will hurt you without helping them.

# # 941 The Complete Woman

Many people hold up the woman described in the book of Proverbs, chapter 31, as the ideal woman. This chapter has often been used as the basis for *limiting,* rather than expanding, a girl's view of her possible future. But as you read it carefully, you realize that this is a picture of a complete woman. Only one of the twenty-one verses concerning this woman relates directly to her role as a mother, and that one simply says, "Her children stand and bless her" (Prov. 31:28, NLT). She is a wife, mother, household manager, teacher, businesswoman, craftswoman, property owner, negotiator, and patron of the poor. Explore the richness of this passage with your daughter.

# Fathers and Sons

# # 942 Not Just Buddies

The problem with father/son relationships is that you can think you have one when really all you are is "buddies." Buddies do things with each other: sports, movies, fishing, games. They hang out. Of course, it's great for you to hang out with your son, but it just isn't enough. It isn't relationship. You can spend plenty of time together and never connect at the heart. Decide with your son that you're going to be true friends, and then do it. There are about one thousand other ideas in this book that might help.

# # 943 I'm Bigger

When your boy starts acting "tough," you, as a father, have three choices for how you'll react. If you let it go or even egg these behaviors on, soon the behaviors will be out of control. Your son can't live successfully without self-control, and he won't like himself very much—or you for allowing it—either. You can also respond to the tough-guy stuff by squelching it with your own warrior spirit: "I'm bigger than you and tougher than you, so I say sit down and shut up!" That's dad control, but it fails to teach your boy self-control. The best way to handle your son is to be an example and show him the tough-and-tender aspects of manhood, then help him develop self-control so he can live them out.

# # 944 Good Hair Days

Guys have certain hair milestones that you and your son can share. You can take your son for his first haircut. Your son's first shave is also a biggie. At the first sight of a whisker (or fuzz), take him to pick up his own razor, smell all the shaving creams, and talk about how it's done. And talk a bit about being a man while you're at it.

# # 945 Shopping

Most men aren't into shopping—especially with women—except for shopping for certain guy things. Get past shopping only for tools and sports equipment. Help each other out on ties and shoes and other personal guy stuff. Go together to pick out each other's cars (Peter has me driving a red-hot convertible). And when he's ready to buy something for that special girl, be there.

# # 946 Not Just Mom

Avoid the all-too-typical dad's problem of letting Mom handle the relational aspects of parenting and home life while he earns money, fixes things, and watches football. You're an individual, not a stereotype. You can choose to be part of the most rewarding aspects of having children. This "soft" side of relating to children may not come naturally to you as a man, but you've got to try. It's sure to get easier as you go along. And why should Mom have all the fun?

# # 947 Make Time

You can be home without really being there. A recent study related to children's performance in school postulated that more single fathers are involved with their kids than dads in two-parent families—46 percent versus 31 percent (*USA Today,* 3 October 1997). Some of these dads in two-parent homes must be either too busy to get close to their kids, or they're dumping involvement in things like schoolwork and household chores off on their wives. You can't delegate connection with your son. Either you're there, or you aren't. Be there.

# # 948 Get Out a Hammer

Get together with your boy and build a giant structure of some kind, one that takes multiple efforts and a long time. It could be out of blocks and take up half a room. It could be a tree house, playhouse, or room addition to the real house. You can use your construction time constructively to discuss your common goal: What it takes to build a relationship that will still be standing years from now.

# # 949 Merry Christmas Decorating

The Christmas season offers many opportunities for you to connect with your son. You'll find boys love to put Christmas lights all over the house. Peter started this when he was about thirteen, climbing up on the roof and sliding along the ridgepole. Last year he and David, twenty and fourteen, took the whole project to new heights (literally). It took them a whole day, and cost . . . a lot. We celebrated with food and hot drinks, and generally had a spectacular day. They get to be macho, and yet the result is beauty. Male togetherness, gorgeous decorations, and just a little bit more connection. You can't beat it!

# # 950 The Talk

Few things dominate the thoughts of most boys and men like sex. We've spent countless hours thinking about it, enjoying it, hating it, resisting its temptations. Unfortunately, many men never really talk about this critical subject with their sons, or they do it about five years after their sons already have the scoop (and plenty of misinformation). Don't let this happen to you and your sons. Men feel uncomfortable discussing the whole issue of sex mainly because their relationship with their sons is too uncertain to handle the introduction of an awkward, embarrassing topic. It takes a lot of vulnerability to discuss a force that can drive you or take you down. It'll take a bit of courage, but it's an incredible way to connect with your son, man to man. If you can be real while discussing this personal subject, the sky's the limit.

# Mothers and Sons

## # 951 Oh, Mom!

At the Relationship Development Center, we've surveyed mothers and sons about their feelings of closeness. When we asked, "When did your boys start to get uncomfortable with your affection?" moms told us it was between the ages of twelve and fourteen (earlier in some cases). No matter how it feels, this is not tragic—it's just reality. Be prepared for the pushing away, and you'll find ways to stay affectionate without making your son uncomfortable. Be sensitive in public places, of course. And you may have to give up cuddling. But you can muss up your son's hair, slap him on the shoulder, pat his cheek. With creativity, you can conquer this man-mountain.

## # 952 Ritual Affection

Be careful not to be so busy being the caretaker that you let your relationship with your son slide. As boys grow and become gangly and uncoordinated and sloppy, you might find yourself spending all morning and evening nagging and squabbling. Then, when you tack on a hug or kiss or "Love you" as they run out the door or go to bed, you'll find you've got the ritual of affection with no actual affection. Drop the disguise; there's nothing worse than not knowing your relationship has fizzled because you've covered it up with this token stuff. It takes time to get inside who this boy really is and what he's thinking and feeling. You have to get inside his heart before you get inside his arms.

## # 953 Smothering

Sometimes it feels pretty good, right now, to have your son rely on you for everything. He's a man, he's helpless, he needs me! But when mothering turns to smothering, true bonding leads to enmeshment and confusion and either a helpless dependency or a "let-me-out-of-here" escape. Your son might let you stay in charge, at least for a while, but eventually he'll resent it because it makes him feel like a wimp. Jesus wouldn't even go out to see his mother at the door when she showed up to challenge and redirect his ministry (Matt. 12:46-50). A son generally seems to have a lower tolerance for this hands-on parenting approach. Hands off, Mom, or you'll lose him in the long run.

## # 954 Worrywart

If you are a worrier who expresses your list of concerns every time you talk with your son, you'll make a nuisance of yourself, and your son won't want to see you, hear from you, talk with you, or take your calls. "Are you drinking your milk? Are you taking vitamins every day? I sure hope you're driving more slowly!" This is the Chinese water torture of mother-son relationships. It has a cumulative negative effect that is huge. It's the umbilical cord that won't be cut. Guys have a very low threshold for caretaking details and hate being nit-picked. Many grown men dread hearing from their mothers, which is probably one reason why they have to be exhorted not to "despise your mother when she is old" (Prov. 23:22). The sad truth is that if you act like a plague, you'll be avoided like one.

# # 955 "It's a Boy"

If you as a woman have preconceived or stereotypical notions about boys, they're going to get in the way of your relationship with your son. Maybe you've always seen boys as entities needing to be organized or as relationally inept without much in the way of feelings. Or maybe because you've failed or been frustrated in your past relationships with men, you're convinced men have relational limitations. Some women panic when they hear the words *It's a boy!* because they have such intense feelings of conflict about men that they're afraid to have a son. Stop thinking of your son first in terms of his gender. Consider his humanity and dignity so that you can relate to the real boy he is and treat him as a one-of-a-kind person. Keep an eye on all that he can become.

# # 956 The Conscience

Have you seen the T-shirts that say, "My mother is a travel agent for guilt trips"? You can't be your son's conscience, no matter how hard you try or how much he needs one. The old Hebrew proverb says that "a foolish son [brings] grief to his mother" (Prov. 10:1). The anticipation of this grief can drive you to crush his foolishness. But if you try to play the role of conscience, you can teach him to be thoughtless about his life because he will think, "Mom will stop me and direct me." And as he gets older, he will resent your role as "cop."

# # 957 "He's Just a Boy"

Mothers who are fond of their son can be prone to excuse their son's bad behavior. "He's just at that stage. He's been sick. I kept him up too late last night—he's tired. He's little—what do you expect? Boys will be boys." If you have low expectations for his behavior or ability to control himself, so will he. It reinforces that perceived need for you to become his mouthpiece. He won't like you or thank you for making excuses for him. Call a skunk a skunk—even though he once was your little white rose.

# # 958 Do the Discipline

For all sorts of reasons, you, as a mother, might want to avoid discipline and punishment of your son or fall back on the "wait till your father gets home" approach. Don't. Your son will perceive this as weakness and take advantage of you. As time goes on, he will lose respect for you. It's impossible to be deeply connected to someone whom you don't respect. Do the discipline.

# # 959 Dominion

God said that human beings were created to have "dominion" over the earth. Whether or not humanity is doing a good job at this, one thing is certain: Boys want "dominion" over their moms. Remember, you weren't given the responsibility of parenthood in order either to dominate him or to be dominated by him. You're here to teach him about self-control and boundaries. Turn his desire to dominate into a practice of controlling himself. Show him how to control his hands and feet when he's little, his mouth when he starts talking (if he's old enough to talk, he's old enough to keep quiet), and his hormones when they try to take dominion over him. You can channel that "dominion mandate."

# # 960 Warrior

King of the hill. Kill the guy with the ball. My dad can beat up your dad. It is no coincidence that men are at the forefront of wars and contact sports and the majority of violence. Some of it is surely cultural, but there is also a definite warrior spirit in boys. What's a mother to do with that? Avoid criticizing or deploring it. Appreciate it, and shape that drive to attack and win toward winning the most important battles of his life. It might even save your life someday. Your son will love you for understanding—and liking—this part of who he is.

# # 961 "After All I've Done . . ."

Every mother feels underappreciated by her son at some point. "What's the matter with him? Doesn't he know what I went through, carrying him, birthing him, caring for him, raising him?" Nope. He probably has no clue, and he doesn't want one either. But don't allow your frustrations to lead you to the ever-dreaded "Is this all I get after all I've done for you?" If he gives in to this manipulating emotional blackmail, his resentment will take off. "You owe me" is the death knell of any relationship. Your appeal has to be based on something other than labors or position—perhaps through real friendship?

# # 962 They're Men

Face the fact that your boys are men-in-process. Whatever you struggle with about men—*whatever*—is all in there. The good, the bad, the courageous, the cowardly. If you can't understand men, you're going to need help with your boys: a pastor, a decent relative, an "uncle" at church, somebody. Find help and understanding, and you can connect.

# # 963 The Ideal Man

Don't try to make your son into your ideal man. You can try to create someone who has none of the flaws of men, none of the flaws of your father or brothers, none of the flaws of your husband or friend. But in trying to deal with this fantasy person, you'll end up not relating to your son's individual bent or personality. For example, you perceive men to be too forceful. Perhaps your father or husband is distant or harsh. So your ideal man is quiet and gentle. You work hard to squish all of that "forceful" stuff out of him—no playing fort, no action movies, no competitive sports. You end up with a young man who can't stand up for himself and resents you for your molding. Utopian schemes never work—at least as intended.

# # 964 Offset

While you can't create your ideal man, you can work to offset the weaknesses he might pick up from the influential men in his life. Perhaps your husband isn't communicative and resists showing emotion. You can help your son develop his relational skills, to talk and freely express his feelings in a genuine and appropriate way. I love the fact that ultra-manly baseball star Mark McGwire cries when he watches *Driving Miss Daisy*. But the key is to do this without setting up a contrast with "manliness"—you want to emphasize that you don't want him to do this to be *different* from men but to be a *complete* man.

# # 965 Looking Good

When a son comes to you and says, "Mom, how do I look?" don't say, "Pretty good, except for ..." Don't criticize. Don't nip and tuck and fuss about the details. Do your best to answer, "Sharp," with two thumbs up. Because in his own eyes he is sharp—or at least hopes he is—or he wouldn't be asking. Your son wants support, not advice.

# # 966 Clotheshorse

For some big occasion, take that boy out and dress him to the nines. Talk about styles, and peers, and what's in and what's out, and go to a lot of stores (to compare styles more than price). Discuss what he likes and why. Ask him what's "nerdish." Let him pick, and don't give anything but compliments and preferences on choices he has already deemed "cool." There is an old joke among boys that says, "You're ugly and your mother dresses you funny." If you want to connect, that's a club to avoid.

# # 967 Quality Review

Take time to tell your sons about their finer qualities (in some cases you may have to imagine more than describe). "I really like how gracious and courteous you are. I appreciate how well you dealt with your sister just now. The world could use more responsible men like you." If you have built a genuine relationship on trust, you'll send their spirits soaring— and flying right into your heart.

# # 968 Larry, Curly, and Moe

In my experience, most mothers don't get the Three Stooges. Now, this isn't a serious, life-threatening problem. But it is a problem. You can see these guys, creating disasters, pounding and insulting each other, doing all kinds of things that would get you arrested anywhere, and fall into criticism: "Would you look at that! That's disgusting! I can't believe you want to watch that. Turn that off." Trust me: Your boys know that you can't and shouldn't do that stuff. That's not the point. The point is that life is tough and confusing and frustrating and just a bit absurd, and, like the court jesters of old, these guys help us laugh about it. They put life in perspective. When you criticize what makes your son laugh at life, you communicate, "I don't understand you at all. We're operating in different universes. You and I are very different." It's hard to get connected when they hear the actual messages behind your words.

# # 969 No Taboo

Be the woman with the listening ear and the good, short, honest answers. Have no taboo subjects with your son. Don't skirt any issues. Talk about real temptations, alcohol and drugs, responsibility to others, sex. Why should he hear about these things from some ill-informed boy or immature girl? Make yourself important as a wise woman, not a maid or janitor. If he knows he can talk to you about anything, he will. And it's hard not to love someone that important.

# # 970 The Big Date

Let that young man know that his mother knows how to have a good time. Teach him how to be a gentleman—to open doors and pay the tab

(even if you have to give him the money ahead of time). If he's got a
healthy relationship with you, he won't be so desperate to find another
one out there. Treat him with all due seriousness and all due joy. And as
you look across that table, see in him the man he is and will become. And
know that this night, you are making him a better one.

# Fathers and Daughters

## # 971 The Marrying Kind

Be the kind of man you want your daughter to marry. Who you are and
the way you are will certainly affect that eventual decision, and you want
it to be a good one. Think of it this way: You'll want your girl to stay
connected to you for the rest of her life, no matter whom she marries. If
she marries someone who reminds her in a positive way of you, she'll
think of you even when she looks at him.

## # 972 Hugs and Kisses

Don't confuse physical contact with relationship; your daughter doesn't.
Just because she'll hug you doesn't mean she loves you and is deeply
connecting with you. Be careful not to let your affection go further than
your real connection. To press for hugs or kisses with a growing daughter
when there is no real relationship is confusing and misleading. It
confuses her by hinting that there's something there when everything
else communicates that there isn't. It misleads her by equating physical
contact with relationship. A close relationship puts the physical affection
in context.

## # 973 Take a Trip

For centuries women didn't go anywhere. Their "place" was so forcibly
the home. Fathers supported this nonsense and raised daughters without
a perspective on the size and shape and makeup of the world in which
they lived. You can do so much better. Widen your daughter's world by
getting out there. Laura and I went on our first trip together to a family
wedding when she was about four. We took a big trip to a conference in
Chicago when she was about twelve. When she was twenty-two, we went
to New York for a holiday and to see *The King and I,* which she was
directing at her college-prep high school. Start early, and the good can go
on and on.

# # 974 Candlelight

Why should some rough-edged teenage boy get the first shot at a candlelight dinner with your girl? You be her first date. Invite her out. Spiff up. Maybe even buy her a corsage. Choose a nice restaurant. "Anything you want, honey!" Treat her like a princess. That future boy will have his hands full, trying to compete with you.

# # 975 Nicknames

Find a name for her that's just yours. I have heard fathers call their girls "Pumpkin," "Bunny," "Scout," "Doll," and "Sweetie Pie." These daddy-to-daughter diminutives can stay in use right on into adulthood (with proper concern about privacy with outsiders). If you start when your daughter is little, she won't know there's any other way.

# # 976 Special Delivery

When she's had some big event or success—graduation, recital, birthday—go nuts! Be the one to send her a card (really mail it), and flowers, and candy, and whatever else you can think of. Girls whose fathers act like they're crazy about them feel much closer to their fathers and much less in need of finding it all "out there." Deliver the goods—along with your heart.

# 25

# Staying Close
# While Far Away

## # 977 Separation

In a recent year I spent twenty-seven full weeks on the road. I was doing what I loved—teaching, helping, caring—but it was keeping me from the *people* I loved. "I use separation as a working definition of death, and I use relationship as a working definition for life," wrote Walter Wangerin in *Mourning into Dancing*. Be aware of it when separation is turning into relational death, and take the steps to keep your relationships alive.

## # 978 Don't Go

Suddenly here it is—a terrific, much-longed-for opportunity has come your way. You *have* to go—right? Well, maybe not. At one point the apostle Paul, one of the greatest missionaries of all time, turned away from a wide-open field because "I did not find my brother Titus there. So I said good-by to them" (2 Cor. 2:13). Don't go, no matter how great the opportunity, if the cost is too high for your relationship.

## # 979 Younger Is Harder

Usually the younger they are, the harder separation from you is going to be for your children. They just don't have perspective; three days can seem like the end of time. A week *is* the end of time. This is another area where connection is not based on equality of treatment. Pour on the time with your little ones. A little less for the older ones will go a long way.

## # 980 Left Behind

When you leave, leave a bit of you behind. Leave a note for your kids to find when you've gone. If they're younger, you can hide the note and then give them "clues" when you talk with them over the phone. Or you can leave some clues that lead them around the house until they find the note. Leave your trail clearly marked.

# # 981 Messages

Try to leave your answering-machine messages in a recognizable pattern, so your kids can enjoy anticipating your calls. Leave a message at a break in the meeting or lunch, so they get it when they get home. They can move right toward that flashing light and know it's going to be you.

# # 982 You've Got Mail

What a great deal. Your kids get to check their electronic mailbox and receive that glorious announcement, "You've got mail!" If you travel very much at all, it's simply a must that you gain E-mail capability. A laptop lets you send personal, detailed messages practically free from anywhere on the planet. If you don't have a laptop or don't carry it with you, you can still access E-mail—by phone. Your messages are converted into voice both ways. Technology helps us go farther faster, but it helps us find our way back home as well.

# # 983 Postcards

Every now and then, postcards can be a delightful break. They invite your children right into your geographical locale. Avoid token messages: "Having a great meeting. Hope all is well." Go for the heart: "I miss you like crazy. I was thinking about how much you mean to me, and . . . Nobody is better than you at . . ." Let them know that where you are would be a lot more interesting if they were there with you in person.

# # 984 Phone Calls

It is really easy to take on phone calls as a duty, to feel that you "owe" them a call. Then when you get on the line, you go right for the practical details: "Anything happening? Are you being good? School going OK?" Perhaps you deliver your own terse reports: "Everything's going fine here. I'm pooped. See you in two days." Take a minute to flop on the bed, kick off your shoes, and determine how you'll customize the call before you make it. Try describing your hotel room and the view out the window. Talk about what they would be doing if they were there. Make plans for when you get back—how you're going to connect like mad. Forget duty. Make it an event.

# # 985 Small Gifts

A big part of the economy must be based on "guilt gifts." It's a common practice to fill the hole of your absence with a present. It's fine to bring your kids a gift, but take the time to make it a personal one (you're going to spend the money anyway; might as well do it right). The gift's price tag isn't nearly as important as the amount of thought you put into getting your kids just the right thing, the gift that says, "See how well I know you; see how much I love you."

# # 986 Animal Rights

Have a small stuffed animal that can go back and forth between you—with them while you're away, with you when you're home. And put a little perfume or aftershave on that duck, so its presence reminds them of you.

# # 987 Prioritize

You can't attend every activity for each of your children, so sit down with your kids and let them have input in creating some priorities. "Which of your events are most important? Which ones should I try to make if at all possible? Are there any that I just can't miss (like their playing the lead in the school play)?"

# # 988 Before and After

If you can't be there for a special event, try to be part of the preparation or celebration—the before or after. Bring refreshments to a practice and visit with the team or cast. Plan the big celebration the next weekend. Plan a video party to watch the tape of the event that someone lovingly recorded for you.

# # 989 Love Letters

If you're going to be apart for days or weeks, hand them a series of letters, with each one dated so they know when to open it. This gets mail out of the hands of the postal service and possibly poorly cooperating ex-spouses, and puts it straight into the hands—and hearts—of your much-loved children.

# # 990 Scrolling Down

If your separation will last a while, prepare a scroll for them to unroll a message per day while you're apart. Write a comment for the last day you'll be away, then roll it up and apply a dot of glue. Then write a

comment for the second-to-the-last day you'll be gone and do the same.
Keep going up to the first day of being apart. Glue or tie up the scroll in
ribbon. It's simply magic.

# # 991 Your Voice in Their Ears

Make sure your kids have access to a tape player, and then record a story
or song for them to listen to whenever they want. That way, whenever
they need or miss you, there you are, a comforting voice against the pain
of separation.

# # 992 Go Hollywood

If you've got a camcorder or can borrow one, record a video of yourself
talking right from the screen into their hearts. Add some drama. Set up a
tripod and record yourself making a meal—one that you're going to
freeze and eat with them when they return. Even if the video isn't of
professional quality, it will still be the blockbuster of the season.

# # 993 Stamp of Originality

Get or make a hand stamp with semipermanent ink. Then print your
name, or both of your names, or a heart with both of your initials in it.
Then stamp it right on her hand. Every time she looks down, she'll think
of you.

# # 994 Dinner Plans

Before your separation, talk about where you'll have dinner to celebrate
being back together again. Let your child pick the place and menu. If you
have more than one child, they can take turns making the selection.

# # 995 Events Planner

Plan for something really special when you get back together—a trip to
the zoo, a terrific concert, a movie you've both been wanting to see. It's
hard to live with separation, but you can always live with anticipation.

# # 996 Phone-Call Plan

Make plans for your phone calls. Agree in advance what you are going to
talk about. Build up the anticipation. "I'm going to give you five smackers
(kisses) when we talk." Make the sounds of hugs and kisses. Call your
child pet names. Crawl right through that piece of technology and right
into his heart.

# # 997 Remembrance

Get your face in front of your child when you're apart. Get a photo of the two of you—just the two of you—that she can put on her dresser. If your child is little, put the picture in a padded frame so she can put it under her pillow when she goes to sleep. Get her a locket with your picture. Have her pillow or pillowcase screen printed with a picture of the two of you on it or stitched with your names. Be creative, and you will be before her always.

# # 998 Parallel Lives

Pick a time of the day when you will both do the exact same thing. "Every morning at 7:30 let's pray for each other. At 3:00 P.M we'll both listen to our cassette of your favorite singer. At 9:00 in the evening, we'll both look at the moon and think about each other." As you stand there gazing at the magnificent moon, your heart will fill as you realize that your very own is looking at that very same sight. Your child will seem very close. And you will seem the same to her.

# # 999 Good Separation

All relationships require some separation to provide breathing room and perspective. When it seems like one of those times has arrived, suggest to your children that you use the separation to search your hearts and relationship and look at what is good and what is better and to look toward the future. Assure them you can grow closer in the spaces in your relationship as well as in times of physical closeness.

# # 1,000 Journey Journal

Try taking a journal on your journey or keeping one while your kids are away. Pour your heart out in it—talk about your youth, explore the struggles of life, philosophize, but make sure it all speaks to their hearts. Either keep a separate journal for each child or designate a trip as "Mary's turn" or "Rob's turn" for the journaling. Hand over the journal when you're reunited, and let your children read what you wrote over days or weeks. I'll bet they'll keep it always.

# Last Thoughts

## # 1,001 Kinds of Parents

There are three kinds of parents: those who make things happen, those who watch things happen, and those who get knocked over the head and say, "What happened?" Be in the first group. Choose the path of connection with your kids. Be proactive and crawl inside their hearts. Decide that nothing in heaven or on earth can keep you from that deep bond—no matter what's gone before today, no matter the failure that litters the path. There is only one way to fail—do nothing. But there are so many ways to connect.

At least a thousand.

# Note to the Reader

*I am honored that you have allowed me to join you on your journey and to share both your load and your joy. If you would like to tell me how you're doing, tell me which ideas were your favorites, or share with me any ideas you have used that are not in this book, you may contact me at*

James R. Lucas
Executive Director
Relationship Development Center
Box 2566
Shawnee Mission, KS 66201 USA
E-mail: JlucasLC@aol.com

For information about seminars/resources call toll-free 1 (888) 248-1733.

# *Other Books by James R. Lucas*

Family and Other Relationships
*Proactive Parenting: The Only Approach That Really Works*
*The Parenting of Champions*

Leadership and Organizational Development
*The Passionate Organization: Igniting the Fire of Employee Commitment*
*Balance of Power*
*Fatal Illusions: Shredding a Dozen Unrealities That Can Keep Your
    Organization from Success*

Personal Life and Growth
*Walking through the Fire: Finding the Purpose of Pain in the Christian Life*

Fiction
*Noah: Voyage to a New Earth*
*Weeping in Ramah*

## About the Author

James R. Lucas is the executive director of the Relationship Development Center, an organization dedicated to helping people with relationship development and enrichment through retreats, conferences, seminars, and workshops. Jim has been active in family and youth ministry for more than twenty-five years. He is also a charter member of the American Association of Christian Counselors (AACC) and speaks extensively in the United States and abroad. He has written numerous books, including *Proactive Parenting* (Harvest House), *The Parenting of Champions* (Wolgemuth & Hyatt), *Walking through the Fire: Finding the Purpose of Pain in the Christian Life* (Broadman and Holman), three books on leadership, and two fiction books, *Weeping in Ramah* (Crossway) and *Noah: Voyage to a New Earth* (Wolgemuth & Hyatt). He is also president and CEO of a leadership consulting group, Luman Consultants International. Jim and his wife, Pam, have four children and live in Prairie Village, Kansas, in the Kansas City area.